Political Ideologies

This informative and widely used text is now available in a third edition. Building on the success of previous editions it continues to provide a clear and accessible introduction to the complexities of political ideologies.

The new edition of *Political Ideologies: an introduction*:

- Introduces and considers the future of the most widely studied ideologies: liberalism, conservatism, socialism, nationalism, fascism, ecologism and feminism.
- Sets each ideology clearly within its historical and political context.
- Includes a new final chapter which examines the end of ideology debates and examines the future of political ideologies in the twenty-first century.
- Has been fully revised and updated and provides an annotated guide for further reading.

The authors are all current or former members of the School of Politics at Queen's University, Belfast.

Political Ideologies

An introduction

Third edition

Robert Eccleshall, Alan Finlayson, Vincent Geoghegan, Michael Kenny, Moya Lloyd, Iain MacKenzie and Rick Wilford

Routledge
Taylor & Francis Group

LONDON AND NEW YORK

First edition published in 1984 by
Unwin Hyman

Second edition published in 1994
by Routledge
11 New Fetter Lane, London EC4P 4EE

Reprinted 1995, 1996, 1998 and 2001
Third edition 2003

Simultaneously published in the USA and
Canada
by Routledge
29 West 35th Street, New York, NY 10001

*Routledge is an imprint of the Taylor &
Francis Group*

© 1984, 1993, 2003 Robert Eccleshall,
Alan Finlayson, Vincent Geoghegan,
Michael Kenny, Moya Lloyd,
Iain MacKenzie, Rick Wilford

Typeset in Century Old Style by
Keystroke, Jacaranda Lodge,
Wolverhampton
Printed and bound in Great Britain by
TJ International Ltd, Padstow, Cornwall

*British Library Cataloguing in
Publication Data*
A catalogue record for this book is
available from the British Library

*Library of Congress Cataloging in
Publication Data*
Political ideologies : an introduction /
Robert Eccleshall . . . [et al.] – 3rd ed.
p. cm.
Includes bibliographical references and
index.
1. Political science. 2. Ideology.
I. Eccleshall, Robert.

JA74 .P63 2003
320.5–dc21   2002036702

ISBN 0–415–23677–0 (hbk)
ISBN 0–415–23678–9 (pbk)

Contents

CONTENTS

The idea of ideology

Iain MacKenzie

What was required was a 'Newton of the science of thought', and it was in this role that he saw himself. Upon his release from prison he pursued this grand project as a member of the Institut National, attempting to create a liberal system of national education that would put into practice his science of ideas.

However, as Napoleon came to power and a new nobility emerged in France, the overt rationalism of de Tracy's science of ideas did not find favour with the increasingly autocratic regime. In the thought of de Tracy, and those who sympathised with him in the Institut National, Napoleon saw a threat to his authority. Their liberal and republican political ideas were to become for Napoleon the source of 'all the misfortunes that have befallen our beloved France', and he dismissively labelled these thinkers 'the ideologues'. Thus, at the very birth of the term, we find that ideology assumed two contrasting meanings: ideology as a science of ideas (de Tracy) and ideology as a set of false, even subversive, ideas (Napoleon). As will become apparent, this dichotomy has dogged the idea of ideology ever since.

While ideology was brought to life in the ferment of the French revolution it matured under different revolutionary conditions. As technological developments in the productive process increased dramatically and the new factories drew ever more people into the burgeoning cities the hitherto disjointed progress of economic modernisation escalated into a full-blown industrial revolution. At the head of this revolution were the new breed of capitalists who owned the means of production and the economists and philosophers who justified their headlong rush towards ever-increasing profit. It was the well documented hardships that capitalism wrought on its work force that provided the impetus and context for a new attempt at demarcating the ideological realm found, famously, in the writings of Karl Marx and Friedrich Engels.

The first truly collaborative work of Marx and Engels was *The German Ideology*, most of which was written in 1845–6 although it was published only posthumously in 1932 after their failure to find a publisher and their subsequent decision to leave the manuscript to 'the gnawing criticism of the mice'. The full text of this work contains long and detailed criticisms of two of Marx and Engels' contemporaries in German philosophy, Ludwig Feuerbach and Max Stirner. The aim of the critique was to expose the false premises upon which these thinkers and others of the German tradition had built their philosophical edifices:

> Hitherto men have constantly made up for themselves false conceptions about themselves, about what they are and what they ought to be. They have arranged their relationships according to their ideas of God, of normal man, etc. The phantoms of their brains have got out of their hands. They, the creators, have bowed down before their creations. Let us liberate them from the chimeras, the ideas, dogmas, imaginary beings under their yoke of which they are pining away. Let us revolt against the rule of thoughts . . . the present publication has the aim of uncloaking these sheep, who take themselves and are taken for wolves; of showing how their bleating

merely imitates in a philosophic form the conceptions of the German
middle class; how the boasting of these philosophic commentators only
mirrors the wretchedness of the real conditions in Germany.

(1974: 37)

Amidst this stinging critique it is possible to discern the various features of
ideology already discussed. First, there is a reiteration, although probably
unwittingly, of the Baconian notion of 'phantoms', of illusions deeply rooted
in the human mind. Secondly, the radical spirit of Enlightenment, the pursuit of
truth in the face of error, shines through their condemnation of German
philosophy. Thirdly, Marx and Engels conduct their critique with all the vitriol
of Napoleon's attack on the 'ideologues' and are similarly concerned that
erroneous ideas spell disaster for national and political culture. Yet within *The
German Ideology* there is also a new approach to the idea of ideology, namely
that false ideas are false precisely because they reflect class interests, in this
case the interests of the German middle class, rather than the interests of all. For
Marx and Engels, therefore, the only way to remove the ideological frameworks
of society is to remove the contradictions of particular class interests inherent
in the economic and social realms. As the Marxist critic Istvan Meszaros puts
it, ideology is 'insurmountable in class societies' and therefore theoretical
reason alone, *contra* de Tracy, will not in itself enable us to overcome false ideas
about the nature of society (1989: 10–11). For Marx and Engels, theoretical
reason must be allied with revolutionary practice aimed at dissolving class
conflict. The contradictions of class-based societies must be overcome in
practice if the reign of false ideas is to be destroyed once and for all.

If we combine this new account of how erroneous ideas emerge with the
claim made by Marx and Engels in *The Communist Manifesto* (1848), that
'the history of all hitherto existing society is the history of class struggle' (2000:
246), then we can discern a full-blown theory of how it is that any particular
society at any particular time comes to have the ideas about itself that it does.
Ideology, in this sense, is no longer simply a science for the generation of true
ideas, or simply a set of false and dangerous ideas, but a general theory of
how ideas emerge from the material base of social and economic conditions. It
is, therefore, an account of how the dominant ideas of our age have come to be
so dominant by virtue of their relationship to developments in the economic
sphere. It is in this sense that Marx and Engels, particularly in their later writings,
view liberalism as an ideology that blinds the populace to the excesses of
capitalist exploitation while also maintaining that liberalism itself is sustained
by the economic forces at work within the capitalist mode of production. The
intimate link between liberalism and capitalism maintains the dominance of both,
making it virtually impossible for the vast majority of people to imagine a world
without either. Such is the force of this ideology, according to many of today's
'anti-globalisation' and 'anti-capitalist' protesters, that it seems easier to imagine
global ecological disaster than to imagine changing the economic, social and
political structures that, arguably, are drawing us ever closer to the collapse of

our biosphere; a failure of the imagination that, it is claimed, must be challenged if humanity is to have a future at all.

After Marx and Engels, but within the tradition of twentieth-century Marxism, the idea of ideology began to take a different shape. Emphasis on the all-encompassing nature of ideology led some Marxists to downplay the notion that ideologies are conglomerations of false ideas supported by class divisions. Instead, many Marxists stressed a view of ideology that conceptualised it as the basis of all social and political action. We can see this in Lenin's analysis of the revolutionary struggle facing Russians at the beginning of the twentieth century. In *What is to be Done?* (1902) he talks of *socialism* as 'the ideology of struggle of the proletarian class'. For Lenin, breaking from the classical conception of Marx and Engels, ideology no longer simply represents the ideas of the ruling class. The crucial factor is the extent to which ideology is an effective weapon in the class war. As Boudon puts it, the novelty of Lenin's approach is that regardless of whether ideologies are true or false they are 'useful' (1989: 18). This addition to the classical Marxist conception opens the way for an understanding of ideology that portrays all forms of action as, in some sense, ideological.

It was a theme picked up in the writings of many subsequent Marxists (for example, Gramsci, Benjamin and Adorno) but it is especially clear in the work of the French neo-Marxist philosopher Louis Althusser. According to Althusser, ideology is the 'cement' that binds human societies together. In this sense, 'ideology is . . . an organic part . . . of every social totality' and 'human societies secrete ideology as the very element and atmosphere indispensable to their historical respiration and life' (1969: 232). The 'ideology of the school', for instance, provides one of the limits of our social interaction. Schools become one medium through which we are socialised into deference towards our 'superiors', in which we are taught to compete against each other and ultimately moulded into the 'good citizens' required by a liberal capitalist society. Furthermore, social and political life is made up of a number of such institutions; not only schools but churches, trade unions and the family all constitute what Althusser calls 'Ideological State Apparatuses'. The usefulness of ideology as a tool of political research is that it helps us understand the ways in which these elements of social life are relatively self-sufficient while nonetheless being ultimately bound together by economic imperatives derived from capitalist productive processes. Importantly, for Althusser, ideology would not disappear in a post-capitalist society – the ideology of the school would still exist but in a form that sought to bolster the bonds of post-capitalist society. He retained, in this sense, the Leninist view that socialism is itself an ideology.

That said, Althusser continued to insist upon the strict separation of ideology and science, in a manner reminiscent of the way classical conceptions of ideology derived their force from the Enlightenment desire to rid social and political life of false ideas. Yet Althusser's rendering of the division between ideology and science remained distinctly Marxist in outlook. The problem he faced was this: if ideology binds social life together and is, therefore, an irreducible element of our political existence, was Marxism itself not just another ideology with no particularly strong claim to being a true account of the way the social and political world operates? His first solution to this problem is the one that he is most known for, although he altered his views on it throughout his career. For the early Althusser, Marx's analyses of the workings of capitalism could be understood as scientific, that is, as not ideological, if they were grounded on the basic premises of Marxist philosophy rather than on a non-Marxist philosophy of science. We can distinguish ideology from science, for Althusser, so long as we construe science as the Marxist science of political economy expressed most clearly in Marx's *Capital*. Marxist philosophy, in other words, is the guarantor of the scientific status of Marxist political economy. This leads Althusser to the claim that Marxism is both a philosophy of science and a science itself; a claim not without a certain paradoxical character, as subsequent commentary has revealed (Callinicos, 1976; Assiter, 1990).

Whether this approach manages to marry together the classical idea of ideology as a set of false ideas with the idea that all activity within social and political life is ideological is open to question. Nonetheless, it provides a glimpse of the deep layers of philosophical inquiry that have had to be unearthed in order for those within Marxism to make sense of the idea of ideology. Recent work, loosely under the banner of post-Marxism, has pursued even deeper geological excavations into the basic strata of ideology such that one is often confronted with the kind of theoretical complexity that leaves one gasping for air with every sentence. Nonetheless, it is the work of post-Marxists like Ernesto Laclau and Slavoj Zizek that has done much to revitalise the idea of ideology in an era dominated by postmodern dismissiveness of all things ideological. As the final chapter in this volume makes clear, their various insights into the nature of ideology serve to remind students of the subject that the legacy of Marx and Engels continues to exert a powerful influence over cutting-edge work in political ideologies.

It would be a mistake, though, to assume that all the interesting work on the idea of ideology has been from a more or less Marxist perspective. Throughout the first half of the twentieth century the concept of ideology quickly spread across theoretical schools and academic disciplines. Even if scholars were not persuaded by the basic economic determinism underpinning the classical Marxist appropriation of ideology the idea that the vast majority of the population held beliefs about social and political life that dominated, in some sense, everyday social and political interaction continued to have resonance and currency within intellectual circles. Within mainstream Anglo-American social science, for example, ideology came to denote constellations of belief such that liberal ideology is understood as a set of interlocking ideas about liberty, equality, justice and the like, while conservative ideology is understood as a different set of beliefs about these key terms. In this sense, ideologies are said to offer contrasting interpretations of *essentially contested concepts*, where an essentially contested concept is one which does not, and could not, have an agreed meaning (Gallie, 1955/6; Connolly, 1983).

We are familiar with the debates around the concept of freedom, for example, between conservatives and socialists; freedom from the state in a market framework versus freedom to fulfil one's creative capacities in a collective setting. This is a staple of British party politics. Are taxes, for instance, an infringement of personal liberty in that they remove the right of individuals to spend their money in the way they see fit? Or are taxes an important form of redistribution that enable people to fulfil their potential as free and equal human beings? Whereas the Marxist tradition of ideological inquiry tended to focus on the underlying realities of such party political debate, endeavouring to unearth the economic substrata upon which these illusory conflicts rested, the Anglo-American approach has always been more concerned with the nitty-gritty of conceptual contestation, looking for the nuances of meaning and understanding that separate and/or link, for example, the feminist idea of equality with that proffered by welfare-oriented liberals.

As Freeden notes, within the Anglo-American tradition of the study of ideology there is a shift away from the idea of ideology to the study of ideolog*ies*:

> No longer is ideology regarded as an aberration of perception or of understanding; instead, a positivist empiricism is harnessed to identify and investigate a widespread social phenomenon: the existence of organized, articulated, and consciously held systems of political ideas incorporating beliefs, attitudes and opinions, though latent beliefs are also included.
>
> (1996: 15)

Furthermore, this emphasis on ideologies within Anglo-American political science also brings with it a certain historical approach that dwells on how and why beliefs about concepts have mutated within and between ideologies. Of course, this is not the Marxist sense of history, where history is governed by the laws of political economy, but a rather more idealist history that focuses on the contributions of great thinkers and politicians within various ideological traditions. For example, where a Marxist might look to understand Tony Blair's advocacy of 'The Third Way' by reference to *the ideology* at work in this new doctrine, political theorists of a more Anglo-American bent would tend to examine 'The Third Way' in terms of the *various ideological strands* that are blended together by its proponents. It may seem like a subtle distinction, but the rift between Marxist and non-Marxist approaches to ideology has deep significance for how we understand contemporary social and political formations. Are the various ideologies that make up our ideological landscape resting on one idea of ideology that can, in principle at least, be unearthed with a view to explaining and possibly removing ideological conflict, as a Marxist might hold? Or, does ideological contestability go 'all the way down' such that we cannot really talk of one single meaning of the term ideology itself? Without hoping to resolve this most difficult issue, it is worth turning our attention to the most systematic account of ideologies within the non-Marxist tradition of recent times, that offered by Michael Freeden in his book *Ideologies and Political Theory* (1996).

The morphology of ideologies

From the outset, Freeden distances himself from Marxist approaches to ideology and places himself firmly within the purview of Anglo-American studies: '[t]he thinking encapsulated in ideologies deserves examination in its own right, not merely for what it masks' (1996: 1). Leaving such Marxist approaches behind, however, Freeden focuses his critical gaze on another form of political theorising that fails to accord ideologies their full due, the Anglo-American tendency to subordinate thinking about ideology to the rigour of moral and political philosophy. For Freeden, scholars tend to miss crucial dimensions of political life if their sole concern is to clarify the logical connections between abstract ideas. In particular, contemporary liberal political philosophy has become overly concerned with delimiting the precise nature of justice, rights, freedom, equality and so on to the detriment of 'our comprehension of political thought as a phenomenon reflecting cultural as well as logical constraints' (1996: 2). Without an appreciation of the cultural life of ideas, he argues, political thought remains a rarified activity with little hope of understanding either the impact of political ideas on political action or, equally important, the impact of political activity on the formation and shaping of political ideas. One cannot simply map out the logical coherence of a solution to a moral dilemma and either expect the populace to fall into line behind the logic of the argument or use philosophical rigour as justification for calling to account those who do not see the logic of the argument. The political realm, for Freeden, is much more complex and demanding than this traditional Anglo-American approach suggests, and in order to understand this complexity it is necessary to examine the realm of ideologies on its own terms. Freeden, in short, wishes to approach the nature of ideologies without subordinating their contribution to political life under either the banner of Marxist political economy or that of analytical moral and political philosophy.

This approach demands both a careful rendering of the ideological domain and a subtle account of scholarly practice in the study of ideologies, such that the complexity internal to that domain is retained and not subordinated to other modes of political inquiry. According to Freeden, ideologies are 'those systems of political thinking, loose or rigid, deliberate or unintended, through which individuals and groups construct an understanding of the political world they, or those who preoccupy their thoughts, inhabit, and then act on that understanding' (1996: 3). In this encompassing definition, packed with the kind of vagueness so abhorrent to those of a strongly analytical bent, Freeden manages to convey the nature of ideologies from the perspective of those who make them what they are: ordinary people engaged in social and political life. As such, Freeden respects his opening intuition that ideologies must be placed firmly in the cultural and not just the logical realm. But how do students of ideology study the cultural life of ideas? What image of scholarly practice is produced as a result of this deliberately open definition?

Freeden acknowledges that scholars of ideologies within the Anglo-American tradition have dwelt rightly on both the temporal and the spatial aspects of ideology; that is, how ideologies change over time (say, the ways in which British liberalism has mutated throughout British history) and how they manifest themselves within different cultures (say, the different emphases found within British and French liberalism). But according to Freeden this is not the whole story. To fully appreciate the role of ideologies within political life one must also look at the morphology of ideologies. Morphology refers to the study of form and structure and it is Freeden's contention that the study of ideologies must address the ways in which ideologies are structured by the linkages between the concepts that make up any particular ideology. He proposes that ideologies can be thought of as assemblages of concepts, some of which will be concepts that form the core of the ideology, while other concepts will be either adjacent to the core or at the periphery of the ideology.

> Central to any analysis of ideologies is the proposition that they are characterised by a morphology that displays core, adjacent, and peripheral concepts. For instance, an examination of observed liberalisms might establish that liberty is situated within their core, that human rights, democracy and equality are adjacent to liberty, and that nationalism is to be found on their periphery.
>
> (1996: 77)

Alongside the temporal and the spatial study of ideologies, Freeden wants to emphasise that concepts change and gain meaning not only through time or cultural setting but also through the ways in which they are related to each other within ideologies. Interestingly, this amounts to an extrapolation of the idea of essentially contested concepts, mentioned above. Where it was traditionally thought that the essential contestability of the concepts that make up ideologies was a product of the intrinsic complexity and value-ladenness of the concepts themselves, Freeden stresses that contestability at this level is itself a product of a deeper contestability to be found in the structure of relationships between concepts that make up an ideology's morphology. The essential contestability of concepts, in other words, is not simply the result of our inability to agree on the meaning of key concepts. Rather, it is derived from the fact that the meaning of concepts changes, depending on the relationships concepts are thought to have with each other. From this perspective, we cannot agree on the meaning of liberty because we cannot agree on its relationships with other concepts such as equality, democracy, rights, justice and so on. Indeed, the study of ideologies is, in large measure, the study of the various ways these and other concepts have been related to each other within the political domain.

Having established the centrality of morphology in the study of ideology, Freeden is quick to point out that this does not mean that any particular ideology – liberalism, say – has a fixed set of core, adjacent and peripheral concepts. On the contrary, he maintains that the study of morphology brings the various changes within ideologies all the more clearly into focus, a claim he makes good in the chapters of the book which deal with liberalism, conservativism, socialism, feminism and ecologism. Moreover the student of ideology should not fall prey to the idea that morphological analyses are somehow divorced from the historical and cultural construction of ideologies. In summing up his argument at the end of the book, Freeden cautions that the relationship between the history, culture and morphology of ideologies must be examined 'without slavishly following any single viewpoint' (1996: 552). And here again we are reminded that Freeden wishes to demarcate the realm of ideologies from both the Marxist tendency to reduce ideology to matters of political economy and the Anglo-American tendency to treat ideologies as forms of sloppy thinking that need to be corrected through the intervention of logical constraints. Ideologies are, in contrast, that particular form of thinking about politics that can be truly said to be political – that is, the changeable and practically oriented thinking of citizens in the social and political world.

Ideologies: some key questions

The Marxist and the non-Marxist accounts of ideology reveal a deep rift in thinking about the nature of ideologies. This apparently unshakable dichotomy often leaves the student of ideology perplexed and unable to judge the claims of various ideologies. Nonetheless, there are a series of key questions that can be formulated which can help to sharpen one's critical focus when faced with the troubling question 'What are ideologies?' The following questions help to bring out the 'big issues' in the debates about the nature of ideologies and can be used both to recap some of the issues that have emerged so far and reveal more clearly the theoretical strata underpinning the ideological landscape.

What relationship do ideologies have to truth? This is probably the trickiest of all problems regarding the nature of ideology because, as Boudon puts it, 'what is knowledge for one person is ideology for another, and vice versa' (1989: 22). Typically, of course, if one is trying to judge, for example, whether liberalism gives a true picture of the social and political world while socialism gives a false one, then the temptation is to resort to empirical examples. Can we not just look at the world around us in a broadly scientific fashion and discover the truth of the matter? Both classical Marxist approaches and many non-Marxist approaches resort to this strategy. The trouble is that ideologies shape what we see when we look at the social and political world. In this sense, the ideological spectacles are already adorned before the social scientific research takes place and it is by no means clear that a method exists which can either remove or even lessen the distorting effects of ideology on social and political research. When it is truth that is at stake, when people disagree about what the truth of a situation really is, the attempt to refer to the facts of the situation is likely to dig us deeper into the ideological mud.

In a useful essay on Marx's concept of ideology, Stuart Hall (1983) argues that the 'problem' of truth and falsity in the classical conception can be abated by refusing to think in such 'all or nothing' terms. He suggests that in place of these tough metaphysical categories we think of ideologies as either 'partial' or 'adequate'. Within non-Marxist literature Boudon also suggests that we need some criterion for judging ideologies even if we will never be able to definitively proclaim one ideology true and the others false. The criterion he plumps for is 'soundness'. It is impossible to prove the truth of an ideology, he argues, but we may assess the soundness of its principles (1989: 202). Interestingly, Freeden's approach to ideology tries to take a step back from even these watered down attempts at assessing the veracity of different ideologies by focusing instead on the idea that ideologies are to be analysed according to the concepts that they allow or disallow as true or false accounts of political reality. Moving away from the idea that ideologies are more or less 'true', 'adequate' or 'sound' attempts at reflecting the social and political world, he proposes instead that the world we inhabit is 'partly the product of those ideologies, operating as ways of organizing social reality' (1996: 4). The student of ideologies, for Freeden, should pursue their morphologies with a broadly detached attitude to questions of truth and falsity. Of course, one might argue that such detachment masks an ideological agenda, one which fails to call to account the false ideas that distort people's view of the social world around them and, therefore, it is an approach which ends up legitimating the *status quo*. Once again, the philosophical depths of ideology theory are quickly exposed.

Will there ever be a time when there are no ideologies? Although the main features of the well established debate around the end of ideologies are outlined in the last chapter, answers to this question depend to a large extent on the answer one would give to the previous question. If it is thought that ideologies are false ideas that can be exposed by one form of analysis or another then the idea of an end to ideology is conceivable. If ideologies are patterns of thought that shape the political world then this would suggest that, if we accept the timeless nature of political engagement, there will always be ideologies.

What is the relationship between ideologies and political activity? There is a tendency to view ideologies as merely constellations of ideas that do not directly impact on day-to-day political activity. However, the picture is more complex than this view suggests. As discussed above, both Marxist and non-Marxist accounts of ideology recognise that ideologies have a role in shaping political activity, often in unconscious ways. Of course, the everyday machinations of politicians may appear unrelated to the admittedly rarified discourses of scholars but this appearance should not cloud the insight that political activity without an ideological frame would be verging on the meaningless. That said, students of ideology should be wary of a straightforward correspondence between the 'reality' of party politics and the various ideologies they appear to represent. For example, to assume that the ideology of conservativism can be mapped neatly on to the day-to-day activities of those who call themselves Conservatives is to reduce the complexity of both conservative ideology and

Conservative party politics to banal caricatures. As discussed in chapter 3, the ideology of conservatism has complex roots in the history of ideas such that many conservative activists versed in post-Thatcherite libertarianism would not be comfortable with the Burkean suspicion of individualism. Similarly the current emphasis within Conservative party politics on the needs of those disadvantaged by New Labour's political agenda would appear to draw heavily on aspects of welfare liberalism also being advocated by many Liberal Democrats. Such complexities are lost if one assumes a simple one-to-one correlation between an ideology and the political party that bears its name.

Are ideologies really just the ideas of ideologues? From the outset, it was noted that those who hold firm to their view of the political world have been labelled ideologues. This claim presupposes that the real activity of politics is best served by compromise, flexibility and openness such that any political actor who does not display these features is merely a dangerous ideologue. Classically, this view is associated with Napoleon's condemnation of de Tracy and with Marxist condemnation of apologists for capitalist liberal democracy. More generally, it is found in arguments against those in political life, be they academics or activists, who endorse to some degree the idea that the social and political world should be made to conform to a ready-made ideal. Many conservatives and some liberals, for example, tend to dismiss other ideologies as the rantings of ideologues while, typically, arguing that their own chosen perspective is non-ideological precisely because it is based on pragmatic politics rather than ideals. There are two problems with such views. First, and as the relevant chapters in this book make clear, both conservativism and liberalism contain ideal visions of the good society. Secondly, the attempt to caricature other political viewpoints as the views of ideologues fails to adequately differentiate those ideological views that are commonly held within the political world from those that are the product of manipulative individuals trying to shape those commonly held views. In other words, all ideologies may have their ideologues, conservativism and liberalism included, but the views of ideologues are only a part of the rich and complex network of concepts and activities that constitute any given ideology.

These questions by no means exhaust the interrogation of ideology but they do serve to remind the student of ideology that the domain of ideologies sits, uncomfortably at times, between the rarified world of philosophical inquiry and the day-to-day machinations of *Realpolitik*. If Freeden is right that it is precisely this condition that makes the analysis of ideologies central to the study of political life then it is important to navigate a clear path between the rocks of Marxist political economy and Anglo-American analytical philosophy.

Conclusion

There are two key features of ideological dispute current in global politics: the gradual coalescence of ideological positions within liberal democracies and the persistent eruptions of ideological fury around the world. In many respects these two phenomena can be explained, at least in part, with reference to the nature of ideology.

While for much of the twentieth century parties that reflected deep-seated class divisions dominated politics in liberal democracies, we are now witnessing a form of dealigned politics which means that each of the main political parties is striving to appeal to all 'the people'. This reflects a change, within both left and right political parties, in their perception of the political terrain. It is no longer possible to gain political power by appealing to one section of the community (the work force, for example) by claiming that the views of the other section (the managers and capitalists, for example) are simply false. There is, in other words, recognition that the political realm is irreducibly marked by competing ideologies and that the task of *Realpolitik* is to construct an ideological vision that encompasses rather than excludes. In the terms outlined above, contemporary liberal democracies reveal a shift from a single account of the nature of ideology to the idea that all political behaviour is, and will always be, shaped by a variety of ideologies. Disputes remain, of course, but these reflect different understandings of the concepts that make up ideologies rather than different understandings of the nature of ideology itself.

In the global arena, though, the political realm is still marked by disagreement over the nature of ideology itself. Even if those involved in the big ideological battles of the contemporary world are rarely Marxist in outlook, the world of international politics is still replete with those political actors determined to reveal the liberal democratic consensus as *the* ideology that distorts the vision of vast swathes of humanity in the service of the imperialistic tendency of international capitalist powers. Most notably, this criticism lurks behind both the criticisms of 'Western governments' in their attitude to non-Western states and in the anti-capitalist protests against multinational corporations. For all the obvious differences between these global movements, both can be said to be pitting a classical conception of *ideology* against the alternative notion of a world of irremovable *ideologies*. If we fail to see this dimension we fail to understand the sources that motivate political actors to turn to radical forms of political expression in pursuit of their objectives. Indeed, that the idea of ideology is still being contested throughout the world reminds us that the consensus within liberal democracies – a consensus that derives in large part from agreement on the nature of ideologies – is by no means the end of the matter.

Further reading

In the last ten years, one of the most significant developments in the study of ideology has been the appearance of Michael Freeden's book *Ideologies and Political Theory* (1996). Although a complicated and demanding text in many ways, the core ideas it contains within are well worth the effort of close reading. The student of ideology would also do well to examine many of the papers that have appeared in the journal initiated and edited by Freeden, *Journal of Political Ideologies*. Of particular interest are Freeden's own editorials, where he clarifies aspects of his own thought as well as summarising and commenting on developments within this field of study. There are also good discussions of the nature of ideology in the following texts: T. A. van Dijk, *Ideology: A Multidisciplinary Approach* (1998); A. Vincent, *Modern Political Ideologies* (1992); S. Malešević and I. MacKenzie (eds), *Ideology after Poststructuralism* (2002).

D. McLellan, *Ideology* (1986), provides a brief yet insightful introduction to many of the issues raised in the introduction, and can be usefully complemented by T. Eagleton, *Ideology: An Introduction* (1991), who undertakes a more wide-ranging analysis encompassing recent trends in social theory. Similarly, J. B. Thompson, *Studies in the Theory of Ideology* (1984) is an excellent guide to traditional debates while also showing how the terms of these debates have shifted in recent years. For a useful survey of the material on ideology see M. B. Hamilton, 'The elements of the concept of ideology' (1987). A very analytical, and at times quite dry, approach to the epistemological problems alluded to above can be found in R. Boudon, *The Analysis of Ideology* (1989). J. Larrain, *The Concept of Ideology* (1979) also provides a study of ideology that is difficult but rewarding. Interesting, and challenging, accounts of the nature of ideology, at both a theoretical and a practical level, can be found in Centre for Contemporary Cultural Studies, *On Ideology* (1978), and also in N. O'Sullivan (ed.), *The Structure of Modern Ideology* (1989).

The literature on Marxism and ideology is vast, often very difficult and related to particular debates within Marxism. However, useful starting points are B. Parekh, *Marx's Theory of Ideology* (1982) and J. Larrain, *Marxism and Ideology* (1983). I would also thoroughly recommend S. Hall, 'The problem of ideology – Marxism without guarantees' (1983). For the more adventurous in this area I. Meszaros, *The Power of Ideology* (1989), is a very long (over 500 pages) Marxist discussion of ideology that can be as rewarding as it is frustrating. On Althusser, a good overall guide can be found in A. Callinicos, *Althusser's Marxism* (1976). An excellent account of Althusser's theory of ideology is C. Williams, 'Ideology and imaginary: returning to Althusser' (2002). A. Assiter, *Althusser and Feminism* (1990), is an ambitious attempt to wed Althusserian Marxism with contemporary feminism.

Approaches to ideology that were not covered in the introduction but would prove interesting in terms of a more detailed look at the debates are: K. Mannheim, *Ideology and Utopia* (1936), who provides a useful link between Marxist and non-Marxist accounts of ideology; and E. Shils, 'The concept and function of ideology', *International Encyclopaedia of the Social Sciences*, VII (1968) argues, to my mind unconvincingly, that scientific knowledge is gradually eroding ideologies.

References

Note. Dates in square brackets indicate date of original publication.

Althusser, L. (1969) 'Marxism and humanism' in *For Marx*, London: Allen Lane.

Assiter, A. (1990) *Althusser and Feminism*, London: Pluto Press.

Bacon, F. (1855) [1620] *Novum Organon*, Oxford: Oxford University Press.

Boudon, R. (1989) *The Analysis of Ideology*, Cambridge: Polity Press.

Callinicos, A. (1976) *Althusser's Marxism*, London: Pluto Press.

Centre for Contemporary Cultural Studies (1978) *On Ideology*, London: Hutchinson.

Connolly, W. (1983) *The Terms of Political Discourse*, 2nd edn, Oxford: Martin Robinson.

Dijk, T. A. van (1998) *Ideology: A Multidisciplinary Approach*, London: Sage.

Eagleton, T. (1991) *Ideology: An Introduction*, London: Verso.

Freeden, M. (1996) *Ideologies and Political Theory: A Conceptual Approach*, Oxford: Oxford University Press.

Gallie, W. B. (1955/6) 'Essentially contested concepts', *Proceedings of the Aristotelian Society* 56, pp. 167–98.

Hall, S. (1983) 'The problem of ideology – Marxism without guarantees' in B. Matthews (ed.) *Marx: A Hundred Years On*, London: Lawrence & Wishart.

Hamilton, M. B. (1987) 'The elements of the concept of ideology', *Political Studies*, 35, pp.18–38.

Larrain, J. (1979) *The Concept of Ideology*, London: Hutchinson.

Larrain, J. (1983) *Marxism and Ideology*, London: Macmillan.

Malešević, S. and MacKenzie, I., eds (2002) *Ideology after Poststructuralism*, London: Pluto Press.

Mannheim, K. (1936) *Ideology and Utopia: An Introduction to the Sociology of Knowledge*, London: Kegan Paul.

Marx, K. and Engels, F. (1974) [1845–6] *The German Ideology* (Students Edition) ed. C. J. Arthur, London: Lawrence & Wishart.

Marx, K. and Engels, F. (2000) [1848] *The Communist Manifesto*, in D. McLellan (ed.) *Karl Marx: Selected Writings*, 2nd edn, Oxford: Oxford University Press.

McLellan, D. (1986) *Ideology*, Milton Keynes: Open University Press.

Meszaros, I. (1989) *The Power of Ideology*, London: Harvester Wheatsheaf.

O'Sullivan, N., ed. (1989) *The Structure of Modern Ideology: Critical Perspectives on Social and Political Theory*, Aldershot: Edward Elgar.

Parekh, B. (1982) *Marx's Theory of Ideology*, London: Croom Helm.

Shils, E. (1968) 'The concept and function of ideology' in D. L. Sills (ed.) *International Encyclopaedia of the Social Sciences*, VII, New York: Macmillan.

Thompson, J. B. (1984) *Studies in the Theory of Ideology*, Cambridge: Polity Press.

Vincent, A. (1992) *Modern Political Ideologies*, London: Blackwell.

Williams, C. (2002) 'Ideology and imaginary: returning to Althusser' in S. Malešević, and I. MacKenzie (eds) *Ideology after Poststructuralism*, London: Pluto Press.

Liberalism

Robert Eccleshall

[Liberalism's] aim is to create a nation, not of humble though kindly treated workers dependent upon a small rich class who alone can enjoy the full benefits of a civilised life; and not of proletarians regimented, controlled, and provided with standardised comforts by a group of dictators or bureaucrats acting in the name of the State; but a nation of free, responsible, law-abiding, and self-reliant men and women – free from the grinding servitude of poverty and (so far as is possible for men) from the tyranny of circumstance; with healthy bodies and alert and trained minds; enjoying a real equality of opportunity to make the most and best of their powers for their own advantage and that of the community, and to choose the way of life for which they are best fitted; having a real share of responsibility for regulating the management of their common affairs and the conditions of their own life and work; and secure of sufficient leisure to live a full life and to enjoy the delights of Nature, letters, and the arts.

> (*The Liberal Way: A Survey of Liberal Policy, published by the authority of the National Liberal Federation*, with a foreword by Ramsay Muir, London: Allen & Unwin, 1934, pp. 221–2)

Problems of definition

Liberalism has a longer history than the other ideologies considered in this book. Its genesis in the seventeenth century coincided with the dissolution of feudal relations and the emergence of modern capitalist society. The earliest liberals were radical Protestants who challenged secular and ecclesiastical hierarchies in the name of individual rights, claiming that ordinary people were competent to judge the affairs of government as well as to choose their own path to eternal salvation. Since that time liberals have been at the forefront of movements to emancipate individuals from political, religious, economic and other constraints on their activities, and they have persistently campaigned for a society that is more open, tolerant and diverse, less paternalist and authoritarian, than one which entrenches privilege and illegitimate authority. As such liberalism provides an ideological map of the major political struggles and developments that have occurred in Britain and elsewhere during the last 300 years.

Herein lies a principal difficulty in identifying the doctrine's distinctive characteristics. In a sense all but the perverse or temperamentally autocratic are now liberals, for few would wish to discard the individual liberties and democratic rights that have been secured in post-feudal society. Liberalism, in everyday usage, often stands for little more than a collection of values and principles which no decent person would reject: a liberal, the economist J. M. Keynes wrote, 'is anyone who is perfectly sensible'. The effect is to lose sight of the doctrine's peculiar perspective on society as well as the boundaries separating liberals from those who belong to rival ideological camps.

One means, favoured by some academic commentators, of bringing liberalism into sharper focus is to characterise it as a bourgeois creed. 'In its living principle,' according to Harold Laski, liberalism 'was the idea by which the new middle class rose to a position of political dominance' (Laski, 1936: 17). Liberalism has been intimately connected with the evolution of the capitalist world, its adherents have endorsed the right to accumulate private property, and until the end of the nineteenth century their assault upon privilege was directed at the power of the aristocracy. The ideology, as Laski indicates, inevitably took shape from the social interests to which it was attached. In characterising the doctrine as essentially bourgeois, however, some commentators wish to depict it as a narrow, excessively individualistic creed which licenses the members of capitalist society to pursue their private interests unrestrained by any sense of duty to co-operate on behalf of the public good.

According to common understanding, then, liberalism is a nebulous doctrine embracing everyone of goodwill, whereas in academic usage it sometimes appears as a coherent but unattractive ideology, unlikely to appeal to anyone with generous impulses. In what follows I suggest that liberalism is neither incoherent nor narrowly individualistic: that what gives the doctrine its distinctive perspective is a strong sense of public duty or citizenship which is linked with the ownership of private property. Liberals, to anticipate the argument, have wished to safeguard individual liberties through a structure of equal rights in the expectation that dutiful citizenship or civic virtue will thereby be enhanced.

An incoherent doctrine?

The adjective 'liberal' has for centuries denoted an open-minded and tolerant disposition. Only from the early nineteenth century, however, was the noun 'liberalism' used to designate political parties and movements, and eventually historians found the term a convenient concept for classifying ideological strands associated with the evolution of post-feudal society.

Liberals themselves often reinforce the impression that their doctrine is little else than the political expression of those civilised values denoted by the adjective 'liberal'. 'To behave liberally,' according to a former leader of the British Liberal party, 'is to behave generously. It implies lavishness. It evokes ideas of breadth and lightness, reason and beauty' (Grimond, 1963: 33). The story which liberals are inclined to tell of their doctrine's history is of a movement for emancipation from successive forms of arbitrary power and outmoded privilege. It is an heroic venture in which bearers of the torch of freedom emerge as magnanimous individuals intent on creating a fairer, more pluralist society that gives individuals ample space to shape their lives according to their own conscience and preferences. Hence a tendency to characterise liberalism as the mobilisation of decent impulses on behalf of social progress: the spirit of 'liberality', as Lord Selborne put it, 'transferred only to the sphere of politics' (Reid, 1885: 82). It is also a success story of battles won against such obstacles to individual liberty as absolute monarchy, religious intolerance, economic privilege, an undemocratic franchise and the poverty flowing from unfettered capitalism. Liberals, on this account, have for three centuries spearheaded the transformation of society from feudal despotism into a structure of liberties equally available to everyone.

This account is not wholly inaccurate. Historically, liberals have indeed been intent on freeing individuals from the clutches of arbitrary power, and as champions of liberty they have advocated the dispersal of authority through society on the assumption that the mass of people can be trusted to act responsibly without interference from the state. The next chapter indicates how Edmund Burke's *Reflections on the Revolution in France* (1790), a classic statement of conservatism, was a reaction to Enlightenment optimism, the belief that in principle all individuals could make sense of the human world and so co-operate to demolish unjust social and political structures. Burke, by contrast, warned of the danger of supposing that society could be dramatically reconstructed in the light of principles that were within the compass of every individual mind. The established order was the product of historical experience, according to Burke, and only arrogant individuals could imagine that their 'private stock' of reason was a more reliable guide in public affairs than the 'general bank and capital of nations, and of ages'. It was naive to suppose that political arrangements should be accountable to reason uninformed by tradition. And the legitimate custodians of tradition were what Burke termed a 'natural aristocracy', 'chieftains' who knew better than the people themselves how they ought to be governed:

> To enable men to act with the weight and character of a people, and to answer the ends for which they are incorporated into that capacity, we must suppose them (by means immediate or consequential) to be in that state of habitual social discipline, in which the wiser, the more expert, and the more opulent conduct, and by conducting enlighten and protect the weaker, the less knowing, and the less provided with the goods of fortune. When the multitude are not under this discipline, they can scarcely be said to be in civil society.

For Burke, then, a properly organised society consists of a hierarchy or chain of command rather than a structure in which individuals enjoy an equal right to be involved in public affairs, or at least to hold government to account through democratic elections.

One expression of those egalitarian assumptions of the Enlightenment which offended conservatives was the Declaration of Independence, by which in 1776 Americans announced that they were no longer a British colony:

We hold these truths to be self-evident, that all men are created equal, that they are endowed by their Creator with certain inalienable Rights, that among these are Life, Liberty, and the pursuit of Happiness. That to secure these rights, Governments are instituted among Men, deriving their just powers from the consent of the governed. – That whenever any Form of Government becomes destructive of these ends, it is the Right of the People to alter or abolish it, and to institute a new Government, laying its foundation on such principles and organizing its powers in such form, as to them shall seem most likely to effect their Safety and Happiness.

Contained in this passage are the principles not only of the Enlightenment but of a progressive liberalism. For besides provoking a conservative ideological backlash, the American and French revolutions stimulated some particularly clear expressions of a liberal perspective: the belief that society is a structure of equal rights in which all are citizens, not a chain of discipline separating a minority of rulers from the mass of subjects; impatience with those like Burke who shrouded political authority in mystery, instead of judging it by principles that are within the grasp of individual reason; and the conviction not only that government should be democratically accountable, but that in large areas of life individuals are responsible enough to manage their affairs without assistance from a paternalist or busybody state. Whereas Burke feared that the 'private stock' of individual reason undisciplined by law and convention would result in the dissolution of 'civil society', Enlightenment liberals argued that civil society would be vibrant only in so far as the state refrained from trespassing upon individual rights and liberties.

A prominent representative of the kind of Enlightenment thinking detested by Burke was Tom Paine (1737–1809), who left England in 1774 to support the American struggle for independence, later joining the French in their revolution against the *ancien régime*. Paine, whose *Rights of Man* (1791–2) was subtitled *An Answer to Mr Burke's Attack on the French Revolution*, was an exponent of the progressive spirit of the age which we now associate with early liberalism. The Burkean appeal to tradition was an attempt to deflect people from questioning their subordination to illegitimate aristocratic authority, according to Paine, and he repudiated conservative inegalitarianism by claiming that individuals are born with a natural right – by which he meant an innate capacity and equal entitlement – to manage their own affairs. This meant that government had to be based upon the consent of those to whom its authority extended, which for Paine entailed regular democratic elections. If individuals were capable of self-government, moreover, the state had a responsibility not to encroach upon private judgement in, for example, matters of opinion or religion. Paine began *The Age of Reason* (1795–6), in which he ridiculed religious orthodoxies and ecclesiastical establishments, by pronouncing that 'my own mind is my own church'.

Burke, comparing the bodies politic and human, likened the 'natural aristocracy' to the head of the human body whose function was to co-ordinate and direct the other members. But for Paine, displaying Enlightenment impatience with traditional vindications of social hierarchy, Burke's paternalist image of political society as a human body writ large was but an attempt to portray aristocratic exploitation of the majority as natural and just. The proper image of a polity was one in which authority flowed not downward to subjects from an unaccountable elite, as Burke suggested, but inward to the centre from the democratic decisions of rational, responsible, essentially self-governing citizens. 'A nation is not a body,' Paine argued in response to Burke, 'the figure of which is to be represented by the human body, but is like a body contained within a circle, having a common centre in which every radius meets; and that centre is formed by representation.' This confidence in the capacity of ordinary people to understand and control the human world, coupled with an urge to topple institutions that failed the test of reason, lay at the heart of Enlightenment liberalism.

One means of highlighting the differences between Burke and Paine is to suggest that, whereas one endorsed the politics of mistrust, the other celebrated the politics of trust. Burke, in characteristically conservative manner, warned of the dangerous political consequences of unrestrained private judgement. Individuals are frail and fallible, according to this pessimistic account of human nature, and left to their own devices they are likely to engage in behaviour that is morally reprehensible and politically disruptive. Hence the need for a disciplinary state which curbs predatory and antisocial impulses through a firm system of law and order. For Paine, in the spirit of Enlightenment liberalism, individuals can by and large be trusted to exercise their judgement in a manner of benefit to themselves and the wider community. Hence the need for a vigorous civil society, immune from state interference, in which individuals may freely associate, formulate opinions, and follow the dictates of conscience in matters such as religion. So perhaps liberals are not inaccurate in depicting their movement as a continual endeavour to create a structure of liberties available to every citizen.

Individual freedom is clearly a primary liberal value. But a commitment to liberty is insufficient to distinguish liberalism from other doctrines. Freedom is one of those elastic concepts whose meanings can be stretched to convey a range of contrary political messages, and as such is prominent in most ideological perspectives on society. Conservatives, particularly those of the New Right or free-market variety, tend to equate freedom with the unhindered pursuit of economic self-interest. Hence their claim in Britain during the 1980s to be liberating the nation by reducing state regulation of the economy. For socialists, however, conservative freedom is licence for a few entrepreneurs to exploit the mass of people, unrestrained by any government responsibility to ensure social justice by redistributing wealth from rich to poor. A free society, according to socialists, is one in which everyone has access to those material resources without which the human potential is thwarted. And this requires the state to combat the inequalities of the capitalist economy through, for example, the provision of a minimum wage and the collective provision of health care and of social welfare.

The difference between these rival conceptions of freedom is often characterised as a debate as to whether liberty is something negative or positive

(Berlin, 1969). Individuals are free, according to free-market conservatives who favour a negative conception of liberty, in so far as they are left alone by government or other external agencies to pursue their private ambitions and shape their lives in the light of particular preferences. But individuals cannot be free, socialists retort, unless government assumes active responsibility for the public good in order to ensure that everyone has access to the necessities of a worthwhile existence.

The problem is that during the course of its history liberalism has encompassed the contrary meanings which conservatives and socialists attach to freedom. In challenging arbitrary power and aristocratic privilege, early liberals sought to push back the frontiers of the state. Individual freedom, they argued, depended upon the enjoyment of certain civil liberties immune from government interference, including the right to accumulate property as well as to express opinions and follow conscience in religious matters. In this sense early liberals would seem to have endorsed the conservative conviction that liberty flourishes in a free-enterprise society which imposes few restrictions upon the pursuit of individual ambition. Towards the end of the nineteenth century, however, many liberals abandoned this ideal of a minimal state in which the right to acquire private property was sacrosanct. The gross inequalities of competitive capitalism, they now acknowledged, impaired the freedom of people whose struggle for survival afforded them little opportunity to make the best of their capacities. These progressive or 'new' liberals, as they are some-times described, advocated political intervention in the economy to eliminate unemployment and low wages, as well as urging public provision of health care and other welfare rights.

In distinguishing themselves from their predecessors, the new liberals sometimes used the terms *negative* and *positive* liberty. Earlier liberals were mistaken, they suggested, in viewing society as an arena of self-sufficient and competitive individuals who were free to the extent that they could pursue private interests without coercion. A less individualistic perspective was now required, according to this argument, one which envisaged society as a collectivity of mutually dependent individuals unable to make the best of themselves unless government assumes responsibility for a public good transcending the private interests of a wealthy minority. Only a more active and interventionist state, then, could make a reality of the right to equal citizenship.

New liberals, in rejecting the faith of their predecessors in unbridled capitalism, concur with socialists that freedom is enhanced rather than restricted by the political elimination of poverty and social deprivation. The link between freedom and the collective provision of the material necessities of life was made by Elliott Dodds in a book which, when published in 1957, was announced as the most comprehensive statement in thirty years of the philosophy of British liberalism.

> We argue that Welfare is actually a form of Liberty in as much as it liberates men from social conditions which narrow their choices and thwart their

self-development as truly as any governmental or personal coercions. At any rate both, in the Liberal view, have this in common that they should be regarded as means to the full and harmonious development of persons. But the 'new' freedoms differ from the old in that they call for positive measures, whereas the 'old' freedoms require simply the abolition of restraints. Their establishment, though in many ways extending the field for free action, involves restrictions which did not exist before.

(Watson, 1957: 17)

But though sharing with socialists a distaste for the gross inequalities of a market economy, new liberals have been reluctant entirely to discard the assumption of their predecessors that a system of economic competition is just in that it distributes rewards on the basis of individual merit. The following passage is taken from Nancy Sear's chapter in the book to which Dodds contributed. If the word 'Liberal' were deleted, her sentiments could be read as a manifesto of free-market conservatism.

The Liberal society cannot be an egalitarian society, since freedom includes the freedom to make headway or to fall back, and liberals cannot agree to restrict the energetic in the interest of the leisurely. On the contrary we should try to ensure equality of opportunity, accepting the implication that those who seize opportunities will go faster and farther than those who do not.

(Watson, 1957: 192)

In some respects, then, modern liberals appear to sit uncomfortably astride the ideological worlds of conservatism and socialism. With conservatives they wish to define freedom as the right of individuals to strive for inequalities of wealth, and yet, like socialists, they want to argue that liberty is diminished unless everyone is given access to the resources necessary for a decent life.

Does the fact that liberalism embraces these conflicting meanings of freedom mean that a firm boundary cannot be drawn between the doctrine and its rivals, and also that the ideology is essentially incoherent? There is a tendency among some academic commentators to depict the transformation of liberalism at the end of the nineteenth century as a seismic shift splitting the ideology into two irreconcilable halves. One argument, favoured by the left, is that liberalism was conceptually robust during its classical phase when the emphasis was upon rolling back the state from civil society in order to eliminate arbitrary power and aristocratic privilege. Liberals had been too energetic pronouncing the desirability of negative liberty to make a plausible case for an economically interventionist state, in this view, and as a consequence their doctrine disintegrated with the passing of the age of *laissez-faire* (Laski, 1940). Arguments of this sort reinforce the impression that there is now little to liberalism beyond those decent sentiments conveyed by the adjective 'liberal', and that the ideology is so nebulous as to embrace all of a generous disposition who favour an open society which tolerates individual differences. A liberal can be expected to dislike authoritarian political regimes, preferring those which give their citizens ample space for self-expression. But does the noun 'liberalism' now signify little else than this disposition to respect individual diversity?

What is clear is that liberty is one of those ambiguous concepts about which there is disagreement as to both its meaning and the social conditions in which it is secured. So to claim that a commitment to freedom is at the core of liberalism is insufficient to identify the doctrine's distinctive characteristics. Of greater analytical value is the recognition that liberalism, in affirming the primacy of freedom, is in a significant sense an egalitarian doctrine. This does not necessarily mean, as one commentator suggests (Dworkin, 1978), that the commitment of liberals to equality takes priority over their attachment to liberty. It does mean that they want freedom to be shared equally through society, for in valuing liberty they commit themselves to the proposition that everyone should enjoy as much of it as possible.

Now the claim that individuals are equally entitled to freedom does not in itself resolve the problem of determining the doctrine's identity. It begs the question of which particular liberties should be made available to everyone. Classical liberals believed that authoritarian government was the greatest threat to individual freedom, and so sought to extend the sphere of civil liberties as a safeguard against arbitrary power; whereas later liberals identify minimal or economically inactive government as an impediment to the equal enjoyment of freedom, and in consequence advocate the collective provision of social or welfare rights. There has been little continuity of agreement among liberals about the policies needed to enhance liberty. What nevertheless emerges from the varieties of liberalism is a persistent image of the good society as an association of free persons who are equal in their possession of basic rights. So the manner in which liberals have tended to couple the concepts of liberty and equality does lend to their doctrine a certain coherence and particular social perspective.

A bourgeois creed?

Historically, then, liberalism can be viewed as having endorsed a succession of strategies for extending the freedoms to which everyone is considered to be equally entitled. But there is a further issue to be tackled in order fully to identify the doctrine's distinctive features. This is the charge of commentators that liberalism is a narrowly individualistic creed which legitimates the maximisation of private satisfactions without regard to the public good. The argument is that, in emphasising the sanctity of individual rights, liberals have an impoverished sense of community and of the requirements of citizenship.

Now in a loose sense liberalism is evidently a bourgeois ideology. From its inception the doctrine conveyed ideas associated with the disintegration of feudal society and the eventual triumph of capitalism, and among its exponents were those who stood to gain from an erosion of aristocratic privilege and the wider accumulation of property. In liberal accounts of the struggle to emancipate individuals from the shackles of traditional society, moreover, the middle classes have not infrequently been cast as the heroes of the story. In *Vindicae Gallicae*, which like Paine's *Rights of Man* rebutted Burke's vindication of the *ancien régime*, James Mackintosh depicted the bourgeoisie as the personification of the values of Enlightenment liberalism:

> The commercial, or monied interest, has in all nations of Europe (taken as a body) been less prejudiced, more liberal, and more intelligent, than the landed gentry. Their views are enlarged by a wider intercourse with mankind, and hence the important influence of commerce in liberalizing the modern world. We cannot wonder then that this enlightened class of men ever prove the most ardent in the cause of freedom; the most zealous for political reform. It is not wonderful that philosophy should find in them more docile pupils; and liberty more active friends, than in a haughty and prejudiced aristocracy.
>
> (Mackintosh, 1792)

For some commentators, however, liberalism is a bourgeois creed in the stronger sense that its adherents celebrate the acquisitive values associated with the pursuit of self-interest in a competitive economy, and in doing so operate with an atomistic conception of the individual. The 'emphasis on the asocial egoism of the individual', according to Anthony Arblaster, 'plays a permanently important part in liberalism. Without taking it into account it is impossible to understand the importance which liberalism attaches to the principles of personal freedom and privacy' (Arblaster, 1984). The basis of this claim is that unlike conservatives such as Burke, who emphasise the inability of people to detach themselves from the traditions and conventions of a particular community, liberals often depict individuals as curiously abstracted from the society they happen to inhabit.

Early liberals challenged arbitrary power by appealing to universal principles. Individuals were said to come into the world with certain natural or inalienable rights, by which was meant an innate capacity and equal entitlement to manage their economic, religious and other affairs. In the words of the seventeenth-century English philosopher John Locke (1632–1704), whose *Two Treatises of Government* (1690) is a classic exposition of this doctrine of natural rights, human beings are born 'in a state of perfect freedom, to order their actions and dispose of their possessions, and persons, as they see fit'. As residents in political society, runs the argument, individuals are entitled to retain their natural freedom in the form of constitutionally safeguarded civil liberties, and this requires a government that is both bound by the rule of law and limited in scope. Its role is that of an 'umpire', as Locke put it, upholding an impartial framework of law and order within which individuals may safely pursue their private concerns. The thrust of the argument was that legitimate government is rooted in the consent of those to whom its authority extends. To cite the *Two Treatises* again:

> Men being, as has been said, by Nature, all free, equal and independent, no one can be put out of this Estate, and subjected to the Political Power of another, without his own *Consent*. The only way whereby any one divests himself of his Natural Liberty, and *puts on the bonds of Civil Society* is by agreeing with other Men to join and unite into a Community, for their comfortable, safe and peaceable living one amongst another, in a secure Enjoyment of their Properties, and a greater Security against any that are not of it.

The inference of this consensual theory of political society is that government ought to be accountable to those whose rights it purports to protect, and the principal message of the *Two Treatises* was that arbitrary power might legitimately be resisted by the 'body of the people'.

So the doctrine of natural rights was a conceptual device by which early liberals challenged political authoritarianism. But the doctrine did tend to view individuals as abstract entities, conveying the impression that what is essential to human existence does not depend upon social relations and, further, that membership of political association is of instrumental value in protecting personal freedoms. This is the basis of the suggestion that classical liberalism was grounded in a form of bourgeois or 'possessive' individualism sanctioning the pursuit of private goals, particularly the acquisition of riches, at the expense of wider social obligations (Macpherson, 1968). The 'great and chief end of men entering into commonwealths and putting themselves under government', according to the *Two Treatises*, 'is the preservation of their property'. There is a sense, then, in which liberalism can be taken to endorse a form of government which permits individuals to accumulate property and indulge in other private pursuits without any obligation to co-operate on behalf of the public good.

The tendency to characterise liberalism as a narrowly individualist creed has been reinforced by some historical scholarship. Historians of political thought such as J. G. A. Pocock distinguish Lockean liberalism from what they describe as a classical republican or civic humanist tradition of political discourse, articulated by James Harrington and others in the seventeenth century and subsequently refined into a condemnation of government patronage and corruption (Pocock, 1975). Whereas, the argument runs, early liberals licensed the pursuit of private goals, radicals of the civic humanist tradition were inspired by the ancient Greek and Roman ideal of a community whose members set aside self-interest by participating in public affairs for the common good. Although many of these radicals concurred with Locke that individuals were entitled to rights against the state, including the right to resist arbitrary power, their emphasis was upon the individual and social benefits of active citizenship. Through participation in public affairs citizens supposedly fulfilled their human potential as well as preventing political corruption. So rivalling the early liberal discourse of natural rights and individual self-sufficiency, according to recent historiography, was one which celebrated civic virtue and communal solidarity.

Like historians of political thought, some political theorists have depicted liberalism as an individualistic doctrine. What has become known as the communitarian critique of liberalism has focused upon John Rawls's *A Theory of Justice*, published in 1971 and regarded as the paradigmatic statement of twentieth-century liberalism. Rawls, an American philosopher, considers what principles of a fair and 'well-ordered' society are most likely to generate widespread assent among its members. His approach is to postulate an hypothetical situation in which free and rational individuals debate the ground rules that would enable them to live together in a polity. Such individuals, according to Rawls, would agree, first, that everyone is equally entitled to basic civil liberties and, secondly, on the desirability of redistributive welfare policies to ensure equality of opportunity. Of relevance is less the consensus about principles of justice which Rawls attributes to the 'original position' – as he describes the natural condition in which individuals discuss the terms of their political co-operation – as the fact that his hypothetical account of the origins of government is in the tradition of Lockean contractualism. This is why the Rawlsian theory of justice is taken by communitarians to confirm that liberalism has a weak sense of society. For both Locke and Rawls consider the foundations of a sound political society by abstracting individuals from it. And in making the self independent of and logically prior to the community in which it resides, communitarians contend, liberals conceive of political association as an instrumental arrangement for people pursuing essentially private interests.

This accusation of asocial individualism can be legitimately made against free-market conservatives who sometimes depict society as a collection of competitive individuals joined by a common desire for security rather than by an awareness of citizenship. 'There is no such thing as society,' Margaret Thatcher pronounced on one occasion, 'there are only individuals'. But there is little evidence, in spite of the communitarian critique, that liberalism is a form of possessive individualism sanctioning the pursuit of private goals without regard to wider concerns. There is a sense of the common good even among those liberals, from Locke to Rawls, who have grounded government in the hypothetical consent of naturally independent individuals. Fair political arrangements are not only the shared achievement of free and equal individuals, according to this theory, they are maintained by vigilant citizenship alert to the danger of arbitrary power. Locke argued that the 'body of the people' had a right to resist unjust government, and later liberals have advocated democratic elections and other forms of public participation. For Rawls the preservation of fair democratic institutions is itself a common good achieved, as he writes in *A Theory of Justice*, 'through citizens' joint activity in mutual dependence on the appropriate action being taken by others'. Among early liberals, too, there was a conviction that a healthy polity presupposes a moral community of public-spirited individuals co-operating in pursuit of common objectives. Historians such as J. G. A. Pocock, we have seen, highlight the existence of two competing political discourses in the seventeenth and eighteenth centuries: the liberal one of individual rights as against the classical republican language of civic virtue. The differences between these discourses have been exaggerated, in my view, because the classical republican ideal of citizen self-government was a hallmark of liberalism itself.

For early liberals this ideal of citizen self-rule was to be achieved through the dispersal of power and authority from existing elites to a much larger body of people. Central to their strategy was a belief in the benefits of widespread ownership of property. Private property, they argued, engenders in its owners the moral discipline and mutual tolerance by which a just society is sustained. In this loose sense liberals did indeed construct a bourgeois ideology, arguing as they did that a well ordered society depends upon virtues associated with the acquisition of private property. In endorsing the spread of bourgeois attitudes through society, however, their wish was to promote, not the asocial egoism of a self unencumbered by public responsibilities, but the virtues of citizens conscious of their obligations within the body politic.

To facilitate this process of *embourgeoisement*, early liberals advocated a twofold strategy that has remained a characteristic of the doctrine. They sought, on one hand, to undermine the power of inherited wealth derived from the ownership of land. The aristocracy was depicted as an idle and parasitic class which reaped an unearned income from rent, and whose privilege and monopolies prevented others from achieving independence. Its ethos of paternalism, moreover, was said to foster among the mass of the population an attitude of deference that was incompatible with a life of autonomy and citizenship. And so, on the other side, liberals wished to make the labouring classes virtuous. In becoming prudent and self-reliant, it was said, the poor would free themselves from dependence on the aristocracy, as well as acquiring those civic virtues which ensured political stability. Historically, then, liberals have been hostile to the undeserved benefits of aristocratic privilege, and also intent on the moral elevation of the poor. This persistent impulse to universalise bourgeois virtues provides a significant clue in the search for the ideology's identity.

The image that emerges from the concern of liberals to make everyone virtuous through the implementation of equal rights is of a one-class society in which, despite inequalities of wealth, there are common habits of self-discipline and responsible citizenship. It differs from the conservative picture of a class or command structure in which the rich and powerful exercise leadership and discipline over the majority, and also from the socialist ideal of a classless society which eliminates the inequalities of economic competition.

A brief history

This persistent ideal of a community of free, independent, propertied and virtuous citizens can be illustrated by glancing at the ideology's evolution in a British context.

In its classical phase, we have seen, liberalism took shape around the idea of natural rights, a concept which was given clear expression during the Civil War period of the 1640s. The conflict between royalists and parliamentarians unleashed a torrent of radical thinking in which the traditional image of society as a rigid hierarchy was displaced by that of a structure of equal rights where individuals exercise autonomy in crucial areas of their lives. Among these radicals were the Levellers, a group formed in 1646, whose extensive programme of political reform took its bearings from the assumption of natural freedom and equality. In *The Freeman's Freedom Vindicated* (1646) a Leveller leader, John Lilburne, articulated the view pivotal to natural rights doctrine: that no form of authority is legitimate unless grounded in the consent of those affected by it.

> Unnatural, irrational, sinful, wicked, unjust, devilish, and tyrannical it is, for any man whatsoever, spiritual or temporal, clergyman or layman, to appropriate and assume unto himself a power, authority and jurisdiction, to rule, govern, or reign over any sort of men in the world, without their free consent.

The 'freeborn' English had been deprived of their fundamental liberties with the introduction during the Norman Conquest of a system of hereditary privilege, according to the Levellers, but the time had come to reclaim those freedoms through the dispersal of power and wealth from elites to the people at large.

Leveller proposals for redistributing authority to ordinary people included a written constitution to protect civil liberties by ensuring that government was bound by the rule of law and also limited in scope. Prominent among these liberties was the right to follow conscience in spiritual matters. Leveller antipathy to religious orthodoxy and ecclesiastical hierarchy derived from the radical Protestant commitment to the priesthood of all believers, which meant that everyone was entitled to choose their own way to truth in a society practising toleration and permitting heterodoxy.

The Leveller programme also advocated the abolition of monarchy and the House of Lords, perceived to be bastions of arbitrary power and economic privilege, and the establishment of a representative Commons elected annually by a larger electorate than before. How large has been a matter of dispute among commentators, deriving from their disagreement as to whether liberalism is a narrowly bourgeois creed. The Levellers appear to have been reluctant to endorse universal suffrage, excluding from their proposals for an extended franchise servants, alms takers as well as women. One explanation is that Levellers were early exponents of a possessive individualism that licensed the pursuit of economic self-interest (Macpherson, 1968). In linking the vote with property ownership, runs the argument, they revealed their conviction that individuals who failed successfully to compete in a market economy thereby forfeited the right to be a citizen. But though Leveller radicalism was certainly moderated by patriarchal and other prevailing assumptions, their caution about the extent of the suffrage did not necessarily stem from an impulse to endorse the inequalities of embryonic capitalism. A more plausible explanation of their readiness to exclude servants and alms takers from the suffrage was the view that, as Maximilian Petty suggested at the time, such 'persons depend upon the will of other men and should be afraid to displease them'. The Leveller objection to aristocratic privilege was that it sustained a hierarchy of social relations – ruler and subject, master and servant – contrary to the natural human condition of freedom and equality. Those at the bottom of the hierarchy, Levellers believed, were unable to make autonomous political choices because of the mechanisms of social control ensuring their subordination to landlords.

The Leveller strategy for restoring the natural condition of freedom and equality was to construct a society in which no one depended upon the will of another. Without intending to 'level mens Estates, destroy Propriety, or make all things Common', as their manifesto, *An Agreement of the Free People of England*, put it, the Levellers nevertheless proposed to disperse property ownership as widely as possible by eliminating economic monopolies, the practice of primogeniture and other bulwarks of landed privilege. In this way those groups dependent on aristocratic paternalism, including servants and alms takers, would eventually disappear, enabling every adult male to enjoy full political rights in a property-owning democracy. Allied to Leveller measures for ensuring the economic self-sufficiency of the poor was an educational plan to make them literate and knowledgeable. A community of educated and masterless individuals would consist of virtuous citizens, according to the Levellers, exercising their birthright as freeborn Englishmen in a civilised manner.

So the Levellers were not narrowly bourgeois ideologues who anticipated a new age of capital accumulation and wage labour. Their ideal was a society of independent proprietors, enjoying ample space within civil society to shape their lives in a responsible manner, respecting the liberties of others, and using their rights as citizens to co-operate in ensuring the preservation of a fair and just polity. Here was the image that recurred in later liberal writings: a one-class community of autonomous citizens, each responsible for his own affairs and making a particular contribution to the common good.

The Leveller conception of democracy was gendered. Women did not need to be enfranchised, even radicals assumed, because their welfare and interests were included in those of their husbands as household heads. This inclination to exclude women from citizenship persisted until the nineteenth century. Not all liberals, moreover, were as eager as the Levellers to redistribute wealth more evenly through the community as a prelude to full citizenship.

In the eighteenth century those claiming to be heirs of the struggles of the previous century against absolute monarchy and religious conformity were the Whigs, who favoured a system of parliamentary government and a degree of religious toleration. They were liberal in endorsing civil liberties, but it was a 'thin' sort of liberalism. As men of wealth and rank, many of them beneficiaries of government patronage, many Whigs neither opposed aristocratic privilege nor advocated democracy, which they equated with rule by the rabble. Government was best left to a propertied minority, they believed, with enough of an economic 'stake' in the community to know better than the masses themselves what was in their political interests. Hence the Whig preference for the English system of mixed government where King, Lords and Commons checked one another against arbitrary power because of their overlapping powers, and in which the 'popular' branch of the legislature was elected by men of substantial property.

These 'conservative' Whigs, embarrassed by that aspect of their ideological legacy which gave credence to demands for political and economic equality, often sidestepped the concept of natural rights. But from the middle of the century, responding to an increasing demand of radicals for an extension of civil and political liberties, they sought to undermine the concept by attacking John Locke as its principal proponent. Having characterised Locke as 'the Idol of the Levellers of England', Josiah Tucker proceeded in *Four Letters on Important National Subjects* (1783) to explain why the mass of people were politically incompetent:

> When a Multitude are invested with the Power of governing, they prove the very worst of Governors. They are rash and precipitate, giddy and inconstant, and ever the Dupes of designing Men, who lead them to commit the most atrocious Crimes, in order to make them subservient to their own Purposes. Besides, a democratic Government is despotic in its very Nature; because it supposes itself to be the only Fountain of Power, from which there can be no Appeal. Hence, therefore, it comes to pass, that this many headed Monster, an absolute Democracy, has all the Vices and Imperfections of its Brother-Tyrant, an absolute Monarchy, without any of the shining Qualities of the latter to hide its Deformity.

Tucker then extolled the virtues of mixed government in which the 'hereditary Nobility' were pivotal in preserving the balance of the constitution.

This vindication of inherited wealth was a world removed from the Leveller assault upon every form of customary privilege. Whig support for limited government and religious toleration provided a tenuous link with the radicalism of the previous century. Yet the liberal kernel – if liberal it really was – of aristocratic Whiggism was contained within a conservative shell. There was a point, probably reached with the denunciation of natural rights thinking, when establishment liberalism – if we can so describe Whiggism – lost touch with its doctrinal roots and shaded into conservatism. Edmund Burke made conformity to tradition rather than natural rights the measure of a fair and just polity, and his eloquent defence of social hierarchy earned him a reputation as a scourge of Enlightenment liberalism and the progenitor of English conservatism. Burke was a Whig.

Although most eighteenth-century Whigs retreated from the radicalism of the previous century, others continued to resort to the idea of natural rights to urge the extension of civil liberties and political rights. In the early decades of the century some of them, disturbed by what they perceived as a tendency to financial corruption and executive tyranny by the Whig establishment, followed the Levellers in advocating a more even spread of private property as a bulwark against arbitrary power. In *Cato's Letters*, popular expressions of radical Whiggism that appeared as newspaper articles in the 1720s, John Trenchard proposed the implementation of an agrarian law to ensure a more equitable distribution of wealth, as well as other measures to extend individual liberties. Economically self-sufficient individuals with a firm sense of their own autonomy within a structure of equal rights, argued Trenchard, would be model citizens alert to the dangers of arbitrary power.

> Every Man's honest Industry and useful Talents, while they are employed for the Publick, will be employed for himself; and while he serves himself, he will serve the Publick: Publick and private Interest will secure each other; all will cheerfully give a Part to secure the Whole, and be brave to defend it.

Here again was the ideal of a community of self-reliant and politically responsible individuals.

The concept of natural rights was also used by dissenters in their bid for greater religious freedom. Their principal target was the Test and Corporation Acts, which entrenched the privileges of the established church by reserving many public offices for Anglicans. A state religion, according to dissenters, violated the natural condition of freedom and equality by infringing the sovereignty of private judgement in spiritual matters. It was the business of government, wrote Richard Price in *The Evidence for a Future Period of Improvement in the State of Mankind* (1787), 'to defend the *properties* of men, not to take care of their *souls* – And to protect *equally* all honest citizens of all persuasions, not to set up one religious sect above another'. A society enshrining natural freedom in its arrangements would consist of religious denominations that were voluntary and equal.

By the time Price was writing radicals such as Paine, we have seen, were demanding equality not only of civil liberties but of political rights by means of manhood suffrage. The failure of Britain to become a democratic republic at the time of the French revolution spurred radicals to use the idea of universal rights well into the next century. The *Nonconformist* weekly, established by the Reverend Edward Miall, campaigned for the disestablishment of the Church of England and the admission of all adult males to the suffrage, depicting the latter as a means of nurturing a virtuous citizenry no longer inhibited by attitudes of deference and subordination. Not only were labouring men entitled to the vote as a natural right, according to the *Nonconformist*, their enfranchisement would be an incentive to acquire those virtues of self-discipline and mutual respect by which a sound polity is sustained. *Reconciliation between the Middle and Labouring Classes* (1842), which consisted of articles printed in the *Nonconformist*, depicted democracy as an educative process of benefit to individuals and the community:

> Only let the poor be taken politically by the hand – placed on a level with other classes – brought forward into association with these whose social

position is above them – and the spirit within them will naturally awake to new life, and become sensible to wants before unknown. Education will not need then to be forced upon the poor. They will pant for education. Man soon accommodates himself to a new sphere, when once he is allowed to move in it – seldom qualifies himself for that sphere before he is called to occupy it. Raise the tone of his self-respect by raising his position, and you awaken in his bosom an honourable ambition to act his part with becoming dignity. The extension to the people of complete suffrage, so far from exciting insubordination, would, calculating upon the ordinary laws of human nature, give a mighty impulse to popular intelligence and morality; and in the course of a short time would secure an amount of education, order, and even religion, which no other means could possibly effect.

The great *consideratum* of society is that all classes should be guided in their conduct by systematic self-government, rather than by the external restraints of law. But men never care to obey, themselves, until they receive from others the respect to which they are entitled. Until then, apart from religion, with which human governments have nothing to do, the grand motive is wanting – the inner spring is sealed up – and men are what they are forced to be, rather than what they wish to be. The way to make them aspire is not to treat them as things of nought – to make them love order and revere law is not to refuse them the benefits of order, and turn law into an engine for their oppression. Place them where they are entitled to be, give them what they are entitled to have, and whilst you take away the main inducement to insubordination, you supply at the same time the main motive to industrious, sober, and peaceable behaviour . . .

So manhood suffrage would provide the poor with that sense of autonomy from which civic virtue flowed.

By this time the case for an extension of individual liberties tended to be made without recourse to the idea of natural rights. The concept did not feature in Adam Smith's *Wealth of Nations* (1776), the classic statement on behalf of a free-market economy. His arguments for a 'system of natural liberty', as Smith described an economy in which individuals can pursue their interests unencumbered by government intervention, are often cited as evidence that liberalism is the narrowly individualistic creed depicted by some commentators, and also that the mantle of the doctrine in its classical phase has been inherited by free-market conservatives. In using the discourse of a competitive economy, however, eighteenth and nineteenth-century liberals were neither licensing the maximisation of private interest without regard to the common good nor defending the inequalities and privileges of capitalist enterprise. The idea of an unbridled economy was a means by which they continued to condemn the privileges of inherited wealth and advocate greater scope for individual autonomy on the part of ordinary people.

The New Right of the 1980s is sometimes said to have been in the tradition of the nineteenth-century Manchester school of liberalism. But members of the

Manchester school, unlike free-market conservatives, were intent on eliminating prevailing inequalities. Some of them were involved in a free-trade movement which culminated in 1846 with the abolition of tariffs on imported grain. The Corn Laws, they believed, inflated the price of domestic bread, and were therefore a form of taxation on the poor for the benefit of landowners. The leaders of the Anti-Corn Law League, Richard Cobden and John Bright, attributed current injustices to the system of hereditary privilege introduced with the Norman Conquest – as the Levellers had done – and they argued that the balanced constitution extolled by mainstream Whigs was designed to preserve the undeserved wealth of the 'great territorial families of England'. Cobden and Bright linked their arguments against economic protectionism with proposals, including household suffrage and an educational scheme, to enable the mass of people to attain that independence on which virtuous citizenship was said to depend. Instead of being used to endorse the acquisitive impulses of competitive individuals, then, the concept of a free economy underpinned the liberal vision of a society of autonomous citizens equal in their possession of basic rights.

The concept of natural rights was absent too from the writings of John Stuart Mill (1806–73), one of the most influential of British liberal thinkers. Mill argued that individuals who were secure in their independence and intent on fulfilling themselves would contribute to the welfare and progress of society, and in this sense his work was a sophisticated expression of the familiar assumption that a sound polity emanates from a virtuous citizenry. Of interest are the novelty of Mill's arguments and his proposals for constructing a community in which autonomous individuals co-operate in the pursuit of shared objectives. *On Liberty* (1859) was in some respects an orthodox, though elegant, argument for limited government that did not encroach upon civil liberties. But whereas earlier liberals had condemned arbitrary government, Mill used the concept of liberty to warn of the danger of the tyranny of public opinion. In modern society, according to Mill, there were growing pressures to conform which inhibited individual spontaneity and cultural diversity. Without the space for individual experimentation with life, however, the human potential would be thwarted and society would stagnate.

Mill's desire for a more open, pluralist society shaped his attitude to democracy. He favoured adult male and, unlike earlier liberals, female suffrage, linking the latter in *The Subjection of Women* (1869) with proposals to secure for women equal legal as well as political rights with men. Mill advocated universal suffrage partly on the ground that the disenfranchised were invariably exploited by those with political power, but also because the virtues of citizenship were cultivated by the exercise of democratic rights. The case which Mill made for democracy in *Thoughts on Parliamentary Reform* (1859) is not dissimilar from that put in the *Nonconformist*:

> It is important that every one of the governed should have a voice in the government, because it can hardly be expected that those who have no voice will be unjustly postponed to those who have. It is still more important

as one of the means of national education. A person who is excluded from all participation in political business is not a citizen. He has not the feelings of a citizen. To take an active interest in politics is, in modern times, the first thing which elevates the mind to large interests and contemplations; the first step out of the narrow bounds of individual and family selfishness, the first opening in the contracted round of daily occupations . . . The possession and the exercise of political, and among others of electoral, rights, is one of the chief instruments both of moral and of intellectual training for the popular mind; and all governments must be regarded as extremely imperfect, until every one who is required to obey the laws, has a voice, or the prospect of a voice, in their enactment and administration.

Although in favour of admitting everyone to the franchise, Mill advocated a graduated suffrage in which additional votes were awarded to those who by their occupation and professional qualifications 'could afford a reasonable presumption of superior knowledge and cultivation'. His intention in wishing to weight democracy in favour of enlightened opinion was to counteract what he described in *On Liberty* as the tyranny of 'collective mediocrity'. A system of plural voting, he hoped, would ensure that legislation reflected informed opinion.

Mill's preoccupation with the stifling of individuality by mass conformity may appear to run contrary to the liberal conviction that ordinary people can be trusted to act in a civilised manner. Like the Levellers, however, he believed that the labouring classes had been inhibited from practising the art of self-government by their subordination to a propertied minority. His strategy, also like that of the Levellers, was for a society in which everyone had both the incentive and the opportunity to be autonomous in a socially responsible manner. He believed that making the number of votes dependent on educational and other achievement would spur the poor to improve themselves. Another proposal, outlined in *Principles of Political Economy* (1848), was for a network of economic co-operatives in which workers themselves would own capital and take managerial decisions. The effect would be a 'moral revolution' providing the labouring classes with a sense of autonomy and of being engaged in the pursuit, not of competing private and sectional interests, but of a common good. Society had advanced to a stage where the poor had to be treated as citizens rather than subjects, Mill wrote in the same book, so that the 'prospect of the future depends on the degree in which they can be made rational beings'. The problem of how to universalise a disposition to intelligent self-government was one to which Mill persistently returned in his writings.

The liberal concern with virtuous citizenship prompted some writers in the decades after Mill's death to provide a sharper, more robust conceptualisation of the common good. In doing so they suggested that the state, as custodian of the public interest, had a responsibility to eliminate social and economic obstacles preventing individuals from making their particular contribution to the well-being of the community. Many of these 'new' or progressive liberals were influenced by the claim of the Oxford philosopher and Liberal city councillor,

T. H. Green (1836–82), that liberty ought to be understood not merely in a negative sense as the absence of external constraints upon individual conduct. Individual freedom was not necessarily secured through competition for scarce resources within the framework of a minimal state confined to preserving law and order. Individuals were free in so far as they fulfilled their potential for rational and moral conduct, according to Green, and for him this meant transcending the narrow concerns of self-interest to participate in a shared way of life. Freedom was to be understood, then, as a positive capacity for citizenship. In a famous lecture, 'Liberal Legislation and Freedom of Contract' (1881), Green said that government should 'maintain the conditions without which a free exercise of the human faculties is impossible' by emancipating the poor from ignorance, disease, squalid housing and exploitation at work. Advocates of a free-market economy believed that regulations of this sort would infringe the property rights of landlords and employers. Freedom, Green retorted, was not a licence for a minority to frustrate the potential of others to contribute to the common good by making the best of themselves.

Green did not think that the state had an enormous amount of work to do in removing social and economic impediments to virtuous citizenship. He believed, like earlier liberals, that most of the ills of British society derived from the system of hereditary privilege established at the Norman Conquest. The persistent influence of aristocratic power explained lingering attitudes of deference and subordination among the labouring classes, according to Green, as well as political reluctance to tackle the evils of landlordism. Once the feudal debris had been cleared by measures such as the taxation of inherited wealth, the poor would acquire the virtues of citizenship within a predominantly competitive economy.

Other liberals, influenced by Green's characterisation of freedom as the positive capacity of individuals to make the best of themselves, were less convinced of the efficacy of unregulated capitalism. What prompted them to formulate the philosophy of an enlarged state was the use made by advocates of a free economy, considered in the next chapter, of the Darwinian discourse of natural selection to contend that society progresses through a competitive struggle in which 'fit' entrepreneurs accumulate riches and the 'unfit' poor suffer the consequences of their incompetence. New liberals responded by formulating their own evolutionary theory to demonstrate that the 'unfitness' of the masses was perpetuated by government inactivity. L. T. Hobhouse (1864–1929), a prolific publicist of the new liberalism, detected in modern society the emergence of a higher form of morality because citizens were increasingly willing to set aside private interests for the sake of the common good. Among the manifestations of social progress was the spread of democratic values, a diminution of class conflicts, and a readiness to embody altruism in public policy through, for example, factory and sanitary legislation.

Hobhouse used his theory of evolutionary collectivism to justify a more extensive programme of social reform than Green had envisaged. In *Liberalism* (1911) he argued that the state ought to establish a 'living equality of rights' through welfare policies financed by taxation. Hobhouse's intention was to vindicate the measures implemented by the reforming Liberal government between 1906 and 1911, including the provision of old-age pensions and an insurance scheme for sickness and unemployment. In arguing for a minimum wage and other social rights, moreover, he discarded the assumption of earlier liberals that a market economy could provide everyone with the material basis of individual autonomy. Poverty and unemployment signified not a moral failure or character defect on the part of individuals, as Social Darwinists claimed, but the structural imperfections of an economy which invariably deprived some people of the necessities of a worthwhile existence. It was the business of government to deal with the flaws of market capitalism by mobilising the 'collective resources and organised power of the community for public needs'. Hobhouse challenged the idea that the rights of private property are sacrosanct by arguing that wealth is neither accumulated nor secured by individuals in isolation from one another. The social dimension of wealth creation entitled government to treat a proportion of individual income as surplus that could be taxed to provide the poor with a basic wage and other benefits.

Hobhouse derived the idea of a surplus from his friend, J. A. Hobson (1858–1940), who argued that the redistribution of wealth into a living wage for the poor would secure economic efficiency by providing them with new purchasing power. In *The Crisis of Liberalism* (1909), Hobson urged a measure of political regulation of the economy as well as welfare policies:

> Liberalism is now formally committed to a task which certainly involves a new conception of the State in its relation to the individual life and to private enterprise. That conception is not Socialism, in any accredited meaning of that term, though implying a considerable amount of increased public ownership and control of industry. From the standpoint which best presents its continuity with earlier Liberalism, it appears as a fuller appreciation and realisation of individual liberty contained in the provision of equal opportunities for self-development. But to this individual stand-point must be joined a just apprehension of the social, viz., the insistence that these claims or rights of self-development be adjusted to the sovereignty of social welfare.

A positive understanding of liberty as a capacity for human fulfilment entailed the public provision of welfare and other social rights, in this view, to achieve the conventional liberal ideal of equal freedom for everyone.

Two men, both members of the Liberal party, are regarded as the principal architects of the welfare or humanised capitalism which prevailed in Britain from 1945 until the ascendancy of the New Right in the 1980s. In *The General Theory of Employment, Interest and Money* (1936), J. M. Keynes (1883–1948) provided the classic vindication of a mixed economy in which the state assumes overall management of investment and consumption, while leaving production in the hands of private enterprise. This kind of hybrid economy preserved personal liberties and cultural diversity, according to Keynes, while eradicating mass unemployment and other social ills which nurtured authoritarian political regimes.

The other man, William Beveridge (1879–1963), an unsuccessful Liberal party candidate, wrote several reports in the 1940s which became the ideological foundation of the post-war welfare state. The business of government was to eliminate deprivation and unemployment, according to Beveridge, through such measures as comprehensive social insurance, free health care, the setting of a minimum wage and Keynesian management of the economy. Liberty, he told the Liberal Assembly:

> means more than freedom from the arbitrary power of Governments. It means freedom from economic servitude to Want and Squalor and other social evils; it means freedom from arbitrary power in any form. A starving man is not free, because till he is fed, he cannot have a thought for anything but how to meet his urgent physical needs; he is reduced from a man to an animal. A man who dare not resent what he feels to be an injustice from an employer or a foreman, lest this condemn him to chronic unemployment, is not free.

So the provision of full employment in a welfare state was another tactic in the liberal strategy to achieve equality of rights.

Conclusion

The principal argument of this chapter is that the coherence of liberalism is to be detected in the way in which a persistent commitment to an equal right to liberty has been given substance in different historical contexts. A related, less explicit, argument is that liberalism is essentially an ideology of the left. Its adherents have endorsed not the unrestrained egoism of enterprising individuals intent on capital accumulation, as commentators sometimes suggest, but the rights of citizens engaged in a mutual endeavour to sustain a just polity. Liberalism has always been a progressive ideology easily distinguished from forms of conservatism.

The final issue to be addressed is the location of liberalism in modern society. In Britain the doctrine has been attached to a political party for a comparatively short period of its history. The Liberal party was formed in the 1850s, began to lose electoral support during the First World War and merged with the Social Democratic party in the 1980s. The disappearance of the Liberal party does not necessarily signify the disintegration of liberalism as a set of principles embraced by people who believe in an equal right to freedom. Liberal Democrats, the name given to members of the party which emerged from the realignment of the 1980s, continue to berate their Labour and Conservative opponents for insufficient commitment to civil liberties and democratic accountability. Also, as in earlier centuries, those whom we identify as liberals may not describe themselves as such. Liberal values can be discerned, for example, in arguments against sexual and racial discrimination, on behalf of minority rights, and in a renewed campaign in Britain since the 1980s to safeguard citizens against arbitrary government through, for example, the establishment of a Bill of Rights or the introduction of a written constitution. Liberalism in a broad sense is diffused throughout society.

There are limits, however, to this diffusion. In the 1980s some conservatives were eager to unfurl the banner of liberalism in their crusade to roll back the state from the economy. But, notwithstanding endorsement from those commentators who depict the doctrine as a form of asocial individualism, the New Right was incorrect in perceiving itself as a reincarnation of classical liberalism. The free market, like the idea of liberty itself, is one of those slippery concepts that has been put to various political uses. Whereas classical liberals honed it into an assault upon every form of privilege and patronage, conservative individualists from Robert Peel to Margaret Thatcher have used it to defend the wealth and authority of a minority. The authoritarian individualism of the right has little in common with any form of liberalism.

Socialists can with greater legitimacy claim to have inherited the mantle of liberalism. With liberals, and unlike conservatives, they believe that a more even distribution of wealth is necessary to secure an equal right to freedom. The difference in the past is that some socialists have assumed that their objectives are incompatible with the continuation of a system of private property. 'We are not among those communists who are out to destroy personal liberty,' wrote Marx and Engels in the first issue of the *Communist Journal* (1847),

> who wish to turn the world into one huge barrack or into a gigantic work-house. There are certainly some communists who, with an easy conscience, refuse to countenance personal liberty and would like to shuffle it out of the world because they consider that it is a hindrance to complete harmony. But we have no desire to exchange freedom for equality. We are convinced . . . that in no social order will personal freedom be so assured as in a society based upon communal ownership.

The problem for socialists, of course, is that public ownership has been discredited by the failure of certain forms of state planning in Western societies and more spectacularly by the collapse from the late 1980s of communist regimes elsewhere. Hence the attraction now of 'market' and other forms of socialism whose adherents advocate a more even dispersal of wealth within a structure of private property and economic competition. But market socialism, though not described as such, has been a feature of liberal thinking since the Levellers.

So perhaps it is not surprising that socialists eager to proclaim the benefits of private enterprise sometimes tap into the narrative of progressive liberalism. After becoming leader of the Labour party in 1994, Tony Blair sought to distance himself from the commitment of the party's founders to Clause 4 state ownership.

Blair's preference, rather like that of J. S. Mill, is for a form of market communitarianism which promotes economic competition while attending to the cultivation of civic virtue. Blair, like liberals themselves, is inclined to depict British history since the seventeenth century as a persistent struggle to give substance to the ideal of equal rights; and, again with liberals, to characterise this process as a staircase to citizenship: 'the century-by-century accretion of civil, political and social rights. The assumptions of hierarchy, deference and status are broken down, and progress to full citizenship is gradually achieved' (Blair, 1996: 7). For Blair New Labour inherits the best of liberalism, and his speeches contain more favourable references to the likes of Hobhouse, Keynes and Beveridge than to the pioneers of the labour movement. Liberals may challenge the claim of democratic socialists to be the flag bearers of a struggle for citizenship that has persisted for three centuries. Blair's efforts to reformulate labourism, however, should alert us to the possibility of finding expressions of liberal principles beyond the confines of any particular political party.

One area in which liberal principles are now fiercely debated is that of political philosophy. The publication in 1971 of Rawls's *A Theory of Justice* marked the rehabilitation of grand theorising in the classical liberal tradition. It became fashionable again to consider, as John Locke and others had done, the universal ground rules for a fair society. We have seen that Rawls's assumption of an 'original position', in which naturally independent individuals reflect upon the terms of their political association, provoked the communitarian critique that his just society is an instrumental arrangement for self-interested individuals with little regard for the public good. The rather sterile debate between libertarians and communitarians is less intense than when the second edition of *Political Ideologies* was published in 1994. A criticism nevertheless persists that the speculative liberalism represented by *A Theory of Justice* fails to confront some of the issues of modern society.

One complaint is that this sort of rarefied philosophical exercise has little practical bearing on how the frontiers of a liberal society are to be preserved and extended. Edmund Burke was critical of Enlightenment thinkers for their abstract universalism. Believing that they had discovered the infallible guidelines for securing freedom and equality, the ideologues of the 'Age of Reason' failed to appreciate the value of diversity and difference either within or between communities. Conservatives continue to castigate liberals for their approval of rationalism in politics – for endorsing, that is, the kind of political activity which rides roughshod over tried and tested practices in an elusive search for the perfect society. Liberals usually dismiss the conservative condemnation of abstract theorising as a bid to gloss over the unfairness and inequalities of existing arrangements. Yet the principal criticism which some liberals make of Rawls is that in effect he is indulging in rationalism. The Rawlsian preoccupation with the universal ground rules of justice, they contend, fails to address the issue of how to give substance to the ideal of equal citizenship within the complex conditions of modern societies.

According to theorists opposed to Rawlsian universalism a formal commitment to a structure of equal rights may stifle the liberal agenda by being blind to the particular needs of disadvantaged groups. Integrating excluded groups such as women and ethnic minorities into the social mainstream entails granting them additional rights and resources. But Rawlsian universalism provides at best weak endorsement of particular group rights. The preference of anti-Rawlsian liberal theorists is for a discourse that seeks to reconcile group rights with the universal aspiration of free and equal citizenship by acknowledging the 'politics of difference'. Whereas women's oppression used to be challenged by appealing to universal rights, for example, feminists are now inclined to emphasise the distinctive contribution which emancipated women can make to the life of citizenship.

The issue of particular group rights has also been prominent in recent debates about multiculturalism. Liberals, in keeping with their commitment to pluralism and toleration, wish to safeguard cultural diversity through laws which interfere only minimally with individual preferences. But are cultural differences to be accommodated merely by the legal guarantee of basic individual rights, or through additional public support for disadvantaged groups? Liberals who emphasise the politics of difference tend to favour affirmative action on behalf of ethnic minorities, including, for example, public funding for Islamic and other faith schools. There is, however, a counter liberal argument. The ideal liberal society – articulated not least by J. S. Mill – consists of critical, autonomous individuals who, in questioning received wisdom, become increasingly public-spirited and tolerant of diversity. Yet single-faith schools may impede the acquisition of the virtues of citizenship by discouraging dissent and curiosity, condemning other beliefs, and by portraying gender and other inequalities as God-given. On this view a liberal polity should foster a socially integrated multicultural community, not by granting disadvantaged groups certain privileges which may entrench ethnic loyalties, but by safeguarding the rights to which everyone is entitled.

Much of the most significant recent writing about issues such as multiculturalism has been by theorists attempting to tease out the implications of liberalism. The fierce controversies which often erupt between liberal thinkers who consider these issues is a sign of the potency of a doctrine which in its various manifestations since the seventeenth century has been committed to the equal rights of citizenship.

Further reading

As he does with conservatism, Michael Freeden brilliantly identifies the ideological features of liberalism in his *Ideologies and Political Theory* (1996), pp. 141–316. Freeden is critical of Rawls and other contemporary theorists for retreating from politics into abstract speculation. Anthony Arblaster, *The Rise and Decline of Western Liberalism* (1984), is a wide-ranging and enjoyable history of the doctrine, even though as a critic of liberalism from the left he depicts it as an individualistic creed which became incoherent at the end of the nineteenth century. A brief but sharp history from Locke to modern liberals such as Rawls is John Gray, *Liberalism* (1986), though like Arblaster – but from an alternative ideological perspective – he portrays liberalism as a 'project of theorising political institutions for the government of an individualist society' which foundered in its post-classical phase. In *Two Faces of Liberalism* (2000) Gray urges liberals to abandon the kind of universal rationalism represented by Rawls. Richard Bellamy, *Liberalism and Modern Society* (1992), is a wide-ranging analysis of the development of liberalism in Britain, France, Germany and Italy from the nineteenth century to the present. His *Liberalism and Pluralism* (1999) is intended as a sequel to *Liberalism and Modern Society*, 'extending the historical argument of that work into the contemporary era'. Amy Gutman, *Liberal Equality* (1980), is interesting on liberal theories of equality from Locke to Rawls. Susan Mendus, *Toleration and the Limits of Liberalism* (1989), focuses on the arguments of Locke and Mill for toleration.

With regard to thinkers mentioned in the chapter, John Sanderson, *'But the People's Creatures'* (1989), is a crisp account of the thinking of the Levellers and other radicals in the 1640s. Richard Aschraft, *Revolutionary Politics and Locke's Two Treatises of Government* (1986), persuasively argues that Locke was far from being the bourgeois ideologue of many accounts. Among the better books on Paine are Mark Philp, *Paine* (1989), and Gregory Claeys, *Thomas Paine* (1989). Richard Bellamy (ed.), *Victorian Liberalism* (1990), includes chapters on Adam Smith, Mill, Green and the new liberalism. An authoritative introduction to Mill's thinking is William Thomas, *Mill* (1985). A book rich with insight into Green's intellectual milieu is Melvin Richter, *The Politics of Conscience* (1964). Good accounts of the new liberalism include Stefan Collini, *Liberalism and Sociology* (1979), Michael Freeden, *The New Liberalism* (1978), Peter Clarke, *Liberals and Social Democrats* (1978), Peter Weiler, *Liberal Social Theory in Great Britain, 1889–1914* (1982), and John Allett, *New Liberalism* (1982). Beveridge is well served by Jose Harris, *William Beveridge* (1977).

On Rawls see Chandran Kukathas and Philip Pettit, *Rawls's* A Theory of Justice *and its Critics* (1990), as well as his own revision of the ideas of *A Theory of Justice* in John Rawls, *Political Liberalism* (1993). Stephen Mulhall and Adam Swift, *Liberals and Communitarians* (1992), provide a clear account not only of communitarian objections to Rawls but also of his own theory. Perhaps the most accessible survey of recent debates within liberalism, focusing on attempts to reconcile particular group rights with traditional universal claims to free and equal citizenship, is Andrea Baumeister, *Liberalism and the 'Politics of Difference'* (2000). Will Kymlicka, himself an advocate of particular group rights, has collected articles by political theorists who explore the issue in an edited book, *The Rights of Minority Cultures* (1995). Perhaps the most impressive attempt to unpick the complex ideas in the debate about the rights of ethnic minorities, particularly the problem of reconciling the liberal ideal of equal citizenship with cultural diversity, is Bhikhu Parekh, *Rethinking Multiculturalism* (2000). Brian

Barry, *Culture and Equality* (2001), is a polemic against Parekh and others who wish to see specific rights granted to minority groups. This book, though often infuriating, is a brilliant attempt to defend the kind of liberal universalism advocated by Rawls.

References

Allett, John (1982) *New Liberalism: The Political Economy of J. A. Hobson*, Toronto: Toronto University Press.

Arblaster, Anthony (1984) *The Rise and Decline of Western Liberalism*, Oxford: Blackwell.

Aschraft, Richard (1986) *Revolutionary Politics and Locke's Two Treatises of Government*, Princeton NJ: Princeton University Press.

Barry, Brian (2001) *Culture and Equality: An Egalitarian Critique of Multiculturalism*, Cambridge: Polity Press.

Baumeister, Andrea (2000) *Liberalism and the 'Politics of Difference'*, Edinburgh: Edinburgh University Press.

Bellamy, Richard, ed. (1990) *Victorian Liberalism: Nineteenth-century Political Thought and Practice*, London, Routledge.

Bellamy, Richard (1992) *Liberalism and Modern Society: An Historical Argument*, London: Polity Press.

Bellamy, Richard (1999) *Liberalism and Pluralism: Towards a Politics of Compromise*, London: Routledge.

Berlin, I. (1969) 'Two concepts of liberty' in *Four Essays on Liberty*, London: Oxford University Press.

Blair, T. (1996) 'My vision for Britain' in G. Radic (ed.) *What Needs to Change: New Visions for Britain*, London: Harper Collins.

Claeys, Gregory (1989) *Thomas Paine: Social and Political Thought*, London: Unwin Hyman.

Clarke, Peter (1978) *Liberals and Social Democrats*, Cambridge: Cambridge University Press.

Collini, Stefan (1979) *Liberalism and Sociology: L. T. Hobhouse and Political Argument in England, 1880–1914*, Cambridge: Cambridge University Press.

Dworkin, R. (1978) 'Liberalism' in S. Hampshire (ed.) *Public and Private Morality*, Cambridge: Cambridge University Press.

Freeden, Michael (1978) *The New Liberalism: An Ideology of Social Reform*, Oxford: Clarendon Press.

Freeden, Michael (1996) *Ideologies and Political Theory*, Oxford: Clarendon Press.

Gray, John (1986) *Liberalism*, Milton Keynes: Open University Press.

Gray, John (2000) *Two Faces of Liberalism*, Cambridge: Polity Press.

Grimond, J. (1963) *The Liberal Challenge*, London: Hollis & Carter.

Gutman, Amy (1980) *Liberal Equality*, Cambridge: Cambridge University Press.

Harris, Jose (1977) *William Beveridge*, London: Oxford University Press.

Kukathas, Chandran and Pettit, Philip (1990) *Rawls's* A Theory of Justice *and its Critics*, Cambridge: Polity Press.

Kymlicka, Will, ed. (1995) *The Rights of Minority Cultures*, Oxford: Oxford University Press.

Laski, H. (1936) *The Rise of European Liberalism*, London: Allen & Unwin.

Laski, H. (1940) *The Decline of Liberalism*, L. T. Hobhouse Memorial Lecture No. 10, Oxford: Oxford University Press.

Mackintosh, J. (1792) *Vindicae Gallicae: Defence of the French Revolution and its English Admirers, against the Accusations of the Right Hon. Edmund Burke*, London: Robinson.

Macpherson, C. B. (1968) *The Political Theory of Possessive Individualism: Hobbes to Locke*, London: Oxford University Press.

Mendus, Susan (1989) *Toleration and the Limits of Liberalism*, Basingstoke: Macmillan.

Mulhall, Stephen and Swift, Adam (1992) *Liberals and Communitarians*, Oxford: Blackwell.

Parekh, Bhikhu (2000) *Rethinking Multiculturalism: Cultural Diversity and Political Theory*, Basingstoke: Palgrave.

Philp, Mark (1989) *Paine*, Oxford: Oxford University Press.

Pocock, J. G. H. (1975) *The Machiavellian Moment: Florentine Political Thought and the Atlantic Republican Tradition*, Princeton NJ: Princeton University Press.

Rawls, John (1971) *A Theory of Justice*, Cambridge MA: Harvard University Press.

Rawls, John (1993) *Political Liberalism*, New York: Columbia University Press.

Reid, A., ed. (1885) *Why I am a Liberal: Being Definitions and Confessions of Faith by the Best Minds of the Liberal Party*, London: Cassell.

Richter, Melvin (1964) *The Politics of Conscience: T. H. Green and his Age*, London: Weidenfeld & Nicolson.

Sanderson, John (1989) *'But the People's Creatures': The Philosophical Basis of the English Civil War*, Manchester: Manchester University Press.

Thomas, William (1985) *Mill*, Oxford: Oxford University Press.

Watson, G., ed. (1957) *The Unservile State: Essays in Liberty and Welfare*, London: Allen & Unwin.

Weiler, Peter (1982) *Liberal Social Theory in Great Britain, 1889–1914*, New York: Garland.

Conservatism

Robert Eccleshall

> The common antithesis between a society organised for the good of all and a society run in the interest of a governing class is a false one. Everyone must agree that society should be organised for the general good, but the whole question is whether it is for the general good that there should be a governing class or not.
>
> (Hollis, 1957: 35)

> Conservatives, if they talk about freedom long enough, begin to believe that that is what they want. But it is not freedom that Conservatives want; what they want is the sort of freedom that will maintain existing inequalities or restore lost ones, so far as political action can do this.
>
> (Cowling, 1978: 9)

Problems of definition

One problem in defining conservatism is the reluctance of some, conservatives themselves, as well as academic commentators, to acknowledge that the ideology poses serious conceptual difficulties. In the commonsense approach the meaning of the doctrine is literally given in the verb 'conserve', and conservatism is taken to be a set of preferences or beliefs regarding social change. Conservatives are said to be sceptical about ambitious schemes for improving the human condition. Instead of speculating about a future earthly paradise, they settle for the benefits of a customary way of life; rejecting the projects of the social planner, they favour the piecemeal reforms that are needed to keep the ship of state on an even keel.

This approach is unsatisfactory for several reasons, not least because self-styled conservatives do sometimes advocate radical change. In the 1980s, for example, the so-called New Right assailed institutions that impeded market forces, justifying their programme of social reconstruction with the sort of abstract ideas which conservatives reputedly abhor. It is of course possible to argue that those who wish to unsettle established institutions are not genuine conservatives, no matter how they designate themselves. Old-style British Tories were inclined to depict the New Right as a throwback to the nineteenth-century Manchester school of liberalism, economic dogmatists who had ideologically misled the Conservative party; and some academics also prefer to describe New Right radicals as old-fashioned liberals rather than conservatives. But this excommunication of avowed conservatives whose views fail to conform to some stereotype is rather arbitrary, as well as being insensitive to the historically varied forms of the doctrine. It seems preferable to recognise that conservatives can be radical or traditional in their attitude to social change, and to characterise the ideology in a manner that accommodates both types.

Sensitivity to historical diversity, however, can create its own kind of conceptual hazard. Some commentators, alert to differences within conservatism, write as if the representatives of its various strands are distant cousins, members of an extended family with nothing in common besides a surname. The effect is to lose sight of the ideology's peculiar characteristics, leaving little sense of the frontiers that separate conservatives from liberals, socialists and others.

In what follows I suggest that there are enough resemblances among members of the conservative family to identify some common ideological traits, and that what distinguishes the doctrine from its rivals is the vindication of inequality. The argument will unfold through a closer inspection of the two alternative approaches just outlined.

Conservatism and tradition

Those who define conservatism as an attitude to change often portray it as superior to rival ideologies. Their argument is that other ideologies encourage impractical schemes of social improvement. Conservatism is said to affirm the value of what has been tested by historical experience, and in doing so it dispels any illusion that the imperfections of human arrangements can be eliminated in some future Golden Age. In making a virtue of what has been called the 'politics of imperfection' (Quinton, 1978), conservatism purportedly corresponds to timeless instincts. In his spirited *Conservatism in England* (1933), F. J. C. Hearnshaw traced the origins of the doctrine to Adam's caution in the Garden of Eden. Eve, according to Hearnshaw, was the first radical: reckless, starry-eyed, easily tempted by the false promises made by the serpent – the latter perceived as a forebear of Karl Marx. Other writers also take the view that conservatism stems from a temperamental preference for the familiar, coupled with a distaste for theoretical speculation. 'Conservatism is less a political doctrine,' wrote R. J. White at the beginning of an anthology first published in 1950, 'than a habit of mind . . . a mode of feeling, a way of living' (White, 1964: 1). Phrases such as these still appear in the opening sentences of some articles and books about conservatism.

The proposition that conservatism is rooted in a natural dislike of change is of negligible analytical value, conflating as it does ahistorical patterns of individual behaviour with the emergence – at a specific moment in Western culture and among particular social groups – of a cluster of ideas about the purposes of government and the organisation of society. Conservatism is to be understood not as the expression of recurring habits and instincts, but as a distinctive perspective on society shaped by the political struggles and class divisions of the post-medieval state.

Nor should much credence be given to the suggestion that conservatism is different from other political doctrines because it belongs outside the realm of ideology. Those who characterise conservatism as a frame of mind often denigrate ideology as a perverted or 'alien' form of knowledge (Minogue, 1985), consisting of speculative notions which foster the illusion that the political order can be dramatically improved. Conservatives, in contrast, allegedly attain genuine understanding of human affairs because of their pragmatic attachment to existing institutions. This insistence that conservatism is not an ideology is itself an ideological ploy by those sympathetic to the doctrine, part of the rough-and-tumble of political argument rather than an analytical exercise.

Not everyone who equates conservatism with opposition to fundamental change is so unsophisticated. S. P. Huntington has made an interesting case for understanding conservatism as a 'positional' ideology, differing from its rivals in not providing an ideal of how society ought to be organised (Huntington, 1957). Whereas other ideologies stand *for* something – a more even distribution of resources, for example, or an extension of civil liberties – conservatism warns *against* dismantling established institutions. If other ideologies are concerned with what should be done, conservatism is about the hazards of doing anything too different from what already has been done.

In a sparkling book, A. O. Hirschman, not himself a conservative, has identified a triad of arguments or theses by which conservatives typically vindicate the *status quo*: the *perversity* thesis, according to which goal-directed or purposive politics produce consequences contrary to those intended, an example of this kind of argument being the contention of opponents of the French revolution that the bid for liberty would backfire into tyranny; the *futility* thesis, by which society cannot possibly be turned upside down, as in the claim that no amount of social engineering will succeed in eliminating inequalities of wealth and power; and the *jeopardy* thesis, which holds that the benefits of radical reform are always outweighed by the costs, an example being the argument of nineteenth-century conservatives that an extended franchise would disturb the balance of the constitution (Hirschman, 1991). In these ways conservatism is a kind of counter-blast to conviction ideologies, its adherents persistently rehearsing the same catechism of objections to promises of a brighter tomorrow.

As a warning against conviction politics conservatism is a reaction to modernity, the belief that communities can be liberated from the superstition and tyranny of the past through social engineering on a grand scale. The optimism of the modern world was expressed in Enlightenment liberalism with its assumption that each individual could in principle make sense of the world, apprehending the rules of a just social order and co-operating with others to make institutions accountable to the tribunal of reason. It was during the Enlightenment, particularly at the time of the American and French revolutions, that many of what are now taken to be classic statements of conservatism were formulated. In America John Adams and Alexander Hamilton advocated a 'natural aristocracy' of wealth and moral leadership as a means of giving to a new society the stability of a semi-feudal state such as Britain. In France Joseph de Maistre and others countered the call for liberty, equality and fraternity with a counter-revolutionary demand for the absolute power of a theocratic state to be restored. England's most notable champion of the *ancien régime* was Edmund Burke, Irish by birth, who vindicated the legacy of the past by challenging the Enlightenment belief in human perfectibility.

Central to Burke's repudiation, in *Reflections on the Revolution in France* (1790), of French Jacobins and their English allies was his claim that historical experience is more reliable than abstract speculation in the conduct of public affairs. Society is the product of organic growth, according to Burke, accumulating the wisdom of generations who had learned what was prudent through trial and error rather than by attending philosophy seminars to discuss the rights of man. The political order exists not to implement universal rights but to secure certain needs such as food, shelter and education, and each community satisfies these needs in a manner appropriate to itself. Burke warned of the dangers of discarding the 'prescriptive' authority of a customary way of life under the illusion that social progress can be deliberately planned, and he predicted that the quest of revolutionaries for liberty and equality would result in forms of despotism and oligarchy more oppressive than any of the inconveniences and imperfections of the *ancien régime*.

Burke also repudiated the assumption of the 'Age of Reason' that the principles of a just political order are within the compass of every individual mind. Individuals are weak and fallible because of sinful human nature, he argued, often passionate instead of rational, prone to selfishness and mistaken judgement, and therefore each in isolation cannot apprehend the complexities of the public interest. Burke contrasted the small 'private stock' of individual reason with the inexhaustible 'general bank and capital of nations, and of ages'. Political practices are the outcome of a traditional and corporate wisdom, the consensus of generations forming a bulwark against the fanciful schemes which emanate from the vanity of individual minds. 'The individual is foolish,' said Burke in his *Speech on the Reform of the Representation in the House of Commons* (1782), 'the multitude, for the moment, is foolish when they act without deliberation, but the species is wise, and when time is given to it, as a species, it always acts right.' If liberalism can be said to endorse the politics of trust – the argument being that society benefits, morally and politically, from the relatively unrestricted exercise of individual judgement – Burkean conservatism emphasises the socially undesirable consequences of private reason undisciplined by custom and convention. And the doctrine of natural rights, in Burke's view, was the product of faulty judgement, formulated by individuals intoxicated with their capacity for abstract thinking disconnected from historical realities.

Burke's distaste for doctrinal simplicity in politics has found frequent echoes in British conservatism. In 1872 Benjamin Disraeli (1804–81), then leader of the Conservative opposition, castigated Whigs for seeking to govern Britain according to intellectual abstractions fashionable in continental Europe – substituting, as he put it, 'cosmopolitan for national principles' – and as a consequence waging 'war on the manners and customs of the people of this country under the pretext of Progress'.

In the twentieth century the case against viewing politics as the pursuit of dogmatic certainty was eloquently made by Michael Oakeshott (1901–90), regarded by many as the finest British conservative philosopher since Burke. Politics, for Oakeshott, 'is not the science of setting up a permanently impregnable society, it is the art of knowing where to go next in the exploration of an already existing traditional kind of society' (Oakeshott, 1962: 58). Wise politicians neither equip themselves with universal, supposedly infallible guidelines such as the 'rights of man', nor set their sights on some ultimate destination – the classless society or whatever. Instead, they become familiar with the conventions of a settled way of life, using their experience to pick up 'intimations' of what to do next amid its shifting complexities. An example he gave of how politicians find their way around was the enfranchisement of women in Britain at the beginning of the twentieth century. Women were granted the vote not because of the compelling logic of some abstract idea such as natural justice or universal rights, but because of their gradually improving legal and social status. In these circumstances the lack of female suffrage was correctly perceived to be an incongruity in the English way of life that ought to be rectified, a mischief that had become apparent through the passage of time rather than by the application of deductive logic.

Oakeshott underlined the folly of misunderstanding politics as the pursuit of doctrinal simplicities by distinguishing two types of knowledge, technical and practical. The former can be precisely formulated into rules – as in the Highway Code, for instance – and learned in advance of an activity. Practical knowledge, on the other hand, is imprecise because acquired by experience rather than learned in a mechanical fashion. The technique of cooking can be learned by reading books, but we become accomplished cooks only by practising the art. Good politicians, like proficient cooks, acquire their skills not by poring over manuals that contain the science of governing, but from immersion in those habitual patterns of conduct which signal 'where to go next' among the uncertainties of the practical world to which politics belongs. In political activity, as Oakeshott put it in an often quoted metaphor of the ship of state:

> Men sail a boundless and bottomless sea; there is neither harbour for shelter nor floor for anchorage, neither starting-place nor appointed destination. The enterprise is to keep afloat on an even keel; the sea is both friend and enemy; and the seamanship consists in using the resources of a traditional manner of behaviour in order to make a friend of every hostile occasion.

Oakeshott's critique of the deficiencies of technical knowledge as a basis for public affairs is another example of the conservative condemnation, persistent since the age of Burke, of those who naively imagine politics to be the pursuit of some metaphysical enterprise.

Oakeshott labelled the disposition to retreat into theoretical abstractions as rationalism in politics. Rationalists are social engineers eager to set in place a deliberately planned society, tidily managed according to the axioms of technical knowledge. Unaware that there can be no ultimate purpose in politics beyond ensuring the continuity of a particular way of life, they dream of finally eradicating poverty and unemployment, of putting an end to war, and so on. But the conduct of human arrangements according to such simple formulas is bound to fail, and like the biblical Tower of Babel every project to build an earthly paradise will eventually collapse.

The Tower of Babel can serve as a metaphor for conservative objections to socialist or liberal programmes of social transformation. Clearly, conservatives have frequently vindicated the latent wisdom of existing institutions, accusing their ideological adversaries of succumbing to the illusion that politics is the science of human perfection. Does this mean that traditionalism is the key to the conservative sanctum, providing a sort of creed which all who subscribe to the doctrine readily profess? There are four related reasons for supposing that the heart of conservatism lies elsewhere.

The first is that conservatives do not invariably shun abstract thinking in favour of a pragmatic style of politics. There are numerous examples of the conservative predilection for 'loose metaphysical' speculation. Benjamin Disraeli, though scornful of Whigs for succumbing to Continental rationalism, was himself prone to ideological flights of fancy. In the 1840s he opposed advocates of a capitalist market economy, among them members of his own party as well as Whigs, by fabricating from 'the principle of the feudal system' an image of an idyllic past: a mythical Merrie England in which the propertied classes had benevolently discharged their custodial responsibilities to the poor, who had reciprocated with affectionate deference.

Among the kind of free-market conservatives whom Disraeli lambasted there is ample evidence of a fondness for dogmatic certainties. Tory opponents of the New Right in the 1980s used to complain that their party had been captured by alien ideologues, as though all former conservatives had quietly practised the art of prudent statecraft without recourse to the certainties of political economy. Yet there have always been conservatives who believed that politics ought to consist in the application of the infallible laws of supply and demand. The Liberty and Property Defence League was founded in 1882, largely by conservatives, with the intention of preventing government from providing welfare or meddling in economic matters. Its principal publicist, Lord Elcho, believed that political economy was 'simply the law of gravitation applied to social matters'. And W. H. Mallock (1849–1923), a member of the League, spent four decades attempting to formulate a 'scientific conservatism' of sufficient theoretical sophistication to combat the superficially persuasive logic of socialism. Mallock's systematic conservatism was intended to demonstrate, by a combination of deduction and empirical evidence, that the mildest deviation from unfettered capitalism would result in economic decline and cultural stagnation. Even Burke, whose writings are supposed to be a clear expression of the conservative aversion to intellectual abstractions, was a dogmatic free-marketeer. Politicians who fancied they could alleviate poverty by ignoring economic imperatives were, according to him, impious. Government was not competent:

> to supply to the poor, those necessaries which it has pleased the Divine Providence for a while to withhold from them. We, the people, ought to be

made sensible that it is not in breaking the laws of commerce, which are the laws of nature, and consequently the laws of God, that we are to place our hope of softening the divine displeasure to remove any calamity under which we suffer.

Conservatives, then, are no less capable than their ideological adversaries of supposing that sound political conduct consists in the application of the correct intellectual formulas.

This inclination to build theoretical castles in the air means, secondly, that conservatives sometimes indulge in their own form of rationalism. Their attraction to purposive politics is obscured by the right's caricature of the rationalist as a starry-eyed optimist on the ideological left, someone naive enough to suppose that a classless society can be delivered by application of the appropriate axioms. But some conservatives also imagine that the ship of state can be guided, contrary to the message of Oakeshott's metaphor, towards an 'appropriate destination'. The New Right was one manifestation of this sort of perfectionism. There was little evidence of distaste for doctrinal certainties in the New Right's flirtation with monetarism and other refinements of the science of political economy, of preference for gradual reform in its crusade to push back the state from the economy, of respect for a customary way of life in its assault upon the post-war settlement, or of an aversion to simplistic solutions in its portrayal of a brave new world of competitive individualism. The ideological right is as capable as the left of utopian speculation.

The third reason why conservatism cannot be equated with traditionalism is that the right is not invariably against radical change. Conservatives certainly possess a stock of arguments, inherited from the counter-revolutionary response of Burke and others to the attack upon the *ancien régime*, by which they have frequently defended the established political order. The point is that these arguments have been used to oppose political programmes of which the right disapproves. On other occasions, as in the 1980s, conservatives can be as fervent as their adversaries in advocating schemes of political reconstruction.

This is so because, fourthly, conservatism is not – contrary to S. P. Huntington – a negative or 'positional' ideology which warns against tampering with the *status quo*, whatever that happens to be at a particular historical moment. Conservatism, like other ideologies, does stand for something in that its adherents have a clear conception of how society ought to be organised. Not every conservative would claim that there is a divine blueprint for social arrangements – as Burke suggested when vindicating the brutalities of an unshackled market economy. Yet all favour a society in which certain inequalities are preserved, and in condemning purposive politics their intention is to ridicule the egalitarian ideals of their opponents. What prompted Michael Oakeshott to identify conservatism with an antipathy to social engineering was his hostility to post-war planning for full employment in a welfare state. When conservatives themselves assume the mantle of rationalism their intention is to reverse the damage done by rival political projects. A principal objection of the New Right to welfare capitalism was that redistributive taxation had deprived the rich of the incentive to create wealth and discouraged the poor from improving themselves. Hence they set sail towards the beguiling horizon of a market economy in order to escape those features of the post-war settlement that had also offended Oakeshott.

Conservatives, then, can vary in their attitude to political change because at the heart of their doctrine is a distinctive image of the sound political order. Whether their political programme is radical or conservative depends upon their intention at any particular moment either, in the words of Maurice Cowling cited at the beginning of this chapter, to 'maintain existing equalities or restore lost ones'.

A plurality of conservatisms?

There is one further conceptual obstacle to be overcome in defining conservatism. It became fashionable from about 1980 to characterise the antinomies of conservatism using aquatic imagery, 'dry' free-marketeers being contrasted with those 'wet' members of the British Conservative party who were not convinced of the benefits of an unfettered economy. The wet–dry dichotomy highlights a disagreement about the proper scope of government that has been present within conservatism since the early decades of the nineteenth century. There have always been squabbles between those representing the libertarian as against the collectivist strands of the ideology – the former arguing that the state should do little more than safeguard property rights, and collectivists believing that government has responsibility to pursue a common purpose that transcends the sum of particular interests. Does this mean that conservatism lacks a core identity, so that instead of searching for a nucleus of beliefs we should convey the ideology's diversity and contrariety?

According to W. H. Greenleaf, a distinguished historian of the British political tradition, we should be wary not only of searching for a cluster of concepts which conservatives share, but of supposing that there are clear boundaries between the ideology and its rivals. This is because the debate within conservatism between libertarians and collectivists has been reflected in both liberalism and socialism. Ideological divergences are sometimes as acute within as they are between political creeds. Instead, then, of fruitlessly probing for the kernel of a political doctrine, we should seek to convey its ambivalence. And this is done by identifying the interplay of antithetical ideas at work within each ideology (Greenleaf, 1983).

An even stronger case can be made for the doctrine's essential disunity. The collectivist and libertarian strands of conservatism tend to be associated with apparently incompatible conceptions of society. One derives from the aristocratic ethos of the eighteenth century when rank was determined primarily by birth rather than individual achievement. In this conception the community is an organic whole bound by a hierarchy of privileges and obligations in which wealth is held in trust for the common benefit, and where in consequence those with power have a responsibility to attend to the welfare of the mass of people. In the other conception, which is rooted in the bourgeois rhetoric of nineteenth-century capitalism, society is a collection of self-interested individuals united by little beyond a common desire for security, and where wealth and prestige are the outcome of individual success rather than the accident of birth. Here the function of the state is not to promote the public welfare at the expense of private interests, but to secure property rights by maintaining law and order. According to Keith Joseph, one of the architects of the New Right, human beings:

> are so constituted that it is natural to them to pursue private rather than public ends. This is a simple matter of observation. The duty of government is to accommodate themselves to this immutable fact about human nature. Their object (and one must assume the original purpose for which they were created) is merely to avoid the inconveniences which attend the uncontrolled pursuits by private individuals of private ends . . . Men have a natural right to their ambitions because it was not for the purpose of abolishing competitiveness that they submitted to government; it was for the purpose of regulating competitiveness and preventing it from taking violent, fraudulent or anti-social forms.
>
> (Joseph and Sumption, 1979: 100–1)

This is a particularly clear argument for minimal government, and most conservatives lack Joseph's analytical precision when identifying the features of a sound political order. Yet the contrasting conceptions of society are implicit in the disagreements among British conservatives since the beginning of the nineteenth century. Is there, then, no common ground where libertarians and collectivists meet?

There is certainly little common ground on the issue of how the powerful should discharge their responsibilities. In the patrician image of society the privileged classes are obligated to attend to what Disraeli called 'the condition of the people' by, for example, the provision of decent housing and adequate welfare. Conservatives often cite Disraeli when urging the aristocratic ethos of *noblesse oblige* to be adapted to modern conditions through state planning for full employment. And they have often used the ideal of beneficent social hierarchy as a stick with which to beat libertarian conservatives for their cruel indifference to the poor. In the early decades of the nineteenth century, for example, Tories opposed to the growth of market capitalism accused free-traders in their party of succumbing to a spirit of acquisitive individualism; Edwardian conservatives lamented the corruption of their party by a new breed of plutocrats who were creating what Lord Henry Bentinck called a 'bagman's Paradise' for the exploiters of the people; while a frequent complaint of Tory 'wets' was that the New Right had abdicated their responsibility for the casualties of a market economy.

Collectivist conservatives, then, have denounced attempts to emancipate the economy from political regulation as a pretext for the rich to exploit the poor.

But libertarians are no less anxious to occupy the high ground of morality, which they do by accusing patrician Tories of obscuring economic realities in a fog of sentimentality. Their argument for minimal government is threefold. There is, first, the claim that a free market is just because rewards of wealth and esteem reflect the diversity of human talent. Unrestricted economic competition results in 'an infinitely mobile society' with 'an infinite number of snakes and ladders', according to Keith Joseph, because individuals are permitted to rise and fall according to merit. An unshackled market, secondly, is said to nurture habits of prudence and self-reliance. If poverty reflects a lack of individual skill and effort, then the indigent will not be prompted to improve themselves unless made to bear some of the consequences of their own failure. The welfare state, in this view, creates a permanent underclass of what Margaret Thatcher called 'moral cripples', people who are induced by a dependence culture to delegate personal responsibility to officialdom.

The third argument against state intervention in the market is that rich and poor alike benefit from the unrestricted pursuit of self-interest. Ultimately there are no losers from competitive individualism because, in leaping ahead themselves, wealth creators drag the poor some way after them. Without the expectation of large rewards, however, entrepreneurial individuals will be disinclined to generate the prosperity which raises the living standards of everyone. At the beginning of the last century John St Loe Strachey was among libertarian conservatives who opposed a policy of redistributive taxation as a means of financing the public provision of, for example, old-age pensions and free school meals for the poor. 'You will never be able to give every man on a hot day a bigger drink of water,' he wrote, 'if you begin by stopping up the pipe that feeds the cistern.' A crude paraphrase of this style of thinking might be: 'I'm a successful entrepreneur because of my flair and energy. You're unemployed and in receipt of social benefits because being lazy you refuse to "get on your bike" in search of a job. And if I'm heavily taxed to enable you to remain a "lounger and scrounger", then I'll no longer bother to create the wealth that eventually trickles down to you.' The rich, then, are creators of prosperity rather than plunderers of the poor, and any attempt by government to curtail their activities will result in economic stagnation.

In the bourgeois rhetoric of libertarian conservatism society appears as a collection of independent individuals, and government has few functions beyond policing the pursuit of self-interest, whereas in the patrician imagery of an organic nation the state can override particular interests to secure the common welfare. Is conservatism, then, marked by an absent centre? Are we dealing with different types of conservatism, perhaps even two conservatisms, with little or nothing in common? Notwithstanding their differences conservatives do share a perspective on society that distinguishes them from adherents to rival ideologies. Running through the varieties of conservatism is the theme of inequality. Conservatives do not object to rationalism in politics *per se* – otherwise we should not be able to explain right-wing forms of radicalism such as the New Right – but to the kind of social engineering intended to level distinctions of wealth and power.

The conservative vindication of inequality is threefold. Human beings are said to be naturally diverse in energy and talents, so that any project to construct a classless society will be futile. Misconceived schemes of social levelling may appear successful for a while, wrote Bernard Braine in *Tory Democracy* (1948), but 'within a very short space of time this new equality will have vanished into the mist. Some men will be rich, some will be poor. Some will be masters, some will be servants. A few will lead, the rest will follow.' Egalitarian programmes, secondly, are dangerous because they entail authoritarian measures which crush individual liberty. And, thirdly, social hierarchy is desirable because the majority benefit from the leadership of a few. The conservative case for inequality was clearly made by Harold Macmillan (1894–1986), Prime Minister from 1957 to 1963:

> Human beings, widely various in their capacity, character, talent and ambition, tend to differentiate at all times and in all places. To deny them the right to differ, to enforce economic and social uniformity upon them, is to throttle one of the most powerful and creative of human appetites. It is wrong, and it is three times wrong. It is morally wrong; because to deny the bold, the strong, the prudent and the clever the rewards and privileges of exercising their qualities is to enthrone in society the worst and basest of human attributes: envy, jealousy and spite. It is wrong practically . . . because it is only by giving their heads to the strong and to the able that we shall ever have the means to provide real protection for the weak and for the old. Finally it is wrong politically; because I do not see how Britain, with all its rich diversity and vitality, could be turned into a egalitarian society without, as we have seen in Eastern Europe, a gigantic exercise in despotism.

Within this general vindication of social inequality there is scope for particular emphasis, and a major point of difference has been the justification of wealth and power.

In patrician language the emphasis is upon the social breeding of those who constitute a ruling elite. The argument is that those who belong to what Burke called a 'natural aristocracy' can acquire knowledge and wisdom, cultivate taste and virtue, as well as being inculcated with an ethos of public service. And owning substantial property – having a 'stake' in the community, as it used to be put – they are unlikely to be excited by the false expectations which prompt others to engage in reckless schemes of political reconstruction. In bourgeois rhetoric, on the other hand, the emphasis is on the contribution of exceptional individuals who ascend the social scale through their own merit. These 'wonderful people' – Margaret Thatcher's description of entrepreneurs and other wealth creators – supposedly possess rare qualities of ambition and vision, so that from their dynamic leadership flows the prosperity which benefits the less energetic majority.

Common to these two strands of conservatism is the image of a chain of social discipline linked by habits of obedience and submission among the majority, as well as by qualities of wise and firm leadership on the part of an elite. As Burke wrote in *An Appeal from the New to the Old Whigs* (1791):

> To enable men to act with the weight and character of a people, and to answer the ends for which they are incorporated with that capacity, we must suppose them . . . to be in that state of habitual social discipline, in which the wiser, the more expert, and the more opulent conduct, and by conducting enlighten and protect the weaker, the less knowing, and the less provided with the goods of fortune. When the multitude are not under this discipline, they can scarcely be said to be in civil society.

The depiction of society as a command structure distinguishes conservatism from the varieties of socialism which advocate at least the erosion of inequalities, and possibly their elimination.

But what of liberalism, particularly as libertarian conservatives are often assumed to be the heirs of classical liberals in endorsing the inequalities attendant upon a market economy? Commentators who suggest that conservative advocates of a minimal state are liberals in disguise tend to forget that the free market is an ambivalent concept susceptible to different ideological meanings. The ideal of a market economy featured in the campaign of nineteenth-century liberals to eradicate aristocratic privilege and extend individual rights, and as such its use was consistent with the enduring liberal ideal of a community of self-governing citizens free of the tutelage of either an elite or an overbearing state.

In conservative usage, however, the concept of unregulated capitalism has been used to justify rather than undermine the authority of both an elite and a strong state. Conservatives are more pessimistic than liberals about the potential of the mass of people for rational and orderly conduct. The diversity of the human condition, coupled with its frailties and 'inherent wickedness', means that not everyone can respond to the imperatives of a self-help society of competitive individualism. Poverty is said to reflect a moral as well as an economic failure, and morally feeble individuals lacking bourgeois habits of self-discipline pose a threat to the stability of the political order. Hence the argument of libertarian conservatives for government that is limited in scope yet firm in maintaining law and order. In campaigning at the end of the nineteenth century for economic individualism, the intention of the Liberty and Property Defence League was neither to diminish the authority of the state nor to subvert ordered hierarchy. Their fear was that government would become incapable of preserving the inequalities of private property because of irrepressible demands from a recently enfranchised working class for collectivist programmes of social welfare. Similarly, the intention of the New Right in rolling back government from the economy was to restore social discipline rather than erode the state's authority. A frequent complaint of the New Right was that the egalitarian policies of the post-war welfare state had created a dependence culture which had sapped the moral energy and self-discipline of many individuals. In pruning the state they sought not only to remove fetters from wealth creators, but also to make it more efficient in curbing socially unruly behaviour. In this sense, the New Right was a variant on the enduring conservative theme that society, properly organised, is a chain of command in which leadership is exercised within the framework of firm government.

A brief history

Some of these conceptual issues can be clarified by glancing at the evolution of British conservatism. The sobriquet 'Tory' was first used to designate a political group in the 1680s, when it became attached to royalists who were opposed to the Whig doctrine that Parliament could correct or depose a tyrannical monarch. In the modern sense, however, the ideology derives from the early decades of the nineteenth century, when the adjective 'Conservative' was attached to a political party and the noun 'conservatism' came to denote the principles of its members. It was during this period, too, that doctrinal fissures between patrician and free-market conservatives began to appear.

The social ideal of Tory paternalists was of a beneficent hierarchy in which a generous exercise of their custodial responsibilities on the part of the privileged was reciprocated with grateful deference by those in their charge. 'As Tories,' William Johnstone wrote in *Blackwood's Magazine* in 1829:

> we maintain that it is the duty of the people to pay obedience to those set in authority over them: but it is also the duty of those in authority to protect the people who are placed below them. They are not to sit in stately grandeur, and see the people perish, nor, indeed, are they ever to forget that they hold their power and their possessions upon the understanding that they administer both more for the good of the people at large, than the people would do, if they had the administration of both themselves.

The objection of Tory paternalists to the Modern Age was that the people were being severed from traditional sources of protection and discipline. Their argument was that some landlords, as well as the captains of a rapidly developing manufacturing industry, had been misled by the 'theoretic folly' of the new science of political economy into supposing that, for the sake of material advance, the emotional ties of benevolent hierarchy had to be displaced by the harsh, impersonal relations of the capitalist market. This abdication of their responsibility for the people was said to be politically dangerous as well as morally reprehensible. 'I wish for reform,' said the poet Robert Southey, 'because I cannot but see that all things are tending towards revolution, and nothing but reform can by any possibility prevent it.' Unless extensive measures were taken to deal with poverty and squalor, warned the great Tory philanthropist Lord Ashley (1801–85), many would fall prey to the 'two great demons in morals and politics, Socialism and Chartism [which] are but symptoms of a universal disease, spread throughout the vast mass of the people, who, so far from concurring in the *status quo*, suppose that anything must be better than the present condition.' Various remedies were proposed. Southey favoured greater public expenditure on poor relief together with a national system of education; Ashley campaigned to improve conditions of work in factories and mines, as well as to provide the poor with education, housing and public health care. Central to this strategy for countering the socially disruptive effects of the capitalist market was a bid to renew the bonds between responsible proprietors and the bulk of people.

Patrician Tories hoped that traditional social relations would stem the growth of mercenary capitalism. For other conservatives, however, the future lay not in a revived partnership between some of the propertied classes and the masses, but rather in a new alliance of aristocracy and emerging bourgeoisie strong enough to withstand democratic and egalitarian demands from below. Foremost among them was Sir Robert Peel (1788–1850), Prime Minister in 1835 and from 1841 to 1846, whom paternalists detested for succumbing to the nostrums of political economy. Peel's recipe for political stability was a free market allied to firm government. He derided Ashley's campaign for factory reform, for example, on the ground that regulation of the hours and conditions of work would reduce productivity. Manufacturers would respond to this breaking of the 'strict rules of political economy' by cutting wages to remain competitive in the world market, and as a consequence labourers rather than capitalists would suffer from the meddling of philanthropists whose grasp of economic realities was obscured by sentimentality. Peel wanted the free market to operate within a strong state, and in a speech of 1835 he urged landed and middle classes to 'protect the interests of order and property' by forming a 'cordial union' against popular pressures to disperse power and wealth. Peel's bid to emancipate the economy from political constraints culminated in his policy of the 1840s to reduce tariffs on imported grain, eventually eliminating them in 1846. His argument against the Corn Laws was partly that protectionism curtailed economic prosperity, but also that a 'continued relaxation of commercial restrictions' would secure law and order by strengthening the alliance of landed and manufacturing interests.

For Tory paternalists, however, the Corn Laws symbolised not the vested interests of land, but the intimate social hierarchy now threatened by the brutalising spirit of commerce. Among opponents of Peel in the 1840s was a group of Tories known as Young England who rhapsodised about an idyllic past of feudal social relations in which, according to Lord John Manners:

> Each knew his place – king, peasant, peer or priest,
> The greatest owned connexion with the least;
> From rank to rank the generous feeling ran,
> And linked society as man to man.

Manners's proposals for retrieving this Golden Age included the revival of holy days, during which the poor would be spiritually edified as well as physically restored through pastimes such as maypole dancing. From 1842 Young England was led by Benjamin Disraeli, who used the feudal ideal – the principle, in his words, that 'the tenure of all property should be the performance of its duties' – to condemn Peelites for reducing the Conservative party to a selfish faction with no regard for the condition of the people. In *Sybil*, one of a trilogy of novels written at this time, he depicted an England divided into two nations of rich and poor, 'with an innate inability of mutual comprehension', because those with power no longer viewed their wealth as in trust for the benefit of all.

The Conservative party was split in two by the repeal of the Corn Laws, regaining a sense of direction only after the Second Reform Act. Disraeli, who now led the party, used the 'one nation' ideal to appeal to an expanding electorate. Conservatives, he said in 1872, would not be deterred by free-market dogma from improving the 'condition of the people' through, for example, slum clearance and public health regulations. Only by means of a programme of social improvement, according to Disraeli, might the privileged classes persuade a mass electorate to endorse institutions of ordered hierarchy. Soon after Disraeli's death his brand of patrician conservatism became known as Tory Democracy, though some who used the phrase were less concerned to advocate social reform than to convince 'the people' of the natural affinity between themselves and men of property.

But even the mildest proposal for social improvement annoyed those libertarian conservatives who in the last decades of the century joined organisations such as the Liberty and Property Defence League. Fearing that power and property would be submerged in a democratic deluge, they denounced Tory Democrats and other proponents of an enlarged state for heading 'straight to State-Socialism'. Many 'individualists', as those who favoured minimal government became known at this time, found inspiration in Herbert Spencer's *The Man versus the State* (1885), which appeared to find in Charles Darwin's theory of natural selection the key to human evolution. Although some commentators doubt that Spencer was a Social Darwinist, he certainly condemned modern government for promoting the 'survival of the unfittest' through misconceived schemes for eliminating poverty. His argument was that society advances by means of a harsh struggle for survival in which the weak and indolent bear the consequences of their imprudence, whereas efficient and talented individuals are permitted to reap economic rewards and social prestige in abundance. Public provision of welfare encourages undesirable moral habits by rewarding inefficient members of society, Spencer believed, and also deters 'fit' individuals by taxing them to subsidise the 'undeserving' poor:

> Men who are so sympathetic that they cannot let the struggle for existence bring on the unworthy the suffering consequent on their incapacity or misconduct are so unsympathetic that they can, deliberately, make the struggle for existence harder for the worthy, and inflict on them and on their children artificial evils in addition to the natural evil they have to bear.

The poor themselves would suffer from misguided philanthropic efforts to mitigate their condition, according to Spencer, because taxation would deprive efficient members of society of an incentive to create the wealth that eventually percolates down to everyone.

Members of the Liberty and Property Defence League often used the Social Darwinist language of *The Man versus the State* when denouncing anyone who wanted government to be extended beyond the mere protection of life and property. One member of the League, however, censured Spencer on the rather peculiar ground that his theory of evolutionary individualism gave insufficient recognition to the 'cardinal social fact' of inequality, particularly the contribution of exceptional individuals to the advance of society. W. H. Mallock attempted to remove what he considered to be the flaws of Spencerite theory by formulating a 'scientific conservatism' intended to refute, by a combination of logic and empirical evidence, every doctrine which disputed the truths of political economy. Mallock's argument, elaborated in numerous articles and books spanning almost forty years, was that society had advanced from barbarity to civilisation because of the persistent influence of a talented minority whose flair and organisational ability had improved economic and cultural standards for all. What prompted the gifted few to exert themselves for the common advantage was entrepreneurial ambition, the expectation of appropriate rewards for rare talent. Enterprising individuals would be deterred by redistributive policies from exerting themselves, and as a consequence society would slide into cultural mediocrity and economic decline. 'The lesson to be taught,' Mallock wrote in *The Limits of Pure Democracy* (1918):

> is that society depends upon the co-operation of unequals – of the few who lead and give orders, and of the many who follow and obey: that this fact reflects itself in the general configuration of society; and that in proportion as the masses of any country neglect it they will, as a whole or sporadically, lose what they have in their efforts to seize more.

His complaint, of course, was that everyone except dogmatic free-marketeers was intent on undermining society's natural command structure.

Mallock's vindication of inequality was similar to that of other individualists, in spite of his criticism of Spencer. His claim to novelty lies in the use he made of his 'scientific' defence of unbridled capitalism to turn socialism on its head. For Marx, according to Mallock, manual labour was the sole source of wealth, and workers were exploited because some of what they produced was hived off as capitalist profit. For Mallock, in contrast, wealth was created by mental labour, and any increase in productive capacity emanated entirely from the economic and social leadership of a gifted elite. The explosion of wealth in nineteenth-century industrial society derived not from the productive energy of manual labour, but from the talent of inventors as well as the acumen of entrepreneurs who grasped the market potential of technical innovations. These people alone were responsible for generating 'surplus value' which, far from intensifying class exploitation, had substantially improved the living standards of the masses. 'Nations now grow rich through industry as they once grew rich through conquest,' wrote Mallock in *A Critical Examination of Socialism* (1908):

> because new commanders with a precision unknown on battle-fields, direct the minutest operations of armies of a new kind, and the only terms on which any modern nation can maintain its present productivity, or hope to increase it in the future, consist in the technical submission of the majority of men to the guidance of an exceptional minority.

So whereas the socialist message is that the masses are plundered by a predatory minority, the reverse is true: the majority, as Mallock put it in his *Memoirs*, 'are the pensioners of the few'. Once deprived of entrepreneurial command, then, the army of the proletariat would soon slip into penury.

In the early decades of the twentieth century libertarian conservatives continued to argue that the poor would become poorer unless the rich were permitted fully to enjoy the rewards of their entrepreneurial endeavours, and also to berate the collectivist wing of their party for treading a slippery slope to socialism. Occasionally Social Darwinism was used to warn that an encroaching state would impede social progress. Dorothy Crisp, for instance, was horrified that some conservatives were disregarding natural selection in their readiness to endorse misconceived schemes of social amelioration. She was particularly incensed by growing public expenditure on slum clearance, and in *The Rebirth of Conservatism* (1931) predicted that new corporation housing estates would deteriorate into a 'garbage heap' because those:

> who sink into slum life are without doubt . . . the weakest and least desirable of the population. To-day the unfit are preserved at the expense of the fit, the deserving pay for the maintenance of the undeserving, and physically, mentally and morally there is a levelling down of the whole race.

The solution lay in heeding the lessons of political economy which taught that society could not prosper, economically or morally, unless individuals bore the consequences of their own faults and misdeeds.

Crisp's book was published in a decade of deep economic recession and massive unemployment. As a corrective to the defects of the capitalist market some conservatives began to advocate an enlarged state, using arguments similar to those of the liberal J. M. Keynes for a mixed economy. The conservative version of planned capitalism is conveyed in the title of an influential book by Harold Macmillan, published in 1938, *The Middle Way: A Study of the Problem of Economic and Social Progress*. The middle way – or 'half-way house', as he sometimes called it – was to be between unfettered capitalism and state socialism. It entailed public ownership of essential industries, government direction of investment, and sufficient expenditure on welfare to establish an irreducible minimum standard of living. Macmillan, who admired Disraeli, presented the middle way as an updated expression of the 'one nation' ideal, a means of attacking 'most vigorously the grosser inequalities which still divide our democracy with what a conservative Prime Minister was the first to call "The Two Nations".' Like Ashley and other nineteenth-century patrician Tories, who fretted that without reform the nation would be engulfed by socialism, Macmillan argued that a managed economy would be an antidote to social unrest. Without a more 'orderly capitalism', according to *The Middle Way*, Britain might succumb to the totalitarianism, whether fascist or communist, sweeping through much of the rest of Europe.

The necessities of the Second World War led to the sort of economic planning favoured by Macmillan. There was an upsurge of Disraelian sentiment among conservatives at this time, a feeling that greater effort was needed to eliminate poverty. In 1943 some of them formed the Tory Reform Committee to campaign for full employment in a welfare state, declaring that 'to follow Adam Smith in the age of Keynes is like adhering to the Ptolemaic astronomy after Copernicus'. Only after the defeat of the party in the general election of 1945, however, were most conservatives gradually persuaded of the need for the sort of 'humanised capitalism' advocated by Macmillan and the Reform Committee. In accepting Keynesianism they were, of course, careful to put their own gloss upon it, arguing that the objective of a planned economy was neither social levelling nor the frustration of individual ambition. A 'Disraelian approach to modern politics' – the title of a lecture given in 1954 by R. A. Butler – did not require conservatives to abandon their traditional vindication of inequality. 'Society is a partnership,' according to Butler:

> and so underlying all our differences there should be a fundamental unity – the very antithesis of the 'class war' – bringing together what Disraeli called the Two Nations into a single social entity . . . But if Disraeli provided us with inspiration, he was no less prescient in warning of the pitfalls . . . He cautioned us . . . that we should seek to secure greater equality, not by levelling the few, but by elevating the many . . . It is no part of our policy to repress the initiative and independence of the strong. Indeed, unless we allow men and women to rise as far as they may, and so allow our society to be served by what I describe as the *richness of developed differences*, we shall not have the means to earn our national living, let alone to afford a welfare state.

This modernised Disraelian strand of conservatism now became party orthodoxy, and for the next twenty years few voices were to be heard proclaiming the truths of political economy.

From the early 1970s, however, a growing number of conservatives urged a right turn from the middle way of economic planning and extensive social welfare. After the election in 1975 of a new Conservative party leader this momentum to restore a purer form of capitalism became known as Thatcherism, about which there is now an enormous body of literature. As a political project

Thatcherism was in some ways startling, vigorously challenging as it did the assumption that conservatives were now permanently resident in a half-way house between individualism and collectivism. In their bid to kill off socialism – by which was meant the post-war settlement put in place by both Labour and Conservative governments – the New Right assailed the institutions of what they considered a bloated and decadent state. Thatcherism was an example of ideological fundamentalism, an acute form of rationalism in politics which wanted society to be reshaped according to a free-market blueprint. The new individualists may or may not have succeeded in burying socialism; but their radical zeal certainly put an end to the assumption that conservatism consists in a Burkean reverence for tradition and a distaste for political upheaval. In one sense, perhaps, the New Right did not break decisively with tradition. There was much talk among them of going backwards to the future – of retrieving, that is, the dynamic spirit of the Victorian enterprise culture in order to restore the British nation to its former glory. But though Thatcherites may have been counter-revolutionary rather than revolutionary, they displayed little respect for a settled way of life in their impatience to dismantle the institutions of what post-war conservatives had hailed as 'humanised capitalism'.

The Thatcherite project was also unprecedented in its political success. In the past extreme individualists, such as members of the Liberty and Property Defence League, had rarely represented the mainstream of conservative thinking. But the New Right – through a network of 'think-tanks' as well as the expulsion from government office of any 'wet' patrician Tory judged not to be ideologically 'one of us' – were soon intellectually ascendant. By the 1980s only stragglers were left on the middle way, and few extolled the virtues of Disraelian conservativism against the 'two nations' approach of the parvenu right. In office through the 1980s, moreover, conservatives did succeed in pursuing a broadly consistent strategy of increasing the scope for capitalist endeavour by rolling back the state from the economy.

Less remarkable than the New Right's political success were its ideas, which combined, as had expressions of individualism since Social Darwinism, libertarian and authoritarian elements. Thatcherites advocated a restoration of both freedom and order, an extension of individual choice coupled with a strengthening of the mechanisms of law and order.

The kind of freedom they had in mind was the opportunity for enterprising individuals to accumulate wealth unhindered by government. Post-war Keynesian techniques of economic management, they complained, had led to a massive concentration of state power with little scope for adventure capitalism. Middle-way conservatives and other collectivists had sought a safe haven somewhere between capitalism and socialism. But the middle way had turned into a slippery slope. The effect had been to replace the pendulum of party politics by what Keith Joseph, in *Stranded on the Middle Ground?* (1976), called a 'ratchet' of increasingly interventionist government. Among the manifestations of an overloaded state were punitive taxation to finance excessive public expenditure, high unemployment, inflation, inefficient labour practices and general economic torpor. The mistake had been to assume that government was capable of eradicating unemployment and poverty by means of economic management and redistributive fiscal policies. 'Making the rich poorer does not make the poor richer,' according to Joseph:

> but it does make the state stronger – and it does increase the power of officials and politicians, power more menacing, more permanent and less useful than market power within the rule of law. Inequality of income can only be eliminated at the cost of freedom. The pursuit of income equality will turn this country into a totalitarian slum.

The solution was to reduce the functions of government to a minimum, recognising that the inequalities arising from a capitalist market are ultimately advantageous to both rich and poor. 'You cannot create a rich society,' argued Geoffrey Howe, 'without allowing some individuals to become rich as well.' The expectation of wealth is the carrot tempting an enterprising minority to generate the prosperity from which everyone eventually benefits.

The New Right was fond of contrasting the enervating culture of the welfare state with what one writer labelled the 'vigorous virtues' of competitive individualism (Letwin, 1992). This is why their project appeared to some extent as a counter-revolution, recalling heroic moments of the past in an effort to drag the nation back to the Victorian Golden Age of self-sufficiency, thrift and rugged adventure. But the recreation of this kind of self-help culture was said to require a strengthening of law and order. Among the manifestations of the dependence induced by welfare capitalism, according to Thatcherites, were a rising crime rate, promiscuous sex, drugs, unruliness in schools, hooliganism, trade union belligerence and other forms of 'permissive' behaviour. Hence the call for a return to a morality based on self-reliance, decency and respect for the rule of law. Hence, too, the need for a state which, though limited in scope, was neither weak nor inactive in discharging its responsibility for public order. Under her leadership, Margaret Thatcher announced in 1989, successive governments had attempted both to revive capitalist enterprise and to push back the permissive society:

> That's why we've toughened the law on the muggers and marauders. That's why we've increased penalties on drink-driving, on drugs, on rape. That's why we've increased the police and strengthened their powers . . . For there can be no freedom without order. There can be no order without authority; and authority that is impotent or hesitant in the face of intimidation, crime and violence, cannot endure.

The economic liberation of individuals, then, had to be accompanied by a restoration of society's traditional structure of command.

Conclusion

In my conclusion to this chapter in the second edition of *Political Ideologies*, published in 1994, I suggested that there were no signs that conservatism was likely to disintegrate or evolve in some fresh direction. With the collapse of communist regimes in Eastern Europe and successive electoral failures of the Labour party, commentators were then wondering whether socialism had a future. There was also speculation about the potential development of the relatively new, still unfixed, ideas which constituted ecologism. Conservatism, however, seemed set to chug along in the same direction. No one seriously contended, as many did with regard to socialism, that conservatism was exhausted – that, having served its historical mission, so to speak, it was drifting into terminal decline. As members of a broad church, I suggested, conservatives would continue to quarrel about the extent to which government should manage the economy and provide social welfare. They would agree, however, about the need for ordered liberty within a state that preserves or restores inequalities while attending to the mechanisms of social discipline.

Since the publication of the last edition of *Political Ideologies*, however, some commentators have written conservatism's obituary. Whereas socialism is now assumed to have some kind of future, and the contours of ecologism have become 'thicker' or more easily identified, there is a sense in academic writing that conservatism is about to expire.

For John Gray, for example, conservatism began its 'end game' by embracing the ideas and policies of the New Right in the 1980s. There are two aspects to the argument. The first is that free-market conservatives abandoned pragmatism for the abstract logic of economic liberalism – though a liberalism spiced with the rhetoric of Victorian values. In pronouncing that human affairs should be conducted according to market principles, the New Right discarded the conventional conservative aversion to social engineering. 'Bourgeois modernisation', on this account, was a project propelled by the alien dogma of Enlightenment rationalism. The success of the project, secondly, served to 'hollow out' those institutions of old Britain with which conservatism had resonated. The pragmatic defence of ordered hierarchy made sense within an *ancien régime* which had unfolded without dramatic interruption over 300 years. There respect for tradition and lingering attitudes of deference had sustained the claim of patrician statecraft to follow the course of history. But the New Right's release of market forces disrupted tradition and dissolved social hierarchies. The effect was to destroy the culture in which cogent conservative thinking and political practice had flourished. In Gray's words:

> In deserting common sense for crankish doctrines conservatism has detached itself from the society for which it once claimed to speak . . . [The Conservative party] cannot hope to put Tory Britain back together. That has been broken into pieces – partly by Conservative policies. Tory Britain is gone for good. With it has gone the future for conservatism.
>
> (Gray and Willetts, 1997: 163)

The New Right, then, waged war against tradition in the name of market fundamentalism, and in doing so deprived its successors of ideological bearings.

Some British conservative politicians have also considered whether their doctrine now rests on shaky foundations. In 2001 the party suffered another major general election defeat. The campaign to find a successor to William Hague, who resigned as leader after the Labour victory, plunged the party into civil war, with rival factions accusing one another of entering a doctrinal cul-de-sac. Some even suggested that without ideological refurbishment the party might become the third force of British politics, trailing in elections behind the Liberal Democrats.

The problem for conservatives is deciding what kind of society they wish to safeguard or promote. If, as John Gray argues, old Britain has been dismantled by market forces, there have been other challenges to the regime which conservatives once cherished. They were always, for example, staunch defenders of the constitutional integrity of the United Kingdom. But what role is there for a unionist party when devolutionary policies are likely to lead to an ever looser political configuration of England, Northern Ireland, Scotland and Wales?

What principally divides conservatives, however, is the issue of Europe. Should they continue to champion the peculiar virtues of a plucky little island race, unconquered for a thousand years, by resisting attempts to dilute national sovereignty in an expanding European Union? Or should a party of capital, inspired by the adventurous spirit of their ancestors which led to the creation of a great empire, now seize the opportunity for fresh markets which full membership of the European Union provides? One side of the debate accuses the other of wishing to submerge what is specifically British in a flood of Eurocratic legislation. The other claims that distaste for the EU is indicative of an attitude that is crudely nationalistic and perhaps somewhat racist in its depiction of foreigners. Each side tends to accuse the other of lacking the ideas for confronting the challenges of the new millennium.

It is, of course, impossible to predict the electoral future of right-of-centre parties in Britain or elsewhere. There are nevertheless reasons for suggesting that commentators as well as some conservative politicians have been too quick to suggest that the doctrine has begun to unravel. First, the New Right were not heretical in deriving their political project from what Disraeli described as 'loose metaphysical' speculation. John Gray perpetuates the myth that conservatives have been disinclined to equip themselves with theoretical justification. Conservatives, as we have seen, have often argued from fundamental principles, and there is no reason to suppose that the New Right preference for market abstractions dealt a fatal blow to the doctrine.

Secondly, those who lament the absence of some overarching idea capable of uniting conservatives on every issue misunderstand how the doctrine operated in the past. Gray is able to portray earlier conservatives as forming a common front by suggesting that the New Right were classical liberals masquerading as conservatives. Yet, as we have illustrated in this chapter, conservative advocacy of the free market did not begin with the New Right. Conservatism has always consisted of diverse strands. In the past squabbles among free-marketeers and champions of managed capitalism have split the Conservative party more severely than recent disputes about issues such as Europe. Conservatives have rarely been bonded by some tight unifying theme. Rather, they have sought their bearings within the contours of an ideal of ordered hierarchy – contours broad enough to allow for plenty of disagreement.

What about Gray's claim, finally, that 'bourgeois modernisation' destroyed the old Britain of tradition and deference from which conservatism drew its appeal? Even if the New Right project of the 1980s did unsettle society, there is no compelling reason to suppose that conservatives have been deprived of a context for constructing plausible narratives of the sound political order. In the future, as in the past, they are likely to call for a society which preserves inequalities while preventing social indiscipline, and in doing so to disagree as to how precisely such an order is to be safeguarded or attained.

Further reading

Michael Freeden, *Ideologies and Political Theory* (1996), the most ambitious book in recent decades to reflect upon the nature of ideological thinking, contains a challenging section of one hundred pages on 'The adaptability of conservatism'. Roger Eatwell and Noel O'Sullivan (eds) *The Nature of the Right* (1989), contains five chapters by Eatwell on the nature of conservatism together with chapters by other authors on particular countries, including France, Germany, Britain and America. Perhaps the most eloquent and interesting general account of conservatism, with chapters on Britain, Germany and France, is Noel O'Sullivan, *Conservatism* (1976), though his characterisation of the doctrine as a 'philosophy of imperfection' inclines him to exclude from the conservative canon writers who properly belong there. More recently the doctrine has been depicted as 'a widening of Burke's indictments not only of the French Revolution but of the larger revolution we call modernity' by Robert Nisbet, *Conservatism: Dream and Reality* (1986). A. O. Hirschman, *The Rhetoric of Reaction* (1991), provides a superb insight into the contours of conservative thinking. Hirschman's approach is to uncover the characteristic rhetorical postures of opponents of reform during the past 200 years, using illustrations from the counter-revolutionary discourse of the French revolution, the anti-democratic movement of the nineteenth century and recent polemicism against the welfare state.

There are two books written from different ideological perspectives which are more concerned with the philosophy than the history of conservatism: Roger Scruton, *The Meaning of Conservatism* (1980), is a brilliant vindication of authority and inequality with interesting comment on Burke and others within the canon; Ted Honderich, *Conservatism* (1991), is a sustained critique of conservative themes. Arthur Aughey, Greta Jones and W. M. Riches, *The Conservative Political Tradition in Britain and the United States* (1992), is an interesting comparative analysis rich in insight.

With regard to some of the thinkers mentioned in the chapter, the most brilliant, though flawed, study of Burke is probably Conor Cruise O'Brien, *The Great Melody* (1993). A short, sharp account of Burke's ideas from a Marxist perspective is C. B. MacPherson, *Burke* (1980). The story of the group to which Disraeli belonged in the 1840s is told with style by Richard Faber, *Young England* (1987). 'Social Darwinism' is well treated in M. W. Taylor, *Men versus the State* (1992); and Kenneth D. Brown (ed.) *Essays in Anti-Labour History* (1974), contains a chapter on Mallock. On Oakeshott see Paul Franco, *The Political Philosophy of Michael Oakeshott* (1990).

There is a vast literature on the New Right. Among the more comprehensive books are two by professors of politics: Dennis Kavanagh, *Thatcherism and British Politics* (1987), and Andrew Gamble, *The Free Economy and the Strong State* (1988); and two by political journalists: Peter Jenkins, *Mrs Thatcher's Revolution* (1987), and the thematically tighter Hugo Young, *One of Us* (1993). Andrew Adonis and Tim Hames (eds), *A Conservative Revolution?* (1994), is helpful on the ideas and practice of the New Right.

References

Adonis, Andrew and Hames, Tim, eds (1994) *A Conservative Revolution? The Thatcher–Reagan Decade in Perspective*, Manchester: Manchester University Press.

Aughey, Arthur, Jones, Greta and Riches, W. M. (1992) *The Conservative Political Tradition in Britain and the United States*, London: Pinter.

Brown, Kenneth D., ed. (1974) *Essays in Anti-Labour History: Responses to the Rise of Labour in Britain*, London: Macmillan.

Cowling, M. (1978) 'The present condition' in M. Cowling (ed.) *Conservative Essays*, London: Cassell.

Eatwell, Roger and O'Sullivan, Noel, eds (1989) *The Nature of the Right: European and American Politics and Political Thought since 1798*, London: Pinter.

Faber, Richard (1987) *Young England*, London: Faber.

Franco, Paul (1990) *The Political Philosophy of Michael Oakeshott*, New Haven CT and London: Yale University Press.

Freeden, Michael (1996) *Ideologies and Political Theory*, Oxford: Clarendon Press.

Gamble, Andrew (1988) *The Free Economy and the Strong State: The Politics of Thatcherism*, Basingstoke: Macmillan.

Gray, J. and Willetts, D. (1997) *Is Conservatism Dead?* London: Social Market Foundation.

Greenleaf, W. H. (1983) *The British Political Tradition*, II *The Ideological Tradition*, London: Routledge.

Hirschman, A. O. (1991) *The Rhetoric of Reaction: Perversity, Futility, Jeopardy*, Cambridge MA: Belknap Press of Harvard University Press.

Hollis, C. (1957) *Death of a Gentleman: The Letters of Robert Fossett*, Glasgow: Collins.

Honderich, Ted (1991) *Conservatism*, London: Penguin.

Huntington, S. P. (1957) 'Conservatism as an ideology', *American Political Science Review*, 51, pp. 454–73.

Jenkins, Peter (1987) *Mrs Thatcher's Revolution: The Ending of the Socialist Era*, London: Cape.

Joseph, K. and Sumption, J. (1979) *Equality*, London: Murray.

Kavanagh, Dennis (1987) *Thatcherism and British Politics: The End of Consensus?* Oxford: Oxford University Press.

Letwin, S. R. (1992) *The Anatomy of Thatcherism*, London: Fontana.

MacPherson, C. B. (1980) *Burke*, Oxford: Oxford University Press.

Minogue, K. (1985) *Alien Powers: The Pure Theory of Ideology*, London: Weidenfeld & Nicolson.

Nisbet, Robert (1986) *Conservatism: Dream and Reality*, Milton Keynes: Open University Press.

Oakeshott, M. (1962) *Rationalism in Politics and other Essays*, London: Methuen.

O'Brien, Conor Cruise (1993) *The Great Melody: A Thematic Biography and Commented Anthology of Edmund Burke*, London: Mandarin.

O'Sullivan, Noel (1976) *Conservatism*, London: Dent.

Quinton, A. (1978) *The Politics of Imperfection: The Religious and Secular Traditions of Conservative Thought in England from Hooker to Oakeshott*, London: Faber.

Scruton, Roger (1980) *The Meaning of Conservatism*, Harmondsworth: Penguin.

Taylor, M. W. (1992) *Men versus the State: Herbert Spencer and later Victorian Individualism*, Oxford: Clarendon Press.

White, R. J. (1964) *The Conservative Tradition*, 2nd edn, London: Black.

Young, Hugo (1993) *One of Us: A Biography of Margaret Thatcher*, 3rd edn, London: Macmillan.

Chapter 4

Socialism

Vincent Geoghegan

Problems of definition

The key problem in defining socialism, as with all ideologies, is that of adequately capturing similarity and difference; showing what unites socialists without minimising the tremendous differences which separate them. Two dangers have to be avoided: 'essentialism' and 'historicism'. Essentialism reduces the richness of the socialist tradition to a few very general 'essential' or 'core' characteristics. These 'essential' characteristics will be few because once one starts eliminating those many areas over which socialists disagree, relatively little common ground will remain. For example, socialists disagree in their conceptualisations of the state, some seeing it as a reformable and ultimately beneficial instrument of social change, others as a prop to capitalist society which will eventually wither away. Attitudes to the state cannot therefore form one of the 'essential' elements of socialism. Likewise, since some socialists look forward to the end of private property, whilst others consider it as a necessary feature of any conceivable society, socialism cannot be defined in terms of a 'core' theory of property. As a consequence very few concepts or beliefs will be left to provide the definition of socialism. Those core ideas that do remain will be at a high level of generality, for, the more specific one becomes, the greater the risk of resurrecting the major differences which separate socialists. Hence it is true to say, for example, that (except for some very early examples) socialists undoubtedly believe in equality, but when asked what they mean by equality, they have responded with a variety of definitions from equality of opportunity to levelling uniformity. Thus whilst it is true to say that most socialists do believe in equality, this bald statement conceals more than it reveals. In short, the desire to find common ground uniting all socialists will often result in a rather meagre collection of very abstract 'essential' propositions.

One reaction to essentialism is a flight into 'historicism': namely the reduction of the socialist tradition to mere historical narrative, where an account is given of all those over the centuries who have called themselves, or have been deemed by others to be, socialists. A procession of utopian socialists, Marxists, Christian Socialists, social democrats and so forth passes by, leaving little sense of what has brought them all together. Difference is registered by this approach, but any attempt to isolate similarities is all but abandoned, and one is left with a mass of dates, personalities and theories.

Any attempt to provide a definition of socialism which avoids the two dangers of essentialism and historicism is inevitably going to involve an element of compromise. It is, in other words, necessary to have a certain definitional modesty. It will not be possible to produce a definition of socialism which does full justice to similarity and difference; generalities will have to be qualified (as in 'this of course does not apply to socialism brand X'); saving phrases will constantly appear (such as 'most socialists', or 'there was a tendency among socialists', or 'socialists by and large'). So long, therefore, as a degree of flexibility is employed, it will be possible to make general statements about socialism without assuming an underlying essential identity. The philosopher Ludwig

Wittgenstein sought to capture similarity and difference with his theory of 'family resemblance'. In an analysis of what united games (board games, card games, ball games, Olympic Games), he concluded that they had a series of overlapping similarities and dissimilarities, which united them into a *family* of games. Family members are not identical, but they clearly belong together: 'games form a *family* the members of which have family likenesses. Some of them have the same nose, others the same eyebrows and others again the same way of walking; and these likenesses overlap' (1972: 17). In a similar fashion one can point to overlapping family resemblances in socialism. Wittgenstein argued that common features could be found in his 'families'; the view taken in this chapter is that, given the compromises mentioned above, it is possible to make general statements about the nature of socialism.

What is socialism?

Let us begin at a very general level. Socialists, along with proponents of other ideologies, are engaged in three fundamental activities: they are offering a critique, an alternative and a theory of transition; that is, they reveal defects in a society, suggest better arrangements and indicate how these improvements are to be achieved. Of course the relative importance of these activities vary among socialists: some, for example have a highly developed critique of capitalism but only a fairly cursory theory of transition; whilst others may have sophisticated analyses of both, but are unwilling to engage in advanced 'speculation' about a future socialist society.

The critique is usually grounded in some form of egalitarianism. Some early socialists were not egalitarian, some socialists have been egalitarian in theory but not in practice, others have considered equality to be a 'bourgeois' value, and yet others have so defined egalitarianism as to allow a deal of inegalitarianism. Nonetheless most socialists have viewed capitalism, which historically has been their main target, as a fundamentally unequal economic system, concentrating wealth and power in the hands of a minority and condemning the majority to absolute, or relative, poverty and impotence. Socialists stress the unacceptable differences between life chances in such divided societies, and contrast capitalist notions of constitutional and market equality with the widespread inequality found in everyday life. They echo Anatole France's remark that 'The law in its majestic equality forbids the rich as well as the poor to sleep under bridges, to beg in the streets, and to steal bread.'

A second element usually found in the critique is a denunciation of those practices and institutions which undermine or stifle sociability and co-operation. Capitalism is criticised for the isolated, selfish individuals it encourages; too little care is shown for others, who tend to be seen as either irrelevant to one's 'private' sphere, and therefore not worthy of genuine concern, or as competitors, and as such a threat. The result is a stunted individual unable to achieve the humanity that only flows from a genuine community. Socialists agree with the words of John Donne:

No man is an island entire of itself; every man is a piece of the continent, a part of the main . . . any man's death diminishes me, because I am involved in mankind; and therefore never send to know for whom the bell tolls; it tolls for thee.

A contrast is thus drawn between the rhetoric of community promoted by capitalism, with its images of togetherness and belonging, and the fact of isolation and marginality.

Thirdly, the critique operates with a conception of freedom which makes it highly critical of liberal free-market formulations. The classical liberal definition of freedom as absence of constraint is deemed to be contradictory and shallow. It is contradictory because the liberty of the free market tends to undermine both the freedom enshrined in constitutional rights and the actual free activity of the individual; poverty flows from free markets, and poor people cannot be fully free. The contrast here is between the complacent claim of the advocates of capitalism that it is a free society and the reality of a large measure of unfreedom in such a society; or, as David McLellan has paraphrased an old sentiment, 'it was no use having the right of access to the Grill Room at the Ritz if you couldn't afford the bill' (1983: 145). It is shallow in that genuine liberty is not mere freedom *from* external pressures but freedom *to* develop fully as an individual among other free individuals; to be not a mere isolated unit ('free' from all that is most satisfying) but a well rounded, fulfilled human being, delighting in the free use of all one's faculties.

Thus in their critique socialists have echoed, and conceptualised in their own particular way, the great rallying call of the French revolution – liberty, equality and fraternity – rendering it into equality, community and liberty. These values are deemed to be both goals to be achieved and individual attributes. A future society embodying equality, community and liberty would simply not be possible if these values were not in some sense grounded in contemporary humanity. In arguing this way, socialists deploy a variety of empirical propositions and ethical characterisations. Thus whilst very few socialists would argue that individuals are equal as regards ability, character, and so forth (i.e. possessing *identical* characteristics), most would posit a common humanity composed of human capacities, needs and entitlements. Shylock's words in the *Merchant of Venice* come to mind: 'Hath not a Jew eyes?/ hath not a Jew hands, organs, dimensions, senses, affections, passions? . . . if you prick us, do we not bleed?' The deep inequalities of capitalism are deemed to be an affront to this fundamental level of equality. Likewise, whilst acknowledging the lack of genuine community in capitalist society, socialists do argue that people are at some basic level social or sociable, or have the ability, or the need to become so. Freedom too, though absent in its full form in capitalism, is held to be a deeply rooted human aspiration or need. Even socialists who are hostile to theories of human nature in which fixed or essential characteristics are assumed, and who stress the changing nature of humanity over history, would nonetheless recognise the continuing presence of the human capacity for equality, community and liberty.

Socialists therefore claim that their critique isn't mere abstract aspiration, but is, rather, rooted in human experience.

The critique is, as we have seen, a far from seamless web. Important differences exist between socialists. What is the status, for example, of the constitutional rights and values of liberal capitalist societies? Many Marxists have considered that the equality, community and liberty offered by such societies is not merely bogus but actually harmful, because it mystifies true relationships and thereby neutralises the revolutionary proletariat; social democrats and democratic socialists, on the other hand, have considered them to be genuine, if flawed, gains which need to be built upon and perfected. Socialists have also weighted these values differently, some emphasising equality and community over liberty (as in certain forms of Asian communism), others liberty over equality and community (as in Western libertarian socialism) and so on. Much of the diversity of the socialist movement arises from these differing emphases.

Tensions between the three values have been identified both within the socialist movement and by critical outsiders. Is it not unfair, it has been argued, to criticise capitalism for failing to combine equality and liberty when any conceivable economic system is likely to have immense problems in reconciling them? Does not the drive for equality act as a drag on the development of freedom? Are the freedom and equality of the employer to count for nothing? Are not community and liberty also pulling in different directions? Is not a vital component of liberty the right to develop apart from or even against the community? When can the needs of the community legitimately override one's individual liberty? These problems have led many to reject the socialist critique – perhaps capitalism if not an ideal system is nonetheless the least worst! They have also prompted many socialists to conclude that some form of accommodation with capitalism is necessary.

Turning from the socialist critique to the socialist alternative, we are again confronted with great diversity. Socialists have found it impossible to function without an alternative but have embraced the activity with varying degrees of warmth. Thus although an outline of communist society can be reconstructed from Marx's writings he was worried that speculation about the future would distract the working class from freely creating such a society themselves. William Morris, on the other hand, was an enthusiastic utopian who thought that it was a duty of socialists to show how and why their alternative was superior to capitalism. A strong rationalist current in socialism has given socialists the confidence to pose alternatives. Reason is deemed to be a faculty and a norm, and therefore people can distinguish truth from error and construct a rational alternative to an unsatisfactory (and therefore irrational) reality. Socialism, like liberalism, is heir to that great period of questioning in the seventeenth and eighteenth centuries which most graphically manifested itself in the Enlightenment and the French revolution. Ideologies such as conservatism which argue that reality is too complex to be adequately grasped by the mere individual (let alone criticised by them) are rejected by socialists as false and repressive. Some socialists, it should be said, do not base their alternatives in rationalism; some have confidence in faculties such as intuition or feeling and develop non-rational (though not necessarily irrational) visions (Sorel's espousal of myth, for example, or the sex/drug-based visions of the US New Left); others look to inspired texts for their grounding, as in certain forms of Christian Socialism.

The many and varied alternatives which emerge from this process necessarily reflect the values underpinning the critique. Socialists have favoured redistribution of wealth or abolition of private property to overcome inequality; various forms of co-operative production and radical town planning have been suggested to overcome competition and isolation; new work and education patterns have been proposed to promote the growth of free individuality. They have varied in degrees of radicalism from reformist amelioration of existing structures to root-and-branch revolutionary transformation, or may take a staged form of a short-term minimum programme leading in time to a more ambitious maximum programme. They are presented in a variety of forms: manifesto commitments, five-year plans, full-scale utopian blueprints, etc.

A recurring theme is the democratic nature of the alternatives – genuine democracy is seen as embodying the unity of equality, community and liberty: all are equal in a democracy; the democratic will is a communal will; and democracy is grounded in the free choice of the individual. In its earliest days socialism was not democratic – many utopian socialists looked to elites such as intellectuals, philanthropists and statesmen to bring about social transformation. Later socialists, especially those who feared the effect of 'bourgeois indoctrination' on the working class, have also been prepared to modify democracy with more authoritarian elements – the Marxist-Leninist organisational principle of 'democratic centralism', for example. These are exceptions to the predominant conception of socialism as democratic to its core.

Many socialists also claim that their alternatives embody the best of liberalism, liberalism at a higher stage, stripped of its association with the worst aspects of capitalism. Eduard Bernstein, for example, when discussing liberalism, asserts that 'socialism is its legitimate heir, not only in chronological sequence, but also in its spiritual qualities' (1961: 149). Socialism is seen as providing a climate in which the great, and historically revolutionary, values of liberalism can flourish, unlike capitalism, which in practice causes these values to wither. This is what Andrew Gamble means when he writes: 'As a doctrine socialism is not so much a call to reject the principles of liberalism as a claim that it alone can fulfil them' (1981: 100) There are of course socialists who are irredeemably hostile to the liberal legacy both in theory and in practice (Pol Pot and the Khmer Rouge, for example) but such intense hostility is an exception. The critique of liberalism, and the routine abuse directed towards it by socialists should not be taken as wholesale rejection.

The criticism directed towards socialist alternatives, especially the most radical of these alternatives, recalls the types of argument long levelled at 'utopian' schemes in general, namely, that they are unpractical and unrealistic.

Often this is couched in terms of theories of human nature: individuals are essentially imperfect as regards intellect and morality and therefore cannot fulfil the sorts of role which socialist society demands. Thus, it is argued, individuals lack the mental ability to plan the immense complexities of a socialist society ('what cannot be known cannot be planned' (Hayek, 1988: 85)), and cannot be trusted to act altruistically in such structures, whereas capitalism, by contrast, with its market converting private greed into public utility, merely requires humans, not angels. Such criticism has drawn sustenance from the sorry record of so-called socialist societies, from the Soviet Union onwards, despite the claims of many that the socialist credentials of these societies were or are bogus. Friedrich Hayek, one of the most influential critics of socialism, sees the socialist project as based on ignorance and vanity, and doomed to failure, owing to the inevitable constraints of the real world:

> The intellectuals' vain search for a truly socialist community, which results in the idealisation of, and then disillusionment with a seemingly endless string of 'utopias' . . . should suggest that there might be something about socialism that does not conform to certain facts.
>
> (1988: 85–6)

The socialist alternative is thus damned as a factual impossibility.

Socialists clearly disagree in their critiques and alternatives, but it is over the question of transition that the greatest and most intense disagreement occurs. Whereas the alternatives do reflect the values of the critique, the theories of transition may have a more complicated relationship with such values. Many socialists believe that there is a continuity of values from critique to transition to alternative. They argue that the socialist end must be operative in the socialist means. Thus since the goal of socialism includes peace, respect for others, truth and integrity, these qualities must be apparent in the transition to socialism. This is justified on both ethical and prudential grounds – socialists *should* incorporate their values in the transformation, and are more likely to be ultimately successful if they do so. Other socialists, however, argue that the resistance to socialism is so great in society that the transformation may require the use of methods which, in the interim, fall short of the value system of socialism. Thus the use of force may be necessary, though the goal is a society without violence; or there may be the need for elite leadership, though a society without elites is desired. The justification is usually in terms of 'political realities'. The goal will never be achieved without the use of 'regrettable' methods: 'One cannot make an omelette without breaking eggs.' The two approaches condemn one another from these perspectives – the latter sees the former as naively idealistic, the former views the latter as cynical and manipulative.

A wide range of transitions have been advocated over the years: among these are general strikes, mass insurrections, parliamentary roads, effected either singly or in concert. Underlying beliefs inform the choice of method. Social democrats have believed that it is possible, through Parliament, to turn the state into the cutting edge of socialism; revolutionary Marxists assumed that ruling classes would use any means to cling to power, necessitating the use of violent revolution; ethical socialists believed that fundamental transformations had to occur in the hearts of individuals; Fabians maintained that, under the guidance of experts, socialism would gradually but inevitably evolve out of capitalism. Some see the political arena as the main site of transformation, others the industrial; yet others seek to combine the two. Some look for transformation top down, via the state, others from the bottom up, via trade unions, co-operatives and other 'grass roots' institutions. The variations and combinations make classification extraordinarily difficult.

The moral and practical problems involved in the various theories of transition are themselves multitudinous. Moral questions come spilling out. When is radical political action legitimate? Can the present generation be sacrificed for the good of future socialist citizens? Conversely, is an ethical, reformist strategy a betrayal of the interests of future generations? When is it right to break the law in pursuit of the socialist goal? When can violence be used? Questions on the effectiveness of strategy and tactics are as old as the ideology itself. Who is to be the transforming agency? The working class; a part of the working class; the working class with sections of the bourgeoisie; 'the people'; 'the nation'? What is to be the role of political parties, or of intellectuals? Can socialism be brought about in one country? Who are the enemies of socialism? Does participation in government de-radicalise socialist parties? Socialists have agonised over these questions from the start.

This therefore is a good point to move from consideration of these more general issues to looking at the actual history of socialism. The focus will be on the British experience.

The emergence of socialism

Socialism emerged with the development of industrial capitalism at the start of the nineteenth century. It is, however, possible to identify precursors in Britain as far back as the fourteenth century which, whilst not socialist, are of interest in that: they represent the earliest radical response to the growth of capitalism in Britain; later socialists have declared an affinity with them, so that under-standing of the former is assisted by knowledge of the latter; and in a striking fashion, they advocate, embody or discuss beliefs and visions which lie at the heart of socialism and are thus of abiding interest. A good starting point would be the Peasants' Revolt of 1381, which formed part of the complex break-up of English feudalism and the emergence of those social relations which would eventually produce industrial capitalism. In the pages of the medieval chronicler Froissart we can read of the radical cleric John Ball and his sermon to the rebellious peasantry at Blackheath on the proverb 'Whan Adam dalf and Eve span wo was thanne a gentilman', with its image of a Golden Age of equality before the Fall. By the sixteenth century the capitalist penetration of agriculture was such as to help stimulate a major critical work: Thomas More's *Utopia* (1516). In this work More developed a trenchant critique of private property, and speculated about an imaginary island where property was common, distribution was based on need, not wealth, and where 'with the simultaneous abolition of money and the passion for money, how many other social problems have been solved, how many crimes eradicated!' (1965: 130). In the following century, during the turbulent events of the Civil War, Gerrard Winstanley proposed political democracy and economic communism, and set up a short-lived 'Digger' colony to put these ideas into practice. 'A man,' he wrote 'had better to have had no body than to have no food for it; therefore this restraining of the earth from brethren by brethren is oppression and bondage' (1973: 295–6).

The words 'socialism' and 'socialist' began to appear in Britain and France from the late 1820s and early 1830s. The earliest use of the term 'socialist' was in an 1827 issue of the *Co-operative Magazine*, a journal associated with the man whom many see as the founder of British socialism, Robert Owen (1771–1858). Owen's life highlights the Janus face of Britain's industrial revolution: from one aspect the tremendous increase in productivity and wealth which enabled Owen, the son of a humble tradesman, to make a fortune as a manufacturer; from the other the human costs experienced by large sections of the population, which propelled Owen in the direction of philanthropy and socialism. The remedy he proposed rested on a small number of basic ideas which he stubbornly broadcast to whomever would listen, certain that he had discovered the fundamental levers of human happiness. Since for Owen character was determined by the environment, he proposed that the environment be manipulated so as to replace its negative traits with positive ones:

> any community may be arranged . . . in such a manner as, not only to withdraw vice, poverty, and, in a great degree, misery, from the world, but also to place *every* individual under such circumstances in which he shall enjoy more permanent happiness than can be given to *any* individual under the principles which have hitherto regulated society.
>
> (Morton, 1962: 73)

Owen attempted to put this theory into practice in a number of ventures: he commenced fairly successfully with a reform of working and living conditions at his New Lanark mill; and much less successfully, in the more ambitious schemes (like the community of New Harmony in the United States) which were envisaged as prototypes for a radically new co-operative form of existence. Owen displayed both a naive rationalism and a deeply engrained elitism. He believed that he could convert conservative governments and landowners, not merely to his minimal quasi-philanthropic enterprises (which could have seemed attractive to ruling circles worried by labour unrest), but to his maximal socialist schemes; ideas of class struggle were alien to his nature. He saw reform in terms of expert planning from above, and ordinary men and women as objects of benevolence rather than as creative subjects.

From the 1830s to the 1880s the energy of the working class was mainly channelled through movements such as co-operation, trade unionism (in both of which Owen played a role) and Chartism. There was little native development in socialist theory, unless one counts the Christian Socialists, a group of pre-dominantly middle-class reformers such as Frederick Maurice and Charles Kingsley, who considered the competition engendered by capitalism to be contrary to Christian principles. Britain did, however, become home to undoubt-edly the most influential theorists in the socialist tradition, Karl Marx (1818–83) and Friedrich Engels (1820–95). In his early work (some important texts of which remained unpublished in his lifetime – particularly the *Economic and Philosophical Manuscripts*, 1844) Marx developed a critical synthesis of German idealist philosophy (centred on the work of Hegel), British political economy (including Adam Smith and Ricardo) and utopian socialism (notably the French theorists Fourier and Saint-Simon, and Owen himself). In the resulting new theoretical system a critique of capitalism was formulated highlighting the deleterious effects of alienation, communism was posited as the alternative, and the proletariat were entrusted with bringing about the transition. In his mature work, much of it growing out of his studies in the British Museum, and part of it published in his lifetime as the first volume of *Capital* (1867), he produced an anatomy of capitalist society intended to demonstrate that the internal logic of the capitalist mode of production was impelling it towards its own destruction.

Engels's residence in Britain pre-dated Marx's arrival. In 1845 Engels had produced *The Condition of the Working Class in England*, which contained a graphic and horrifying account of the physical and mental suffering inflicted on working people by industrial capitalism. As a member of a German mill-owning family with a factory in Manchester, Engels proved a valuable collaborator for Marx in his studies of capitalism (though the precise nature of the Marx–Engels theoretical relationship is the source of scholarly controversy). Their most influential collaborative political text, the *Manifesto of the Communist Party* (1848), was confident that 'what the bourgeoisie . . . produces, above all, is its own gravediggers. Its fall and the victory of the proletariat are equally inevitable' (McLellan, 2000: 255). Engels produced a number of independent texts which developed, popularised (and some would say distorted) what was becoming known as Marxism; after Marx's death in 1883 he was of great importance in the burgeoning Marxist movement. In the wake of the failure of the 1848 revolutions London had become a centre for exiled revolutionaries, and it was there in 1864 that a body seeking international working-class unity, the International Working Men's Association (the First International) was established; Marx's inaugural address ended with the rallying call 'Proletarians of all countries, unite!' This organisation, which lasted until 1876, provided an arena for the development and propagation of socialist ideas, strategy and tactics; and also the forum for a vicious ideological battle between Marxism and anarchism.

During the last two decades of the nineteenth century, in a climate of periodic slump and depression, Britain experienced a socialist renaissance.

A number of theorists, most notably William Morris, Eleanor Marx and Edward Carpenter, sought to broaden socialists' concerns to include areas of human experience relatively neglected in earlier theorising. William Morris (1834–96) infused his socialism with insights drawn from his experiences as an artist and art critic. Capitalism, he argued, condemned the bulk of the population to labour which is fundamentally dehumanising; only in a socialist society could genuine creative activity be generalised. He drew on Victorian medievalist notions to compare the days before the triumph of capitalism when 'all men were more or less artists' (Morton, 1973: 61) with current conditions in which the instincts for beauty were thwarted. Lack of fulfilment was not confined to the working class, though they were the most abject victims – the aristocracy's idleness and the sham work of the bourgeoisie were part of a pervasive condition of waste and ugliness. He had no inhibitions about depicting a future socialist society, and when the American Edward Bellamy envisaged an influential, high-tech, centralised utopia, in *Looking Backward* (1888), Morris responded with *News from Nowhere* (1890), which combined respect for the supposed simplicity and creativity of the past with the political and economic arrangements of the Marxist vision of communism.

Marx's daughter, Eleanor (1855–98), jointly with her lover, Edward Aveling, produced work on the relationship between capitalism and the exploitation of women. Socialist feminism had emerged in the days of Owen, and included the Irish socialist William Thompson (1785–1833) and a number of women connected with the Owenite movement whom feminist historians are now beginning to bring to light: Anna Wheeler (1785–?), Fanny Wright (1795–1852) and Emma Martin (1812–51) (see Taylor, 1983). By the time Eleanor Marx and Aveling came to write 'The Woman Question from a Socialist Point of View' in 1886 the Owenite feminists had been forgotten. This article, which was a review of August Bebel's *Woman in the Past, the Present and the Future*, drew explicitly on the Marxist perspective of this work, and of Engels's *Origins of the Family, Private Property and the State*, to point to the ultimately economic basis of women's oppression in capitalism and to argue that the need for women to organise themselves was a necessary component of the struggle for human emancipation: 'both the oppressed classes, women and the immediate producers, must understand that their emancipation will come from themselves' (1886: 21). In a socialist society (which, like many of the Marxists of the time, they saw as an inevitable, certain event) men and women will communicate as equals; women will have the same educational and other opportunities as men; marriage – in its present commercial form – will disappear; sexuality will lose its burden of shame, and prostitution will vanish. In short: 'there will no longer be one law for the woman and one for the man.'

An even more radical perspective is to be found in the work of Edward Carpenter (1844–1929). His vision of socialism is of a society in which people have not merely overcome economic and political oppression but also the sexual and emotional repression which permeates capitalist society. Carpenter, however, unlike Eleanor Marx and Aveling, who spoke of the 'natural horror' people experienced on encountering 'the effeminate man and masculine woman', displayed much greater sensitivity to the diversity of human behaviour and relationships. Carpenter's defence and advocacy of same-sex relationships (a brave act in the wake of the Oscar Wilde scandal) was one aspect of a call for individuals to regain their sensuous/spiritual unity. He therefore saw such relationships (which he termed the 'Uranian spirit', emanating from 'the intermediate sex') as a type of vanguard in the struggle against capitalist society: 'the advance guard of that great movement which will one day transform the common life by substituting the bond of personal affection and compassion for the monetary, legal and other external ties which now control and confine society' (1984: 238).

This period also saw the emergence of socialist groups and parties. One might note the role of Henry Mayers Hyndman (1842–1921), whose contribution lay not in the field of theory (his was a rather undistinguished and highly derivative mixture of Toryism and Marxism) but in the foundation in 1884 of Britain's first modern socialist party – the Social Democratic Federation. Morris, Eleanor Marx and Aveling were all sometime members (Carpenter had some association) and although splits occurred (partly owing to Hyndman's high-handedness) a climate was created in which socialist theory, strategy and tactics could be discussed and, to a limited extent, put into practice.

The year 1884 also saw the foundation of the Fabian Society, an exclusive debating and propaganda group whose cultured and highly individual membership (including George Bernard Shaw, Sidney and Beatrice Webb, Annie Besant, and Graham Wallas) defies easy characterisation. The Fabians were committed to a policy of gradualism, which was evoked in the society's name and motto (part of which read: 'For the right moment you must wait, as Fabius did most patiently, when warring against Hannibal, though many censured his delays'). They stressed steady, piecemeal progress, the gradual replacement of capitalist institutions by socialist ones, and eschewed revolutionary, catastrophic conceptions – 'the inevitability of our scheme of gradualness', as Sidney Webb put it. Although committed to democracy, the Fabians were strongly elitist, viewing themselves as an intellectual vanguard: not a mass political party, but a powerhouse of select socialist thinkers, whose role was to inculcate sound scientific views which would promote rational action by a benign state. The second part of the Fabian motto, 'but when the time comes you must strike hard, as Fabius did, or your waiting will be vain, and fruitless', prompted George Lichtheim to remark that there was no historical record of Fabius having ever 'struck hard', and that 'malicious critics of Fabianism have been known to hint that there may have been something prophetic, or at least symbolic, in this misreading of history' (Lichtheim, 1975: 65).

The twentieth century

In the spring of 1902 Lenin (1870–1924) arrived in London for what turned out to be a year's stay. The previous year Eduard Bernstein (1850–1932) had returned to Germany after spending more than a decade in the British capital. Lenin gained no new insight from his visit. London merely confirmed his views of the stark class division of capitalism – his commitment to revolutionary Marxism was not affected. Nadezhda Krupskaya, his wife, recalled visits to areas in which squalid and lavish housing coexisted, where Lenin 'would mutter through clenched teeth, and in English: "Two nations!"' (1970: 65). Bernstein, by contrast, was changed by his period of residence and, although Rosa Luxemburg's remark that 'Bernstein has constructed his theory upon relationships obtaining in England. He sees the world through English spectacles' (quoted in McLellan, 1979: 23) is an exaggeration, it is true that his experience in Britain was an important factor in the development of his 'revision' of Marxism. These two men were to be significantly associated with what became the two dominant forms of socialism in the twentieth century – communism and social democracy.

Controversy has long raged on the nature of the relationship between Marx, Lenin and Stalin. Whereas anti-Marxist critics portray a malign trinity, Stalinists arrange the three into a form of revolutionary apostolic succession. Marxist anti-Bolsheviks distinguish the admirable Marx from the corrupting duo of Lenin and Stalin, whilst Bolshevik anti-Stalinists reject any continuity between the monstrous Stalin and revolutionary founders Marx and Lenin. In the case of Lenin the debate has been fuelled by the theoretical diversity of his voluminous writings and the complexities of his political life. These complications make it very difficult, or even impossible, to portray an essential Lenin; however, and ironically, the very boldness of some of his statements and acts encourages people to do precisely this (especially when important interests are at stake). Communism (known also as Leninism or Marxism-Leninism) was developed under Stalin's aegis, and drew much of its theoretical sustenance from the events surrounding, and the ideas expressed in, Lenin's *What is to be Done?* (1902). In this work Lenin had argued for a tightly disciplined, exclusive party of professional revolutionaries dedicated to bringing socialist consciousness to, and helping to organise, a working class who, unaided, would merely develop sub-socialist trade-union consciousness. It was at the 1903 Second Congress of the Russian Social Democratic Labour party (held in Brussels and London) that Lenin had eventually managed to get a majority for his conception against a much broader conception of the party developed by Martov. (Lenin's group thus got the name 'Bolsheviks' or Majoritarians, while Martov's group acquired the name 'Mensheviks' or Minoritarians.) This conception became the centrepiece of Stalinist communism, though used in a way Trotsky had feared in 1904:

In the internal politics of the Party these methods lead . . . to the Party organisation 'substituting' itself for the Party, the Central Committee substituting itself for the Party organisation, and finally the dictator substituting himself for the Central Committee.

(n.d.: 77)

Lenin attempted to combine discipline with democracy in the party's organisational principle of democratic centralism: relatively free discussion and criticism until a decision is taken, when it becomes binding on the party. The failings in Lenin's own use of this principle were dwarfed by those of Stalin, who merely paid it lip service; in reality the democratic element was dissolved. Stalin, via a cult of the leader, came to dominate party, class, state and international communism. Drawing on an idea of Marx, Lenin had, prior to the 1917 October revolution in Russia, argued for a temporary proletarian dictatorship after the revolution in order to root out residual hostile elements. He had, however, conceived this dictatorship as distinct from the party. Stalin's equating of the two (anticipated, let it be said, by developments while Lenin was in power) generated a party state. The party also came to control the world communist movement via the nominally independent Third International, enforcing the Bolshevik party model and the latest Moscow line.

The Communist Party of Great Britain, founded in 1920, for the first two decades of its existence shared the Soviet party's hostile stance on 'the parliamentary road to socialism'. The Second Congress of the International (Comintern) explicitly rejected a parliamentary road, considering that, at best, Parliament was an arena for propaganda and agitation, whereas socialism, as in Russia, was to be brought about primarily by insurrectionary means. The Communist Party of Great Britain did, over the years, attract militant elements of the working class, and, in the 1930s, numbers of anti-fascists. It also had internal factions and oppositional currents. But although the party was able to foster a lively intellectual culture, including an influential and distinct school of socialist historians (among others, Christopher Hill, E. P. Thompson and Eric Hobsbawm), party ideology, in the hands of Central Committee/Politburo members such as R. Palme Dutt (1896–1974), largely consisted of theoretical and policy acrobatics to shadow developments in Moscow: most dramatic of these was the rapid *volte-face* on fascism in the wake of the Nazi–Soviet pact of 1939. With the death of Stalin in 1953, and in the cold light of revelations of the grim, inhuman past of Stalinism, and the continuing oppressive present (witnessed in the invasion of Hungary in 1956), democratic currents within many Western communist parties became much more prominent. In the 1970s Eurocommunism represented an attempt, by principally the French, Spanish, and Italian parties, to develop a strategy which took democratic, parliamentary aspirations into consideration. By the 1980s time was running out for the world communist movement. The coming to power of Gorbachev in the Soviet Union in 1985, with his watchwords of *glasnost* (openness) and *perestroika* (restructuring), saw a final, doomed attempt to reform Soviet communism from within, which actually led to the complete unravelling of the Soviet system in the USSR and Eastern Europe. In Britain the party – whose journal *Marxism Today* had been part of a desperate search for a reinvigorated Marxism in the 1980s – shattered into hard-line splinters and a 'democratic left' residue which sought to jettison all the remaining baggage of the communist period – and, not least, the thoroughly compromised name 'communist'.

In conceiving of the Third International, Lenin had sought a radical replacement for the Second (founded in 1889), which had effectively collapsed amid the ferocious jingoism at the start of the First World War. Prior to this debacle, however, the Second International had been convulsed by the revisionist controversy; superficially a mere squabble within Marxism but in fact, among other things, a landmark in the development of social democracy. Eduard Bernstein, the most notable exponent of revisionism, developed a critique of a number of Marxist orthodoxies which involved rejecting revolutionary insurrectionism in favour of a gradualist, parliamentary approach. The beast capitalism, he argued, was being tamed: property holders and shareholders were increasing; small and medium agriculture was growing; wages were rising and prosperity was becoming more widespread. All this was reflected in an increasingly complex class system which belied orthodox expectations of polarisation between a small, wealthy bourgeoisie and a massive, impoverished proletariat. At the political level, the working class was gradually, through Parliament, gaining a say in the organisation of society. In short, Bernstein held that a bloody revolution was not only unlikely but unnecessary. He emphasised present realities and the foreseeable future; and sought achievable, if unspectacular, advances and not some supposed, fanciful millennium. Moreover the liberal notions of freedom with which he was imbued made political democracy valid in absolute terms, and not merely as a tactic; further, this democracy enjoined both limitations on majorities and respect for minority rights; proletarian dictatorships were entirely ruled out: 'In this sense one might call socialism "organising liberalism".'

Much of this type of thinking has informed modern social democracy. The British Labour party (founded in 1900 as the Labour Representation Committee) has always been a broad church, but this very breadth, in so far as it reflects underlying social realities, has encouraged a social democratic approach among its leadership. According to Ramsay MacDonald the fact that the party was called 'Labour' and not 'Socialist' indicated the parameters within which any sensible left-wing party would have to operate for the conceivable future: 'Under British conditions, a Socialist Party is the last, not the first, form of the Socialist movement in politics' (quoted in Crick, 1987: 70). It was not, of course, German revisionist Marxism but existing native reformist currents, including Fabianism, which provided the main intellectual input into British social democracy, and made most of the running.

Between the two World Wars, Labour could point to successes and failures. Its goal of using the existing rules of the parliamentary game to win power was achieved, and the Fabian Sidney Webb could enjoy Cabinet office under Ramsay MacDonald. Once in power, however, the party found itself in a double bind: not only did it face the classic socialist dilemma (its state role was to stabilise society, and therefore capitalism, whilst its party role was to overcome capitalism) but this dilemma was aggravated by its unwillingness to depart from narrow constitutionalism and by its desperate desire to be seen as a 'respectable' party. The world economic depression brought matters to a head in 1931, when Ramsay MacDonald formed a National Government with Tories and Liberals to introduce cuts in pay and unemployment benefit demanded by international bankers – but opposed by important sections of his own party. The ensuing election saw the Labour vote plummet, leaving the party in opposition for the rest of the decade.

In the period of economic prosperity between the 1950s and the early 1970s, the 'revisionism' of Anthony Crosland (1918–1977) represented a highly optimistic reformulation of the social democratic case. It was a theory appropriate to reformist practice – Labour social democracy had given up the idea that socialism was fundamentally distinct from capitalism, in favour of the notion of the interpenetration of the two. Crosland argued in *The Future of Socialism* (1956) that, in Britain, 'Capitalism has been reformed almost out of recognition'. There was now a caring and effective state, strong trade unions, businesses increasingly run by socially aware managers rather than bloated plutocrats, and the likelihood of continuous and largely crisis-free prosperity. The existence of private ownership of the means of production was no longer to be seen as a barrier to socialism; remaining inequalities and social injustices could be removed in the context of a mixed economy and a parliamentary democracy – thereby reconciling equality with liberty and efficiency.

With the collapse of economic prosperity in the 1970s, Croslandite optimism became unsustainable. The New Right onslaught, enshrined in government from 1979, left the Labour party badly split. The social democrats, too, split. A resurgent left drove frightened social democrats like Shirley Williams and David Owen out of the party altogether, and into attempts, via the Social Democratic party, at restructuring the centre-left in Britain; ultimately, most regrouped with their natural ideological allies in the Liberal party. Under Neil Kinnock and John Smith the Labour party began a process of 'modernisation', which sought to update party policy and structures, and thereby make Labour more electable. The left was marginalised, and, at the policy level, there was a good deal of implicit acceptance of elements of the Thatcherite agenda. Under Tony Blair (b. 1953) this overhaul of the party gathered even greater momentum. In a sustained charm offensive, reassurance was the fundamental objective. The markets were to be convinced that the party was not hostile to their interests, but rather welcomed a healthy private sector. Previously supportive social groups which had defected to the Conservatives were to be won back, new bases of support acquired, and bedrock support retained. To carry off this ambitious project, particularly nimble ideological and rhetorical footwork was required. Appeals to social justice rubbed shoulders with 'prudent economics', toughness on crime with toughness on the causes of crime, minimum wages with welfare reform. From the perspective of the left, and even among some social democrats, Blair's plans for 'New' Labour involved a clear distancing from socialism. Blair himself argued that his policies were rooted in the traditional socialist values of the party, but that modern problems require modern methods; he portrayed himself as a principled pragmatist. The most notable, sympathetic attempt to give this new direction a degree of theoretical coherence was to deem it a 'Third Way' between social democracy and neo-liberalism. It proved to be a winning strategy – four straight electoral defeats gave way to two crushing victories.

Some, however, might wish to press the claims of an earlier and very different 'third way' – democratic socialism – distinct from both communism and social democracy. Not all commentators would accept the validity of this procedure. Anthony Wright, for example, has been sceptical about the distinction between social democracy and democratic socialism, viewing it as a largely untheorised piece of Labour left rhetoric:

> the distinction . . . was not accompanied by any serious attempt to explore the theoretical pedigrees of these traditions in order to establish what distinction (if any) there actually was, apart from the fact that one sounded more muscular than the other.
>
> (1983: 24)

Bernard Crick (1987), on the other hand, subsumes much of what would be considered social democratic into a very broad category of democratic socialism, including, among others, Anthony Crosland, Ramsay MacDonald and Beatrice and Sidney Webb. Undoubtedly problems do exist in maintaining this distinction. Can one describe as a democratic socialist someone who patently did not use the term as a self-description? Furthermore, how is a history to be written of a tradition that was not really aware of itself as a tradition? There will also be the inevitable boundary disputes as to where social democracy ends and democratic socialism begins. Nonetheless the distinction is worth persevering with, for it does help to illuminate genuine points of difference in the socialist movement.

Democratic socialism can be seen as trying to steer a third way between communism and social democracy; an attempt to synthesise the best elements of the two other traditions, whilst rejecting the objectionable features of both. Democratic socialism shared with communism (or, more precisely, with the Marxist core professed by the adherents of communism) a similar analysis of the basic anatomy of capitalism. Democratic socialism therefore criticised social democracy for its naive reading of capitalism – for its blindness to entrenched interests and the inherent instability of the system. This, it argued, issued in a shallow liberal conception of the institutions and personnel of exploitation and oppression. On the other hand, democratic socialism shared with social democracy a thoroughgoing critique of the authoritarianism of communism – the rhetorical praise for, but actual stifling of, genuine participation at all levels of society. Democratic socialism could therefore be seen as a form of synthesis of these two strands or traditions: namely an attempt to combine a real move towards socialism with authentic democracy. In the British context this involved a combination of radical social analysis with genuine respect for the strengths of the liberal constitutional system.

Within the British Labour party a fierce attack on social democratic assumptions was precipitated by the 1931 crisis. The whole episode served to confirm to democratic socialist critics just how capitalist interests could successfully protect themselves against a Labour government – a situation which called for a hard look at traditional Labour views. This stance was adopted by a body within the party called the Socialist League and in the writings of one of its leading members – Harold Laski (1893–1950). Laski's work provided a critique of both social democracy and communism. In *Democracy in Crisis* (1933) he argued that vested economic interests prevent the people from advancing from formal political control to real economic and political power. Using Marxist conceptions of state and society, Laski rejected the thesis that the great institutions of society (the courts, the press, the educational system, the armed forces, etc.) were genuinely neutral, as opposed to merely formally so; they were firmly in a bourgeois camp which showed every willingness to resort to whatever means were required, including force, to protect its privileged position. Laski feared that people's understandable frustration would lead to violent revolution, resulting in either defeat and chaos or in the establishment of a Soviet-type dictatorship which would be essentially alien to British liberal democratic traditions. Instead he hoped that a future Labour government would push through a thorough socialist transformation. However, the crisis of 1931, and the rise of fascism, had demonstrated how ruthless capitalist interests could be; and thus a radical Labour government would have to be prepared to make a significant departure from traditional constitutional practice to protect its policy: it 'would have to take vast powers, and legislate under them by ordinance and decree; it would have to suspend the classic formulae of normal opposition' (1933: 87). This theme was reiterated by another prominent Socialist Leaguer – Sir Stafford Cripps – who envisaged a Labour government placing before Parliament 'an Emergency Powers Bill to be passed through all its stages in one day' which would allow rule by ministerial orders 'incapable of challenge in the Courts or in any way except in the House of Commons' (quoted in Bealey, 1970: 137–8). The Laskian perspective graphically demonstrates both the character of, and the problems inherent in, British democratic socialism. A radical (in Laski's case, Marxist) analysis of capitalism is combined with a profound belief in the continuing utility and validity of liberal democratic values and institutions; yet these latter can be preserved only by actions which would appear, to many, to be a flagrant violation of liberal democracy. Laski himself was on the National Executive of the Labour party, and, owing to the complexities of Labour party organisation and certainly not to any hegemony in the party, found himself chairman of the Labour party during Labour's 1945 landslide election victory. The new government rapidly found its party chairman's radical criticisms an embarrassment, resulting in Attlee's famous rebuke that 'a period of silence on your part would be welcome'!

A more recent expression of democratic socialism can be found in the work of Tony Benn (b. 1925). At the height of his influence among the Labour left, in the late 1970s and early 1980s, he produced a stream of essays reflecting on the state of British society, and British socialism. Reflecting on his time as a Cabinet Minister in the 1970s, he recalled a Cabinet meeting at which Anthony Crosland reluctantly accepted the humiliating terms set by the International Monetary Fund as the price of assistance; this, Benn argued, displayed the utter bankruptcy of Crosland's social democratic vision of a humanised capitalism: 'That was the moment when social democratic revisionism died in the Labour Party. It was killed, not by the Left but by the bankers' (1982: 33). Of particular concern for Benn was Britain's imperfect democracy – its formal inadequacy, covert checks and external constraints – all major obstacles to the achievement of socialism. Formal problems included 'the unfinished business of 1688', for example, the lack of a written constitution, the powers of the House of Lords and the residual personal prerogatives of the monarch plus new impositions such as the growth of ministerial and prime ministerial government at the expense of Parliament. To this is added the effect of powerful vested interests, the civil service, the judiciary, the armed and security services, the media, the City, and others who directly and indirectly sabotage socialist initiatives. Finally there are the external pressures from the United States, international capital, and, a particular *bête noire* of Benn's, the European Economic Community. Like Laski, Benn wished to see the election of a government committed to a radical socialist agenda. Legitimate extraparliamentary activity included: (1) the right of the labour movement to organise itself to promote a Labour victory at the polls; (2) the right to limited civil disobedience where ancient and inherited rights are threatened; and (3) the right to protect a Labour government from a *coup*, by force if necessary. If the Labour party was to be successful it had to reform its own internal structure, particularly in the area of inner-party democracy; higher levels of the party had to become accountable to lower, and all had to become accountable, whether in power or opposition, to the electorate. It was therefore none too surprising that Benn's brand of democratic socialism won him few friends among the great and the good in the Labour party. He viewed this growing marginality as an opportunity to speak out, untrammelled by party institutional constraints.

Conclusion: socialism in the twenty-first century?

By the mid-1990s claims that socialism was dead or dying were common. Socialism was deemed to be an exhausted ideology totally lacking any significant electoral appeal. Diagnoses varied, but four themes predominated: changes in the working class, globalisation, the collapse of communism and postmodernism. As regards the working class, it was claimed that significant sections had abandoned socialism, and that the class itself was declining in both numbers and social significance. Socialism was therefore losing its social base. In the case of globalisation the claim was that national states could no longer develop truly independent policies. This was considered particularly damaging for socialism, for capital would withdraw its resources from states that attempted to introduce socialist policies. Thirdly, the abject failure of 'actually existing socialism' in the

Soviet Union and Eastern Europe, as well as the scramble for capitalist relations of production, also took their toll. The bitter Soviet joke '"What is socialism?" "The long road from capitalism to capitalism"' hit a nerve. The collapse of communism, it was argued, put a question mark over the whole ideology of socialism. Finally, influential postmodernist perspectives claimed that the great 'modernist' ideologies, which included socialism, were no longer credible. Socialism, with its grand theoretical claims, was a dinosaur, the product of an age surpassed. All four of these explanations pointed in one stark direction – socialism's day had gone. As Joseph Stiglitz wrote in 1994: 'if I were to claim that socialism as an ideology can now be officially declared dead, I do not think it would be an exaggeration' (1994: 279).

This rather gloomy appraisal, however, did not have the field to itself. Not everybody found the various explanations convincing. Doubts were cast on the extent of the decline of the working class, which, it was claimed, retained a significant presence in modern society. Furthermore, socialism, it was argued, had never been able to take working-class support for granted, and in Britain had always had to battle for it against the rival charms of liberalism and conservatism. Nor had socialists rested content with wooing merely the working class: the importance of cross-class support had not been lost on earlier generations. Necessarily so, for, outside Britain, the manual working class had never been a majority of the work force. Socialism from its inception had to deal with sociological and ideological changes in the working class, and this had acted as a spur to theoretical and strategic innovation. In the case of globalisation there was some scepticism as to the power and penetration of this phenomenon: the fact that there were some global checks on domestic policies in no way implied that social democratic states had no basis for constructive economic policy. In addition, it was argued, the inflated claims for globalisation ignored the pragmatic nature of capital, which is driven by the need for profit, not ideological purity, and that corporations may actually prefer a social democratic state if their plants require an effective infrastructure and a healthy and educated work force. For some forms of socialism, notably Marxism, globalisation seemed to confirm theoretical assumptions; capital had indeed become global, and if centre and periphery were now more closely integrated, there was also the possibility of the periphery significantly striking back. As to the collapse of communism, much of the damage by association for socialism pre-dated the collapse; indeed, the right lost a valuable weapon in its ideological onslaught on the left; whilst in the East itself the experience of the brutal realities of the rapid introduction of markets was to give a new lease of life to socialist parties. Finally, the postmodern critique was challenged as inaccurate and of very limited impact. It was charged with caricaturing modernity, including socialism, and of having little explanatory or predictive power.

Socialism therefore may not be dying but changing. Like all long-established ideologies, it has had a protean quality. Major challenges in the past encouraged premature obituaries for the whole ideology: the defeat of the revolutionary wave of 1848, the collapse of the Second International in 1914, the neutralisation of socialism by prosperity in the early 1960s seemed, to some, to sound the death knell of socialism itself. In each case socialism re-emerged, having learnt valuable lessons from its trials and tribulations. Future changes cannot be predicted with any confidence. Were a crystal ball available, much of the change would probably seem only distantly related to current understandings of socialism, as much contemporary socialism would appear to a resurrected Owenite. Perhaps the entire ideological landscape is irrevocably changing, and all the familiar patterns and labels will mutate or disappear. The historical socialist tradition may fragment into new clusters, new ideological formations, new forms of radicalism, where the term 'socialism' is entirely absent. This, however, would not be death but transformation.

Further reading

General

The classic history of socialism is G. D. H. Cole, *A History of Socialist Thought* (1953–60), although its five volumes go only up to 1939; while a fine concise history is provided by George Lichtheim, *A Short History of Socialism* (1975); see also on European socialism *One Hundred Years of Socialism* (1996), by Donald Sassoon, and *Modern European Socialism* (1994), by Lawrence Wilde. Good discussions of the basic themes of socialism are: R. N. Berki, *Socialism* (1975); Bernard Crick, *Socialism* (1987); Anthony Wright, *Socialisms: Theories and Practices* (1987); chapters 11 and 12 in Michael Freeden's influential book *Ideologies and Political Theory* (1996); and Donald Sassoon's article 'Socialism in the twentieth century: an historical reflection' (2000). An old history of British socialism, which is very good on origins, is Max Beer, *A History of British Socialism* (1929; an illustrated one-volume edition was published by Spokesman in 1984); a more recent history can be found in John Callaghan, *Socialism in Britain since 1884* (1990).

Texts

A wide range of British extracts, with a useful introduction, can be found in Anthony Wright, *British Socialism* (1983). On individual authors: Robert Owen: *A New View of Society and other Writings* (1991); Karl Marx: D. McLellan (ed.) *Karl Marx: Selected Writings* (2000); William Morris: A. L. Morton (ed.) *Political Writings of William Morris* (1973); Edward Carpenter: *Selected Writings I, Sex* (1984); the Fabians: G. B. Shaw (ed.), *Fabian Essays in Socialism* (1889); V. I. Lenin: *Selected Works* (1969); Eduard Bernstein: *The Preconditions of Socialism* (1993); C. A. R. Crosland: *The Future of Socialism* (1956); Harold Laski: *Democracy in Crisis* (1933); Tony Benn: *Arguments for Socialism* (1980).

Commentaries

For Owen and Owenism see J. F. C. Harrison, *Robert Owen and the Owenites in Britain and America* (1969), and Gregory Claeys, *Citizens and Saints* (1989); from the vast literature on Marx, Engels and Marxism three good introductions are: George Lichtheim, *Marxism* (1961), David McLellan, *The Thought of Karl Marx* (1971), and Lesek Kolakowski, *Main Currents of Marxism* (3 vols, 1978); William Morris is served by E. P. Thompson, *William Morris* (1977), Edward Carpenter by Chushichi Tsuzuki, *Edward Carpenter, 1844–1929* (1980), and Eleanor Marx by the two-volume Yvonne Kapp, *Eleanor Marx* (1979); for the Fabians there is A. M. McBriar, *Fabian Socialism and English Politics, 1884–1918* (1966).

A good commentary on Lenin is provided by N. Harding, *Lenin's Political Thought* (1983), and on Bernstein by Peter Gay, *The Dilemma of Democratic Socialism* (1962); for Crosland see David Lipsey and Dick Leonard (eds), *The Socialist Agenda* (1981), for Laski, Isaac Kramnick and Barry Sheerman, *Harold Laski* (1993), and for Benn, Jad Adams, *Tony Benn* (1992). From among the plethora of literature on Blair, New Labour, and the Third Way see Mark Bevir, 'New Labour: a study in ideology' (2000), and Michael Kenny and Martin J. Smith, 'Interpreting New Labour: constraints, dilemmas and political agency' (2001); also Anthony Giddens, *The Third Way* (1998). On the 'death of socialism' debate see the first three chapters in *Socialism after Communism* by Christopher Pierson (1995); also Vincent Geoghegan, 'Has socialism a future?' (1996).

References

Adams, J. (1992) *Tony Benn: A Biography*, London: Macmillan.
Bealey, F., ed. (1970) *The Social and Political Thought of the British Labour Party*, London: Weidenfeld & Nicolson.
Beer, M. (1929) *A History of British Socialism*, London: Bell.
Benn, T. (1980) *Arguments for Socialism*, Harmondsworth: Penguin.
Benn, T. (1982) *Parliament, People and Power*, London: Verso.
Berki, R. N. (1975) *Socialism*, London: Dent.
Bernstein, E. (1961) *Evolutionary Socialism*, New York: Schocken.
Bernstein, E. (1993) *The Preconditions of Socialism*, Cambridge: Cambridge University Press.
Bevir, M. (2000) 'New Labour: a study in ideology', *British Journal of Politics and International Relations*, 2 (3), pp. 277–301.
Callaghan, J. (1990) *Socialism in Britain since 1884*, Oxford: Blackwell.
Carpenter, E. (1984) *Selected Writings I, Sex*, London: GMP.
Claeys, G. (1989) *Citizens and Saints: Politics and Anti-politics in early British Socialism*, Cambridge: Cambridge University Press.
Cole, G. D. H. (1953–60) *A History of Socialist Thought*, 5 vols, London, Macmillan.
Crick, B. (1987) *Socialism*, Milton Keynes: Open University Press.
Crosland, C. A. R. (1956) *The Future of Socialism*, London: Cape.

Freeden, M. (1996) *Ideologies and Political Theory*, Oxford: Clarendon Press.

Gamble, A. (1981) *An Introduction to Modern Social and Political Thought*, London: Macmillan.

Gay, P. (1962) *The Dilemma of Democratic Socialism: Eduard Bernstein's Challenge to Marx*, New York: Collier.

Geoghegan, V. (1996) 'Has socialism a future?' *Journal of Political Ideologies*, 1 (3), pp. 261–75.

Giddens, A. (1998) *The Third Way: The Renewal of Social Democracy*, Oxford: Polity Press.

Harding, N. (1983) *Lenin's Political Thought*, London: Macmillan.

Harrison, J. F. C. (1969) *Robert Owen and the Owenites in Britain and America: The Quest for the New Moral World*, London: Routledge.

Hayek, F. (1988) *The Fatal Conceit: The Errors of Socialism*, London: Routledge.

Kapp, Y. (1979) *Eleanor Marx*, 2 vols, London: Virago.

Kenny, M. and Smith, M. J. (2001) 'Interpreting New Labour: constraints, dilemmas and political agency' in S. Ludlam and M. J. Smith (eds) *New Labour in Government*, Basingstoke: Macmillan.

Kolakowski, L. (1978) *Main Currents of Marxism*, 3 vols, Oxford: Clarendon.

Kramnick, I. and Sheerman, B. (1993) *Harold Laski: A Life on the Left*, London: Hamish Hamilton.

Krupskaya, N. K. (1970) *Memories of Lenin*, London: Panther.

Laski, H. (1933) *Democracy in Crisis*, London: Allen & Unwin.

Lenin, V. I. (1969) *Selected Works*, London: Lawrence & Wishart.

Lichtheim, G. (1961) *Marxism*, London: Routledge.

Lichtheim, G. (1975) *A Short History of Socialism*, Glasgow: Fontana.

Lipsey, D. and Leonard, D., eds (1981) *The Socialist Agenda: Crosland's Legacy*, London: Cape.

McBriar, A. M. (1966) *Fabian Socialism and English Politics, 1884–1918*, Cambridge: Cambridge University Press.

McLellan, D. (1971) *The Thought of Karl Marx*, London: Macmillan.

McLellan, D. (1979) *Marxism after Marx*, London: Macmillan.

McLellan, D., ed. (1983) *Marx: The First 100 Years*, London: Fontana.

McLellan, D., ed. (2000) *Karl Marx: Selected Writings*, 2nd edn, Oxford: Oxford University Press.

Marx Aveling, E. and Aveling, E. (1886) 'The woman question from a socialist point of view', *Westminster Review*, 49, pp. 207–22.

More, T. (1965) *Utopia*, Harmondsworth: Penguin.

Morton, A. L. (1962) *The Life and Ideas of Robert Owen*, London: Lawrence & Wishart.

Morton, A. L., ed. (1973) *Political Writings of William Morris*, London: Lawrence & Wishart.

Owen, R. (1991) *A New View of Society and other Writings*, Harmondsworth: Penguin.

Pierson, C. (1995) *Socialism after Communism*, Oxford: Polity Press.

Sassoon, D. (1996) *One Hundred Years of Socialism*, London: Tauris.

Sassoon, D. (2000) 'Socialism in the twentieth century: an historical reflection', *Journal of Political Ideologies*, 5 (1), pp. 17–34.

Shaw, G. B., ed. (1889) *Fabian Essays in Socialism*, London: Fabian Society.

Stiglitz, J. E. (1994) *Whither Socialism?* Cambridge MA: MIT Press.

Taylor, B. (1983) *Eve and the New Jerusalem: Socialism and Feminism in the Nineteenth Century*, London: Virago.

Thompson, E. P. (1977) *William Morris: Romantic to Revolutionary*, London: Merlin.

Trotsky, L. (n.d.) *Our Political Tasks*, London: New Park.

Tsuzuki, C. (1980) *Edward Carpenter, 1844–1929: Prophet of Human Fellowship*, Cambridge: Cambridge University Press.

Wilde, L. (1994) *Modern European Socialism*, Aldershot: Dartmouth.

Winstanley, G. (1973) *The Law of Freedom and other Writings*, Harmondsworth: Penguin.

Wittgenstein, L. (1972) *The Blue and Brown Books*, Oxford: Blackwell.

Wright, A. (1983) *British Socialism: Socialist Thought from the 1880s to the 1960s*, Harlow: Longman.

Wright, A. (1987) *Socialisms: Theories and Practices*, Oxford: Oxford University Press.

Nationalism

Alan Finlayson

You are a nationalist. You may or may not have a strong sense of belonging to a particular country but you are still a nationalist. You may like to think of yourself as a twenty-first-century citizen of the world. Perhaps you use the internet to chat with people from the United States or the Ukraine, speak several languages and feel more attached to Manchester, Glasgow, Cardiff or Belfast than to England, Scotland, Wales or Ireland. But you are a nationalist alongside those who openly claim to prefer 'our' ways to 'theirs' and relish the opportunity to wave a national flag and sing an anthem.

At a time of much discussed 'globalisation', when nationally based governments seem to have less power than a century ago, culture is increasingly dominated by largely American 'global' media and many people travel freely across borders, the world is still largely nationalist. The independent and largely homogeneous nation with its own state is still the primary shape of the otherwise varied political structures under which most of us live. Our cultural habits and attitudes may increasingly be fluid but arguments about them still take place within and between nations. Perhaps most obviously, though still significantly, we think of the world largely in terms of nations and national peoples. Our 'mental map' of the world generally divides it into sovereign states and classifies people, albeit loosely, according to their nationality.

Nationalism is not just something that happens 'over there' in places you only ever hear about on the evening news. It is not just something that involves warfare and atrocity. Nationalism has shaped, and continues to shape, many aspects of the political make-up of our continent and country. For these reasons, because of all these facts, you and I are nationalists.

But, despite this fundamental significance and ubiquity, the phenomenon of nationalism presents something of a challenge to theorists and analysts of political ideology. It does not offer a clear, systematic body of doctrine that can be transplanted and reapplied wholesale from one context to another. By its very nature, the claims of nationalist ideology vary according to the location in which they are found. They are concerned with the singular nature of an individual nation. An ideology such as socialism has been thought about, reflected upon, revised and developed by theorists in many different historical, cultural and geographical contexts, each seeking to draw on an initial body of theory and to apply or develop it in accordance with their particular circumstances. But nationalism, which has also been thought about and practised in many different places, is not so clearly based around core themes and propositions as something such as socialism. It does not immediately lend itself to the kind of excavation of ideas and their historical development and deployment that one may undertake with regard to other political ideologies. Indeed, nationalism, until relatively recently, has been somewhat neglected by political theorists (at least explicitly) and has more often been investigated by historians and sociologists, who tend to understand it as a form of social or political movement or a general idea rather than a political ideology.

This chapter will examine nationalism in a way that leads us into wider questions about the nature of ideology and the ways in which it may be conceptualised. We will begin by looking further at some of the things analysts have said about nationalism as an ideology and the different interpretations they have advanced. Then we will consider some of the ways in which nationalism has been understood as the product of a particular kind of historical period or epoch. The third section will consider more broadly the relationship between ideologies and social movements and look at the way ideologies such as conservatism or socialism often combine with nationalism to produce powerful and successful political movements. It will also look at some recent developments in political theory which have posited it as a viable way of providing solidarity or community within a polity. By way of conclusion we will consider the question of whether or not nationalism is likely to recede in the face of so-called globalisation.

Nationalism as ideology

As you will have seen in earlier chapters of this book, looking at ideologies such as socialism, conservatism or liberalism, it is not difficult to pull out the main tenets of such philosophies; to establish how they understand human nature, the role they believe the state should take, their moral values and so forth. There may be much dispute as to how these things are understood within an ideology, maybe even a large degree of confusion, but nevertheless they form points of reference, co-ordinates perhaps, within which are shaped the kinds of debates that occur within that ideology, the points of principle over which adherents may squabble. They will also shape and clarify points of disagreement with other ideological configurations. But one would be hard put to find within those writings considered purely nationalist the clear expression of a configuration that could be said to belong purely to nationalist ideology. On the whole, nationalists the world over don't hold colloquia or congresses, form think-tanks or create international confederations dedicated to sharing, refining and spreading the doctrine of nationalism. Certainly leaders of nations may get together and discuss tactics if they believe they share some common problems or foes (such as the meetings of African or European nations). But they don't do so in order to discuss the finer points of nationalist reasoning.

However, some have undertaken to interpret nationalism as a more or less fixed constellation of political ideas. According to Elie Kedourie:

> Nationalism is a doctrine invented in Europe at the beginning of the nineteenth century . . . the doctrine holds that humanity is naturally divided into nations, that nations are known by certain characteristics which can be ascertained, and that the only legitimate type of government is national self-government.
>
> (Kedourie, 1960: 12)

This is helpful as a starting point. If we were to try and reduce nationalism to a straightforward doctrine we would have to include something like the claim to national self-determination and the view that nations are a natural unit of social and political organisation. But this sort of view suggests that a kind of 'universal' claim lurks within nationalist thinking. That is to say, a claim that can, and should, be applied to all peoples and that is equally valid for everyone. Certainly there is a part of nationalist ideology that often implies and sometimes explicitly advances such a claim. But it is not really what nationalist politicians or ideologues, with some notable exceptions, are primarily concerned with. The nationalist is concerned with his or her own nation more than with anyone else's. It may make political sense to link a claim about the rights of a people in one place to the rights of people in another. Those experiencing subjugation by a colonial power would be entirely sensible to forge connections with those also under such unwelcome rule, and to use similar motivating arguments and assumptions. But such strategic alliance is not the same as constructing a theory intended to have a general relevance to diverse peoples.

Nevertheless, something like the doctrine described by Kedourie could be said to have shaped the way we think about international politics. Organisations such as the United Nations and the frameworks of international law base themselves, in large part, on just such an assumption. International relations are often conducted as if nations can be treated as individual agents, the basic units of world politics. It is the breakdown of this kind of arrangement, the increased salience of supra-national and sub-national organisations, and of direct region-to-region relations, that has led some to speak of a 'post-nationalist' world order. But peoples in search of some kind of freedom, or simply looking for someone to blame for what they regard as their poor political or economic condition, still seek national self-determination, the right to form their own state based on the integrity of their putative nation and to be free from the interference of others. Furthermore, nationalist ideology, as Kedourie points out, holds nations to be identifiable by specific characteristics. Certainly it is part of our everyday common sense or mental shorthand to speak of 'the French' or 'the Germans' or 'the Russians' as meaningful entities with national characteristics of which we are all, supposedly, aware.

But it is not clear that the general view that the political world consists of nations with obvious characteristics is an ideology in the same sense as other 'isms'. For one thing the ideologies of conservatism or liberalism are quite likely to share such a belief and even those socialists keen to emphasise the importance of an international structure of class oppression can happily support struggles for national independence, as may environmentalists, who likewise take a global perspective on things.

Because of this Michael Freeden has argued that nationalism should be thought of as a 'thin' ideology. It is not entirely substantial in itself but it can function so as to maintain 'host' ideologies. For Freeden, ideologies 'enable meaningful political worlds to be constructed' (1996: 749). They produce identifiable sets of meaning or 'conceptual configurations'. Nationalism doesn't provide a unique constellation of such concepts, nor does it provide a broad range of answers to political questions. It often holds to a 'restricted core' and a 'narrower range' of political concepts but is also often just a component of other ideologies, something that complements them in some way.

Freeden attempts to isolate a core of concepts or claims that may always be found within nationalism: that nations are central to human relationships and a particular nation is particularly important; that this should result in a proper state for each nation (or at least some kind of institutional guarantee of its continuance) for example. He also argues that nationalism is always marked by strong emotionalism and attachment to the ways in which history can be seen as a story about the continuous existence or persistence of a people, and to a particular territory – the place where that history has been, and should continue to be, played out (1996: 751–4).

But the way in which these components are organised and configured may vary across cases. As Freeden shows, 'each core concept of nationalism . . . logically contains a number of possible meanings . . . [and they may be] attached to as many adjacent and peripheral concepts as there are interpretations of nationalism'. Furthermore 'the core concepts of nationalism cannot rival the possibilities available to mainstream ideologies such as conservatism, liberalism or socialism – all of which have core conceptual structures which permit a far fuller range of responses to socio-political issues' (1996: 752).

We seem to face a paradox. On the one hand we have an ideology that is so weak and thin that it offers little in the way of a comprehensive political or social philosophy. Yet it is able to inspire the most emotional of commitments and seems to shape our very consciousness of how the international order functions. It is a particular doctrine that forms the primary animating force of certain political movements *and* it is a more general framework that helps make sense of the world for many different social and political actors at both an international and everyday level. It is quite possible for politics (as well as you and me) to be shaped by the latter even if we have little regard for the former. Whatever it is, nationalism is not a body of thought easily assimilated into a taxonomy of ideologies. Perhaps then we should be wary of thinking of nationalism as an ideology at all.

Benedict Anderson opens his renowned and important study of nationalism by declaring that it is less like ideologies such as liberalism or fascism than like 'kinship or religion'. He goes on to suggest that we should define the nation as 'an imagined political community – imagined as both inherently limited and sovereign' (Anderson, 1992: 5). It is imagined because its members cannot possibly know or even hear of all their fellows 'yet in the minds of each lives the image of their communion' (1992: 6). It is limited because all nations consider themselves to have boundaries beyond which are other nations (perhaps against which the nation is defined) and sovereign because they demand to occupy the centre of political arrangements, to stand in the place where once we would have found divinely ordained monarchs. In short, the modern world imagines itself to be made up of nations and makes them the centre of its political arrangements. Rather than a single coherent, doctrinal ideology, nationalism is perhaps a kind of governing principle for the organisation of modern sociality.

In defining nationalism against ideology Anderson may seem to be making it into a subjective phenomenon, something that exists just when a bunch of people think it does. The analysis of nationalism is haunted by this tension between objective and subjective definitions. As the historian Hugh Seton-Watson has declared, in a tone that sounds somewhat exasperated: 'All that I can find to say is that a nation exists when a significant number of people in a community consider themselves to form a nation, or behave as if they formed one' (1977: 5). This is the basis of a widespread division in the field. Some seek to emphasise the objective features of the phenomenon of nationalism – the social facts considered necessary for its emergence. These may include a shared language, fixed territory, certain historical conditions and so forth. Others emphasise more 'subjective' aspects such as belief, commitment, will and imagination. The classic example of this latter approach is probably that of Ernest Renan, who, at the end of the nineteenth century, asked the question 'Qu'est-ce qu'une nation?' 'What is a nation?' and answered that 'a nation is a spiritual principle', constituted by 'possession in common of a rich legacy of remembrances' and by 'the desire to live together, the will to continue to value the heritage which all hold in common'. For Renan a nation is founded on a 'tangible deed' of consent which he famously called 'a daily plebiscite' (Renan, 1990). A plebiscite is a referendum, a popular vote. Renan is suggesting not that we really do vote to accept our nationality but that there can be nations and nationalism only because the people of a given nation continually accept it. It is something to which we affirm our allegiance in our everyday actions.

Probably the best contemporary exponent of such an approach is Walker Connor. For Connor the essence of a nation is 'a psychological bond that joins a people and differentiates it, in the subconscious conviction of its members, from all other people in a most vital way'. 'What ultimately matters,' argues Connor, 'is not *what is* but *what people believe is* . . . a nation is a matter of attitude and not of fact' (1994: 93). In other words being a nation does not necessarily mean that a people are all of the same genetic stock or share exactly the same history but it does mean that they act as if, or believe, that they do.

It is not the case that those who emphasise the subjective aspect of nations are abandoning the possibility of an objective analysis, even less that they are endorsing all the claims of nationalism. Rather, one of the things that nationalism is is the subjective attachment to certain ways of experiencing the world. We might say that nationalism is itself a kind of social theory – a kind of theory about how the world works, of what gives us a place in it, how we should think of our relations with other people and of how it should be politically organised. And in this sense we might argue that nationalism is definitively an ideology. But it is peculiar among ideologies in that its subjective and emotional aspects are foregrounded. Other ideologies certainly inspire emotional attachment and even a partisan sense of belonging. But they tend to suppress these in place of forms of rational argument, claim and counter-claim. At the level of formal argument nationalist ideologues are more than capable of attempting to be calmly rational in their argument. But they also acknowledge that sentiment and emotion are important bases of political life while the supporters of nationalism are most often likely to make their fervour both known and noticeable. As Freeden points out: 'All ideologies . . . carry emotional attachments to particular conceptual configurations, both because fundamental human values excite emotional as well as rational support, and because ideologies constitute mobilising ideational systems to change or defend political practices' (1996: 754). For this reason nationalism perhaps has much to teach us about ideology. Where others suppress their emotional rhetoric when they advance philosophical arguments, nationalism makes a virtue of them. And where other ideologies may be portrayed as aloof from the world, offering a distanced but rational comment and guide, nationalism makes a virtue of being supposedly embedded in our sense of what we are.

Perhaps this is one of the key things that ideologies do – provide us with a sense of who we are and then make us feel proud of it. Ideologies are not just ways of thinking about the world but ways of being within it. They give us a sense of what is going on, organise our perceptions of certain things and orient us in certain directions. This is a broader sense of ideology than is perhaps usual and it does suggest that we all, in a sense, 'live' in ideology. But it is also a way of thinking about ideology that can help us make sense of nationalism.

However, we need not neglect the attempt to understand the kinds of objective conditions that make it more or less likely (or even make it possible) that people will develop a nationalist sensibility. We know that ideologies such as socialism and liberalism have their roots in certain social conditions, that they emerge at reasonably clear moments in history, although this is not always seen as part of the way in which we should make sense of these ideologies. But, with nationalism, questions as to its origin are the main ones that have been investigated.

When was nationalism?

There is a common assumption that outbursts of nationalist fervour are indicative of a kind of latent tribalism, a primordial or atavistic trait of human nature, something that has been with us for ever. While there may be a case to say that some sort of group loyalty has always been intrinsic to human social organisation it is much less clear that nationalism, as we know it, is such a perennial feature. For many historians it appears to be a specifically modern phenomenon, emerging out of the social transformations of seventeenth and eighteenth-century Europe. For example, Seton-Watson declares that 'the doctrine of nationalism dates from the age of the French Revolution' (1977: 27).

Greenfeld suggests, and with some good reasons, that the 'original modern idea of the nation emerged in sixteenth-century England, which was the first nation in the world' (1992: 14). For Greenfeld, what makes the concept of the nation new in sixteenth-century England is its use as synonymous with 'the people'. Thought of as a nation, the idea of 'a people' loses the negative connotations of terms such as 'rabble' or 'mob'. It also removes the implication that a people is a group which is not part of the ruling elite, nobility or monarchy. Instead the people-as-one-nation become a kind of elite. Because they are part of the nation they share in something that elevates them, that makes them, in some sense, chosen (see Greenfeld, 1992: 7):

> The assertion of the nationality of the English polity went hand in hand with the insistence on the people's right of participation in the political process and government through Parliament. In fact in this case 'nation', England's being a nation, actually meant such participation. The representation of the English people as a nation symbolically elevated it to the position of an elite which had the right and was expected to govern itself, and equated nationhood with political citizenship.
>
> (Greenfeld, 1992: 30)

Nationalism then, was fundamentally related to the idea of popular sovereignty or democracy.

However, despite the clear ways in which concepts of nationhood acquire a specific and 'new' meaning in the modern period there is no uniform scholarly opinion on just how new it is or on how much emphasis we should give to the novelty and pure 'modernity' of nationhood and nationalism. In fact there is considerable argument about its emergence into history and the status to be attached to its possible precursors.

The key to such debates is the claim that nationalism has to be understood as rooted in social and economic transformations and not just political or intellectual ones. Many claim that nationalism is the result of 'modernisation'. This is nothing to do with the policies of the Blair government, although these are often declared to be connected with 'modernisation'. Nor is it to do with being particularly contemporary. When social scientists talk of modernisation or modernity they mean the shift from simple and traditional forms of social organisation to industrialised societies based around the complex interaction of the economy, large-scale state bureaucracies and mass communication systems that bring larger and larger groups of people into contact with each other. As such, modernisation is not a moment in history but a process. It is also something that may take place at different times in different places. Indeed, some places on our planet have not become fully modernised (perhaps they have been prevented) while others, it has been claimed, are now postmodern.

So how might nationalism be connected with this process of modernisation? In essence the argument is that under the conditions of upheaval and dislocation wrought by modernisation the reproduction of everyday social life and culture cannot be 'taken for granted'. The ways in which people are used to doing things, their habits, their traditions, their prejudices, are all thrown off kilter. This could lead to a total breakdown in society. But nationalism serves to reintegrate populations into this new social context.

Ernest Gellner (1983), for example, traces the sources of nationalism to the transformation from predominantly agricultural to industrial society, a transformation that significantly alters the relationship between culture and politics. He characterises agrarian societies as predominantly local in their orientation, hierarchical in structure and, crucially, semi-literate. That is to say, they were fairly closed and rigid forms of social organisation with limited variation between people in any particular social unit. Literacy is a skill monopolised by religious clerics and the ruling class exists in rigid separation from the peasantry. People are limited in their social as well as geographical mobility. They cannot move up or down the social ladder.

Industrialisation alters all this. People move through society and get mixed up much more. Industrial society, unlike agrarian society, is open-ended and always developing, demanding flexibility. For Gellner, nationalism 'is rooted in a certain kind of division of labour, one which is complex and persistently, cumulatively changing' (1983: 24). This necessitates a change in the place of culture in social organisation. No longer confined to single craft-based or agricultural occupations, but rather moving about and having to fulfil numerous different tasks, people require a basic training in literacy and numeracy. This makes their mobility possible:

> in industrial society notwithstanding its larger number of specialisms, the distance between specialisms is far less great. Their mysteries are far closer to mutual intelligibility, their manuals have idioms which overlap to a much greater extent and re-training though sometimes difficult is not generally an awesome task.
>
> (1983: 26–7)

The generation of a widely shared 'high' culture becomes necessary, since, without some basic homogeneity between people, society cannot function. Only widespread educational systems can accomplish this and they in turn require a state large enough to organise them. Thus culture and the state become linked. If cultures are to survive they need to have their own 'political roof', their own state. This, for Gellner, is the origin of nationalism. Its genesis as a cultural principle of social organisation lies in this transformation of social structure.

This is what scholars call the 'modernisation thesis' of nationalism. While Gellner is an exemplar of this approach he is not alone in arguing for it. Many social scientists and political theorists have adopted something like a modernisation-based approach, though their precise rendition of it may vary. For many Marxist theorists, for example, capitalist modernisation generates nations because, for example, it standardises languages (in order to increase the size of available markets and so to make obtaining profit easier) and it uses nationalism as a way of providing legitimacy for an oppressive state, obscuring what should be the international consciousness of the working class (see Nimni, 1994).

But there are a number of criticisms that may be made of the modernisation thesis. Not the least is that such theories are often taken to imply that the era of nationalism has passed. This may have looked like the case at one stage but it certainly doesn't look like that now that nationalist and ethnic conflicts have become such a part of Central and Eastern European politics. But modernisation theorists might claim that this is in fact symptomatic of a form of new modernisation happening as a result of the collapse of Soviet domination.

It is not always clear though, whether nationalism is to be understood as a result of modernisation or as a necessary condition. Does it make it possible for societies to industrialise or is it something that industrialisation produces? The modernisation thesis is a very general theory of nationalism that needs supplementing with more detailed analysis of any particular example. Even if it is entirely correct it may not tell us very much about how nationalism works as a political ideology. Things are always more complicated than epochal descriptions of social change allow.

But perhaps the most serious challenge to the modernisation thesis is the argument that historically nationalism has not emerged alongside industrialisation. The historian Marc Bloch has argued that national consciousness is apparent in France and Germany as far back as 1100 – long before 'modernisation'. By contrast Eugen Weber (1979) has demonstrated that some people living in rural France did not consider themselves French as late as the end of World War I. They lived in isolation from the rest of the country, spoke distinct regional vernaculars and generally had little to do with urbanised 'modern' France. As Connor concludes, it is hard to date the precise emergence of a nation, since an elite may be attached to national consciousness long before there is any record of what the mass of people thought. A nation is formed through a long process and there is no single point when it turns into a nation (see Connor, 1994: 210–26; also Williams, 1991).

Anthony Smith stresses the necessity for modern nationalism of a prior 'ethnic core'. Although notions such as self-determination may be recent, nations have roots going much further back. We must be careful, Smith urges, not to confuse *state* formation with *nation* formation. Accepting that national*ism* as an ideology may be said to emerge in the eighteenth century, Smith stresses the significance of historic *ethnies* (French for 'ethnic communities') in making later nationalisms possible. They form the basis of deeply held nationalist sentiments. Historical factors such as prolonged warfare with other ethnic groups produce a strong bond of ethnicity and a sense of belonging to an immemorial community. Smith is not arguing that nations are formed out of actual ties of kinship: '*Ethnies* are constituted, not by lines of physical descent, but by the sense of continuity, shared memory and collective destiny' (Smith, 1986). This leads him to stress, in a way that the modernisation theorists tend not to, the importance of myths, collective memories, persistent traditions and shared symbols in the constitution of ethnic identifications. These can in turn provide the resources for modern nationalists to shape nationalisms: 'if nationalism is modern and shapes nations . . . then this is only half the story. Specific nations are also the product of older, often pre-modern ethnic ties and ethno-histories' (1998: 195). *Ethnies* compete with other modes of organisation for the basis of people's identity and sense of history, space and place (for example, social class, city, etc.) and are often very successful. The sheer number of such ethnic groups, their obvious presence and the plethora of material evidence from the past up to the present attest to the validity behind Smith's argument. Clearly, for example, though there is much truth in the claim that ethno-religious identification in Northern Ireland persists because of the instrumental manipulation of political elites, it is also obvious that history has bequeathed to that region the basis of such identities, which, although they are not unchanged over time, are something that is really there (see Whyte, 1990).

This is a good corrective to the more cavalier modernisation theories that can be too general in their search for laws of development rather than ways of looking at the importance of contexts that are not simply incidental. As Smith (1998) makes clear, it is not impossible to combine a modernisation thesis with the recognition of historicity. It does not mean we have to abandon questions as to the extent to which a shared ethnic memory is something that is reinvented or reworked. Nationalist intellectuals and activists may expend a great deal of effort recovering (perhaps inventing) traditions, folk tales, languages, songs and so forth (see Hobsbawm and Ranger, 1992). But it is not possible for them to invent absolutely new ethnic identities where there was no prior basis at all. Perhaps this is true of all ideologies – none can take root where there is no fertile ground in the first place or, rather, when ideologies do take root they do so in specific contexts and they will be altered by, and adapt to, those contexts. All ideologies are the result of the long historical effort of human beings to try and make sense of, and have an impact upon, the natural and social world in which they find themselves. Each of us has to do this but we can only ever do it against the backdrop of the history that has brought us to where we are and the ideologies which those before us have constructed.

Political movements, political ideologies and nationalism

We have seen how, in the sixteenth and seventeenth centuries, nationalism, or at least nationality, was closely linked with democratic sentiments – with the idea that 'the people' should have some say in their own government. In order to 'think' democracy people also needed to think of themselves as already united and connected with each other. Imagining themselves to be part of an ancient nation with ancient rights helped them do this. Thus the ideologies of democracy and nationalism were, for a time, inseparable and mutually supporting. Indeed, nationalism rarely travels alone. It always works with other ideologies, other kinds of political ideal, and these may be of the left as much as of the right. This raises the difficult question of whether nationalism is taking the leading or supporting role in its own political dramas. As Freeden asks, 'are democracy and community glosses on nationhood, or are nationhood and nationalism more generally, a gloss on ideologies in which democracy and community play a crucial part?' (1998: 759).

Elements of nationalism can contribute to other ideologies, giving them a much needed context and legitimacy. As Breuilly shows, nationalism 'arises out of the need to make sense of complex social and political arrangements' (1982: 343). Since the modern state developed by basing its claims to legitimacy on the sovereignty of the people, rather than of the monarch, the problem arose of which people exactly were sovereign, and 'Once the claim to sovereignty was made on behalf of a particular territorially defined unit of humanity it was natural to relate the claim to the particular attributes of that unit' (1982: 343). In other words, to justify political arrangements by finding them to be in accordance with the nature or spirit of the people, the national community. Thus, while nationalism may always need a 'host' ideology, it is also possible that other ideologies find a useful 'host' in nationalism – that they can enhance their persuasiveness by being associated with a supposed national character or sentiment. In fact this could be a way in which an ideology can make itself appear 'natural'. This is not to suggest that nationalism is always consciously employed by unscrupulous and manipulative politicians as a strategy for maintaining power. It may just be that politicians or ideologues, in trying to make sense of the world and to sustain their own arguments, find themselves seeing things in national terms. Just think of the extent to which British politicians routinely refer to the good of the nation or the national interest; the way they portray themselves as being more in tune with the national spirit than their opponents. This may not be nationalism in the sense of a singular and clear doctrine but it is national-ism in the sense that it draws on implicit assumptions about the naturalness of nations and uses them to articulate a political case (see Billig, 1995). In this way the claims of, say, conservatism (which often advocates an organic notion of some sort of unified community to which we owe allegiance) may combine with nationalism (which of course also advances a notion of a naturally unified community). But socialism too can combine with nationalism, particularly in the case of populist anti-colonial nationalisms, where both ideologies share a notion of the people as the source of all that is legitimate and true. We might also make mention of ecologism, which, given that it seeks in part to protect the landscape, is quite capable of being used by nationalism and of using nationalism and national sentiment as justification for opposition to certain kinds of social change.

There is also a relationship between feminism and nationalism. Feminism, like nationalism, often functions within the context of a relationship to an ideology such as liberalism or socialism. But the claims of feminism are sometimes related to those of nationalism, especially in the context of national liberation struggles, in which women (especially in non-Western contexts) often play a crucial part. We might also think of the use of aspects of gender and gendered symbolisation within nationalism which have been astutely analysed by feminist scholars. Nations are often imagined in mythic form as female figures. We speak of

Britannia and paint her as a woman. In France, Joan of Arc is a key female national icon and France itself is imagined as female. But this often means that the land or the country is being figured as a nurturing, mother figure whose sons must always be ready to defend her. Her daughters can consequently be instructed to continue the work of reproducing the nation both biologically and culturally. In fact a whole range of gendered and sexualised imagery almost always goes along with nationalism (e.g. Yuval-Davis, 1997; Walby, 1996; Mosse, 1985) and appeals to nationhood may be one way in which a certain form of anti-feminism is constructed.

What we are seeing here is the way in which ideologies combine and recombine with each other and with other political ideas in the attempt to forge a political belief system that seems both coherent and natural. Ideologies are not just about constructing doctrinal positions. They are also about establishing the legitimacy of one's own political claims and the illegitimacy of one's opponents'. One of the best ways of doing this is to suggest that your own views are not an ideology – they are normal and obvious – while everybody else's views are foolish philosophy. Conservatism very often makes this sort of claim. But nationalism and nationality can lend this naturalness to a range of ideologies because nationality seems a part of the everyday, natural world. Even if we consciously reject our nationality and claim to be global cosmopolitans it is still clear to us what it is we are rejecting, just as it will be clear to many other people what nationality it is we think of ourselves as trying to get away from.

So far, in looking at the interaction of political movements and ideologies with nationalism, we have not thought about liberalism. Since liberalism claims to champion the individual, to protect her or his liberty from the impositions of collectivist ideologies and always to promote tolerance, we might well presume that nationalism and liberalism are antagonistic ideologies. Certainly, nationalism generally has not been much admired by liberal political theorists. Isaiah Berlin, for example, while he understood the potency of the romanticist ideal of the organic community, criticised nationalism precisely because of the way in which it privileges the interests of the supposedly organic community over those of smaller groups or individuals. It can thus be despotic and oppressive (Berlin, 1979: 333–55). But Berlin makes the common distinction between national*ism*, the ideology, and nationality or 'mere national consciousness – the sense of belonging to a nation' (1979: 346). And it is nationality and liberalism that have often combined.

As we have noted, nationalism makes it possible to imagine a kind of community between people that has been important in sustaining claims about rights and legal equalities and useful in making government seem legitimate. Liberalism has long known this. J. S. Mill, the archetypal liberal thinker, noted that free government was virtually impossible in multinational states. It was, he thought, necessary for a governed people to feel some connection and solidarity with each other. Increasingly, contemporary liberal political theorists and ideologists are beginning to see ways in which a sense of nationality may be important for them. In part this has been stimulated by the criticisms of what is known as communitarianism. Communitarian thinkers have argued that liberalism is insufficiently attentive to the need of individuals to be part of a wider substantive community. They argue that values such as tolerance, justice, fairness and so forth take on meaning for people only within the context of an embedded, shared culture within which they can feel themselves a part of something (see Mulhall and Swift, 1992). As a result of this debate (and also perhaps because of actual problems of solidarity and civic commitment in many liberal democratic polities) some theorists have begun to think about the importance of the 'principle of nationality' to life in a good polity.

One thing that some liberals have done to effect this connection is make a distinction between good and bad nationalisms. This builds on a distinction that other scholars have established between what have been termed 'civic' and 'ethnic' conceptions of the nation (see Geertz, 1963; Plamenatz, 1976; Ignatieff, 1993) For the former the nation is primarily a 'political' unit with some sort of civic tie between a set people. This fosters duties, rights, responsibilities and obligations. By contrast 'ethnic' nationalisms are understood as interpreting the nation as bonded through some kind of blood tie or through a powerful shared historical or cultural consciousness. Through this distinction liberals try to distance themselves from the more aggressive aspects of nationalism. This distinction can be found, in varying forms, throughout writings on nationalism. Sometimes it is mapped on to a distinction between Eastern and Western nationalisms, where the latter are civic and democratic, the former cultural and authoritarian (see Kohn, 1944; Plamenatz, 1976). Other times the division is labelled 'civic–territorial' and 'ethnic–genealogical' (Smith, 1991) or 'individualistic–libertarian' and 'collectivist–authoritarian' (Greenfeld, 1992).

David Miller (1995) rejects such an easy distinction but instead defends what he calls 'a principle of nationality'. He argues that it need not be irrationally indefensible to claim that national identity is a part of one's identity. Nations are ethical communities (though this need not mean that we owe no ethical obligations to those beyond our nation or no special ethical obligations to a smaller unit such as our family). This in turn means that there should be some right to self-determination, though not necessarily to a sovereign state. For Miller this last claim is important, for it is in part the autonomous and self-determining nature of nations that makes their meaningful ethical status possible.

Miller's position is in part motivated by a sort of realism. He just thinks it unlikely that people will suddenly decide that their sense of nationality was a big fiction and so give up on it. Better then to think within nationality and see how it may fit with liberal, civic, principles. In any case many political philosophers already assume something like a national community, a body of people with a sense of shared history, continuity and so forth, when they begin to theorise about the nature of justice or rights and so forth. It is possible, Miller avers, to develop a sense of nationality that contributes to, rather than detracts from, a shared commitment to the civic principles of the liberal state. But this has implications for issues such as multiculturalism. Ethnic or cultural minorities within a liberal state have a right to expect that the state will make some effort to accommodate them but they too must accept their responsibility to be loyal to the national state. For Miller a politics of nationality is opposed to a narrow 'politics of identity'. A civic national identity does not impose itself upon other identities. Rather, it is a kind of framework for a common identity within which other identities may make legitimate claims.

Miller's arguments have come in for criticism on the grounds that they tend to lead to support for the *status quo* and thus downplay the extent to which the grievances of a minority may be severe and rooted in the unjust nature of present political arrangements. It has also been argued that Miller does not fully appreciate the interrelationship of civic and ethnic conceptions of nationalism, the fact that they provide each other with support (see O'Leary, 1996; Smith, 1998).

We can perhaps see that, whatever our initial feelings about nationalism, it is a kind of fundamental political ideology. This is not necessarily because that is how it has to be or can only be. It may simply derive from the ways in which people in the past have developed ideas and practices that helped explain to them why they should feel about each other in certain ways, how we should answer certain sorts of difficult political question. It is also, of course, the result of certain past political victories and disputes. It may be objected that in making this claim I am conflating those general sentiments of nationality with full-blown nationalism. But unless we recognise that the sentiment of nationality in the West comes from (and has been historically sustained and propagated by) what were once nationalisms – full-blown movements for national unity or liberation – we cannot understand the nature of nationalism as an ideology. It is not just or only a doctrine comprised of certain core claims. It is a set of general ideas that contribute to a larger 'world view' and which may be drawn on by a range of political actors and thinkers in different ways, at different times and in different contexts.

Conclusion

In this chapter we have looked at nationalism in a slightly unusual way. Rather than treat it as an isolated political doctrine we have considered the interaction of nationalism with other ideologies and touched on what this may tell us about the nature of ideology. Instead of reviewing studies of virulent and violent ethnic nationalisms we have been concentrating on the place of nationalism in our general political thinking and particularly in our ideas about democracy. This is not to ignore the instances of nationalist or ethnic conflict. Rather it is to stress that we need to take nationalism seriously as a political force and that means thinking about how it is part of 'us' and not just part of 'them', over there, somewhere, engaging in what we think of as unthinkable. Nationalism was a

European invention and it was Europe that exported it across the globe (see Chatterjee, 1986).

As one would expect of an ideology, nationalism offers answers to the big questions of social and political life. It makes a claim as to the basis of human sociality and relationships. It gives reasons for why we should (or shouldn't) feel obliged to others. It advances a case for what makes the best form of legitimate government and suggests something about citizens' relationship to the state. But it does not necessarily always say much more. When it comes to advancing a case about the distribution of wealth, for example, or about the way in which an economy should be run, nationalism alone is pretty useless. It may imply a kind of equality between all fellows but it may also advocate a hierarchical and authoritarian form of government in the interests of that national equality. Nationalism always needs to be in connection with wider social philosophies. This may be indicative of, as Freeden claims, how thin nationalist ideology is. It may also show how simplistic it is. But this may also be evidence of the fact that nationalism is, in a sense, a more fundamental ideology than others. It is successful to the point where we do not really notice many of the essentially nationalist assumptions we all make.

But for how much longer can nationalism function in this way? What happens to it in the face of globalisation? We are seeing something like the erosion of nation states or at least the growing separation of the national part from the state part. Supra-national political institutions such as the European Union are taking power away from single nations. Increasingly, non-governmental organisations such as worldwide pressure groups, multinational corporations and so forth move between and above national sovereignty. And there is also cultural globalisation. It is unlikely that the people within a single nation will partake in the same forms of cultural experience all the time or that they will even share in their own national culture. They may buy food from all over the planet, eating Chinese one day, Italian the next. They very probably travel to other countries and may even have jobs that necessitate them speaking to or visiting other nations very regularly.

People in the United Kingdom may well watch nothing but American or Hong Kong action movies on their televisions or DVD players manufactured in Taiwan. This may be a very important influence on the future directions of national sentiment. Human collectivities have always grasped their sense of being a collective through forms of artistic dramatisation and expression and the (often ritualised) public act of observing and maybe participating in them. The ancient Greeks, and especially the Athenians who lived in what many regard as the first democracy, regularly held festivals and competitions for everything from sport and athletics to drama and poetry. These were occasions when the collective, the 'imagined community' in Anderson's phrase, could experience itself as such and have its being reaffirmed. When it came to the dramatic festivals, the dramas themselves touched on and explored the question of what it was to be an Athenian citizen and held up ways in which the community might like (or might not like) to think of itself (see Goldhill, 1986). In our own time we still engage in such collective rituals though their place in our lives, and the extent to which they can be contained within singular collectivities, have certainly changed.

Scholars of nationalism have often pointed to the importance of communication systems in enabling people to develop a sense of shared culture and belonging. Anderson argues that the emergence of nationalism was closely related to the spread of trade in printed matter. In order to create viable markets this trade assembled varied dialects into more homogeneous languages, creating a bridge between elite clerical Latin and diverse popular vernaculars. For Anderson, it was this convergence between capitalism and the technology of printing that made it possible to begin imagining the national community. But, as Deutsch shows, communication entails not only language but also 'systems of writing, painting, calculating etc. . . . information stored in the living memories, associations, habits, and preferences . . . material facilities for the storage of information such as libraries, statues, signposts and the like' (1966: 96). The predominantly national basis of media institutions has made them of tremendous importance in the maintenance of national communities. Television has been understood by its own practitioners and professionals as a means of integrating millions of domestic family units into the rhythms and experiences of a national imaginary (Ang, 1996: 5). The media, far from simply reflecting national experiences, create them by their presence as recorders of events. Be it the coronation of a monarch, the swearing in of a president or the creation of a 'national' tragedy (such as the sudden death of a princess in a car crash or a football team in a penalty shoot-out) media events 'integrate societies in a collective heartbeat and evoke a renewal of loyalty to the society and its legitimate authority' (Dayan and Katz, 1992: 9). The mass media have, in a way, replaced the ancient festivals, and it is these forms of instantaneous electronic media that offer the rituals of collective life. But the media are increasingly internationalised and fragmented. It is now less and less likely that people will all simultaneously watch the same event at the same time, despite wide access to such media.

This sort of cultural 'globalisation' may already be having an impact on the way we experience nationality. But what we are seeing is not the development of an overarching cosmopolitan or 'world' identity. Rather we are seeing the proliferation of 'new' or resurgent nationalisms. In the United Kingdom, for example, devolution in Scotland and Wales is actually reinforcing certain kinds of nationalism or national sentiment. On the continent of Europe smaller regions such as the Basque country in Spain continue to fight their cause. Other regions, some spurred on by their capacity to address the European level of government directly, are growing in confidence and may begin demanding more power. In the United Kingdom this is represented by those calling for assemblies in the north of England. In Italy one can look at the (fluctuating) support for the separatist Northern League, motivated by resentment and prejudice towards the south of the country. Alternatively, we may look at the attempts by some supranational organisations to try and generate a supranational identity. The

European Union has tried to develop common cultural and media policies and seeks to fund, for example, film projects which it hopes may add to a sense of shared culture and identity across the countries of Europe. In a sense this reproduces the activities of the nation state, as understood by someone such as Gellner, in developing a shared 'high culture' across a territory. But we should also remember the persistence of nationalism and nation states. Even when people do travel widely and consume many forms of culture they are capable of reining them in to their national perspective. It does not follow that these things automatically erode a sense of nationality. Indeed, the growth of communication technologies makes it possible for peoples to maintain their sense of cultural identity and specificity regardless of territorial factors. Those in an ethnic diaspora can continue to keep up with news and culture from their home country and with their fellow nationals. They may even be an important force in maintaining separatist movements (see Seaton, 1999: 258). For this reason, cultural globalisation is as much a force for sustaining ethnic and national groups as a cause of the decomposition of nations from both above and below.

What we are also seeing, thanks in large part to computer technologies allowing the fast movement of information from one place to another, is the growth of global networks of political organisation. As political problems and issues begin to take on a global scale (as with environmental crises, for example, or the management of the capitalist economy) those involved begin to organise globally. So it is that we have seen the global co-ordination of oppositional campaigns to match the globalisation of economic power. Some argue that we need to develop a form of global civil society capable of responding to such phenomena (see Archibulgi *et al.*, 1998). Undoubtedly there are trends towards a reconfiguration of international political, economic and cultural space but whether or not things are moving inexorably upwards in scale remains to be seen.

In assessing the likely prospects of nationalism we should perhaps try to remember what it has been for. Nationalism is an ideology the central function of which is to provide an incontestable answer to the question of why we should think of ourselves as living together in certain ways rather than separately and of providing one part of a way in which we might do so. This, surely, is the fundamental question of any political theory. Indeed, it is perhaps the most fundamental aspect of all political ideologies, even if it is so fundamental that we hardly ever actually see it and think about it. But what is our relationship to each other? Why should I want to have anything to do with you? How is it even possible that I can have anything to do with you? On what basis can I trust you or enter into any sort of collaboration with you? Without an answer to these questions there can be no society. Political theory has provided answers to these questions in ways that are different from nationalism. In world history there have been other solutions to them too. Because nationalism answers these questions in ways that are often exclusivist, hostile to some people in order to favour others, some have sought to establish better and more open ways of answering these fundamental political questions while others have tried to 'co-opt' nationalism to their cause. Perhaps in the future we will develop yet more answers. If our world is to become more successful in managing interdependence between the varied peoples of the globe it will need to think of ways of understanding that interconnection that do not just rely on homogeneity, exclusivity and territorial boundaries. But, because no other ideology has yet succeeded in providing, on its own, an answer of sufficient emotional force, of institutionalising it and making it last, we are all, still, nationalists.

Further reading

The issues raised here are very much alive in a number of respects. For this reason students might be advised to look at the growing literature on globalisation and international governance. Aspects of this debate are considered in the essays that make up *Re-imagining Political Community* edited by Daniele Archibulgi, David Held and Martin Kohler (1998). Andrew Linklater's *The Transformation of Political Community* (1998) also looks at these issues.

On nationalism itself a good overview by a master of the field is Anthony D. Smith's *Nationalism and Modernism* (1998). This looks at all the theories considered here, as well as others. A useful reader with short extracts from many of the major writers on this topic is also edited by Smith along with John Hutchinson: *Nationalism: A Reader* (1994). The debate stimulated by David Miller's endorsement of the 'principle of nationality' is well represented by the special issue of the journal *Nations and Nationalism*. See Brendan O'Leary (ed.), 'Symposium on David Miller's *On Nationality*' (1996).

References

Anderson, Benedict (1992) *Imagined Communities*, 2nd edn, London: Verso.

Ang, Ien (1996) *Living Room Wars: Rethinking Media Audiences for a Postmodern World*, London: Routledge.

Archibulgi, Daniele, Held, David and Kohler, Martin, eds (1998) *Re-imagining Political Community: Studies in Cosmopolitan Democracy*, Cambridge: Polity Press.

Berlin, Isaiah [1979] (1997) 'Nationalism: past neglect and present power' in *Against the Current: Essays in the History of Ideas*, London: Hogarth Press.

Billig, Michael (1995) *Banal Nationalism*, London: Sage.

Breuilly, John (1982) *Nationalism*, Manchester: Manchester University Press.

Chatterjee, Partha (1986) *Nationalist Thought and the Colonial World*, London: Zed Books.

Connor, Walker (1994) *Ethnonationalism: The Quest for Understanding*, Princeton NJ: Princeton University Press.

Dayan, Daniel and Katz, Elihu (1992) *Media Events: The Live Broadcasting of History*, Cambridge MA: Harvard University Press.

Deutsch, Karl (1966) *Nationalism and Social Communication*, Cambridge MA: MIT Press.

Freeden, Michael (1996) *Ideologies and Political Theory*, Oxford: Oxford University Press.

Geertz, Clifford (1963) 'The integrative revolution: primordial sentiments and civil politics in the new states' in C. Geertz (ed.) *Old Societies and New States: The Quest for Modernity in Asia and Africa*, New York: Free Press.

Gellner, Ernest (1983) *Nations and Nationalism*, Oxford: Blackwell.

Goldhill, Simon (1986) *Reading Greek Tragedy*, Cambridge: Cambridge University Press.

Greenfeld, Liah (1992) *Nationalism: Five Roads to Modernity*, Cambridge MA: Harvard University Press.

Hobsbawm, Eric and Ranger, Terence (1992) *The Invention of Tradition*, Cambridge: Cambridge University Press.

Ignatieff, Michael (1993) *Blood and Belonging: Journeys into the new Nationalism*, London: Chatto & Windus.

Kedourie, Elie (1960) *Nationalism*, London: Hutchinson.

Kohn, Hans (1944) *The Idea of Nationalism: A Study of its Ideas and Background*, New York: Macmillan.

Linklater, Andrew (1998) *The Transformation of Political Community: Ethical Foundations of the post-Westphalian Era*, Cambridge: Polity Press.

Mill, John Stuart (1861) *On Representative Government*, Oxford: Oxford University Press, 1995.

Miller, David (1995) *On Nationality*, Oxford: Clarendon Press.

Mosse, George (1985) *Nationalism and Sexuality: Middle Class Norms and Sexual Morality in Modern Europe*, Madison WI: University of Wisconsin Press.

Mulhall, Stephen and Swift, Adam (1992) *Liberals and Communitarians*, Oxford: Blackwell.

Nimni, Ephraim (1994) *Marxism and Nationalism: Theoretical Origins of a Political Crisis*, London: Pluto Press.

O'Leary, Brendan, ed. (1996) 'Symposium on David Miller's *On Nationality*', *Nations and Nationalism*, 2 (3).

Plamenatz, John (1976) 'Two types of nationalism' in Eugene Kamenka (ed.) *Nationalism: The Nature and Evolution of an Idea*, London: Edward Arnold.

Renan, Ernest (1990) 'Qu'est-ce qu'une nation?' in Homi Bhaba (ed.) *Nation and Narration*, London: Routledge.

Seaton, Jean (1999) 'Why do we think the Serbs do it? The new "ethnic" wars and the media', *Political Quarterly*, 70 (3), pp. 254–70.

Seton-Watson, Hugh (1977) *Nations and States: An Enquiry into the Origins of Nations and the Politics of Nationalism*, London: Methuen.

Smith, Anthony (1986) 'The myth of the "modern nation" and the myths of nations', *Ethnic and Racial Studies*, 11, pp. 1–26.

Smith, Anthony D. (1991) *National Identity*, London: Penguin.

Smith, Anthony (1998) *Nationalism and Modernism*, London: Routledge.

Smith, Anthony and Hutchinson, John, eds (1994) *Nationalism: A Reader*, Oxford: Oxford University Press.

Walby, Sylvia (1996) 'Woman and nation' in G. Balakrishan (ed.) *Mapping the Nation*, London: Verso, pp. 235–45.

Weber, Eugene (1979) *Peasants into Frenchmen: The Modernisation of Rural France, 1870–1914*, London: Chatto & Windus.

Whyte, John (1990) *Interpreting Northern Ireland*, Oxford: Clarendon.

Williams, Glyn A. (1991) *When was Wales?* Harmondsworth: Penguin.

Yuval-Davis, Nira (1997) *Gender and Nation*, London: Sage.

Fascism

Rick Wilford

> Fascist movements and regimes were characterised more by what they were against than what they were for – a Manichean division of the world into the forces of good and evil.
>
> (Eatwell, 1995)

More than half a century after the end of the Second World War would seem a secure vantage point from which to pen an epitaph on fascism. The dictatorial regimes that constituted the Axis were utterly defeated and their satellites or puppets vanquished, while the leaders of those regimes took their own lives, were executed, imprisoned or, in some cases, fled under assumed identities.

Militarily, it was a consummate victory for the allied forces and yet, while the fascist regimes were crushed, the ragbag of ideas upon which they were based continued to be – and indeed still are – peddled by their adherents. This adherence takes a variety of forms. The desecration of Jewish cemeteries in Belgium, arson attacks on immigrant hostels in Germany, the bombing of a gay bar in London's West End, are all symptoms of the continued existence of neo-fascist groups and their propensity to engage in antisemitic, racist and homophobic violence.

The literature of 'Holocaust denial', a virulent cottage industry of historical revisionism, is another indication of fascism's apparent resilience. However, the purveyors of such material suffered a massive setback in 2000 when one of their number, David Irving, lost a libel action against Deborah Lipstadt (and her publisher), author of *Denying the Holocaust: The Growing Assault on Truth and Memory*. Irving had claimed that the book represented him as a Nazi apologist, an admirer of Hitler who had resorted to the distortion of facts and to the manipulation of documents in support of his contention that the Holocaust did not take place, thereby seeking to destroy his reputation as a historian. In summing up, the judge in the libel case, Mr Justice Gray, issued a withering condemnation of Irving, both as an historian and as a man. He had, said Gray, 'for his own ideological reasons persistently and deliberately misrepresented and manipulated historical evidence . . . and portrayed Hitler in an unwarrantedly favourable light, principally in relation to his attitude towards and responsibility for the treatment of the Jews'. Effectively stripping him of the status of an historian, the judge revealed Irving as an apologist for Nazism, no more than a propagandist and a polemicist. Turning to Irving's character, Gray was even more coruscating: 'He is an active Holocaust denier, antisemitic, racist and associates with right-wing extremists who promote neo-Nazism.' Irving, who was later to lose his appeal against the judgement, emerged as a financial and a moral bankrupt (see Evans, 2001).

More worryingly, across Europe, including in countries subjugated by Nazism, neo-fascist and extreme right parties attract high levels of electoral support. Such parties, which articulate xenophobic, exclusive forms of nationalism, include France's *Front National* (FN). In 1995 the FN candidate and party leader, Jean-Marie Le Pen – who has described the Holocaust as 'a mere detail in history' – polled 15 per cent of the national vote in the first round of the presidential election. In 2002 he increased his vote share to just under 17 per cent, coming second in the poll ahead of the Socialist candidate, thereby guaranteeing him a straight fight with the incumbent, Jacques Chirac, in the second and final ballot. The result stunned France and Europe.

The electoral surge of neo-fascist parties is not confined to France. In Austria the Freedom Party – established by a former member of the SS – was led by Jorg Haider, a man who has extolled the employment policies of the Nazi era. In 1999 it emerged as the joint second largest party in the national election with almost 27 per cent of the vote, a level of support that enabled it to form a coalition government with the Austrian People's Party. Meanwhile, in the UK general election of 2001, the neo-Nazi British National Party contested seats in, among other places, Oldham's two constituencies. In one, it polled 11 per cent of the vote and in the other just over 16 per cent, coming third with just under 500 votes less than the Conservatives and comfortably ahead of the Liberal Democrats' and the Green party's candidates. In the local government elections of May 2002 the BNP saw three of its candidates elected in Burnley.

Such evidence makes it clear that any obituary of fascism would be premature. Thus, while this chapter cannot conduct a post-mortem on the moribund body of the doctrine, what it can do is explore the lineage of an ideology that benighted much of the twentieth century and which still poses a political threat to freedom and democracy. But why, for some, does such a discredited ideology continue to have an appeal?

'Appeals' of fascism

Part of the answer lies in the ability of fascists to simplify the complexities of political life. Characteristically, its ideologues divide peoples and nations into two irreconcilable camps: 'them' and 'us': those who are not of, or for, 'us' are the enemy. 'They', whether Jews, Blacks, Muslims or 'foreigners' in general, are responsible for the ills besetting 'us'. This feature of the doctrine alerts us to its exclusivity, its 'either–or-ism'. But this is more, much more, than a simple dualism. The bifurcation is predicated upon a hierarchy of value: 'they' are not just different from, but inferior to, 'us'. The notion of superior and inferior peoples – in Nazi terms, *Übermenschen* and *Untermenschen* – justified a relationship of domination and subordination that led, ultimately, to the death camps of Europe. Whether couched in terms of a superior state, as in Mussolini's Italy, or a 'master race', as was the case in Hitler's Germany, fascism was and is both exclusivist and inegalitarian.

Among other things, the stress on superiority rather than difference distinguishes fascism from nationalism, with which it does have an affinity. But, whereas nationalism (see Chapter 5) can be inclusive, coexist with other doctrines, whether socialism, conservatism or liberalism, and respect the integrity of other self-governing nations, fascism neither tolerates ideological competitors nor recognises fundamental equality among nations. This basic intolerance is also signalled by its celebration of aggression. Fascism is a belligerent form of nationalism, contemptuous of the rights of both individuals and other nations, seeking proof of its vitality in the ability to subject others to its thrall. The pursuit of its goals – whether national glory or racial supremacy – is conducted not through the power of argument but rather by the argument of power.

Fascism did of course flourish in the inter-war period, initially in Italy and subsequently in Germany, and was mimicked by parties and movements elsewhere in Europe, including Britain. To that extent it appeared as, and according to many of its exponents was, the new doctrine for the New Age of the twentieth century, a thoroughly modern ideology. It was represented by its exponents as a break with the past, consigning competing doctrines to the dustbin of history. Yet, while extolling its novelty, the ideologues of fascism were also mindful of the past. It is a Janus-like doctrine, looking both forward and backward, seeking to revivify some imagined, pre-industrial sense of community and belonging, whether it was the romanticised Roman empire or the image of a sylvan medieval Germany. Fascism was – and is – also a counter-revolutionary ideology, seeking to subvert the civilising effects of the Enlightenment that had displaced myth and superstition, installing rationalism and secularism in their stead.

Already we can sense something of the duality of fascism's appeal. While celebrating those aspects of the re-imagined past which fascist thinkers considered inspiring, it also rejected other traditions and ideas that encumbered its primary mission: that of national redemption. Conservatism, while sensitive to the past, was regarded by fascists as unequal to the task of national reawakening and rebirth. While a hierarchical doctrine, the attachment of conservatism to emergent democratic norms and institutions rendered it powerless to confront the universalising ambitions of competing ideologies. The task of national regeneration required the defeat of conservatism and its vested interests because they were perceived as a brake on the wheel of history. Moreover, service in the cause of national reawakening required not the pursuit of individualism prescribed by liberalism, nor the realisation of an egalitarian society promised by socialism, but the rebirth of the nation as the living community to which all true people belonged. A recovered national identity thus transcended the individual and united all classes in a common enterprise.

Beset by liberalism and socialism, proto-fascists in the nineteenth century believed that the prospect of a recovered national solidarity was threatened by self-serving individualism, on the one hand, and the promotion of class conflict which threatened to set nationals against one another, on the other. To combat these doctrinal opponents the advocates and practitioners of fascism sought to reinvent and reinvigorate a common national identity and to eliminate all competing ideas. To adopt the metaphor of the school yard, fascism strutted in the playground of ideas as the sadistic bully. The doctrine was, and is, as Sternhell (1979: 368) observes, 'a vision of a coherent and reunited people [and] waged an implacable war against anything which stood for diversity or pluralism'.

Problems of definition

Though we inevitably associate fascism with the regimes of Hitler and Mussolini, it did not emerge entirely unannounced with Mussolini's march on Rome in 1922, but from an eclectic range of ideas that long pre-dated the twentieth century. This chapter attempts to trace the provenance of those ideas that were moulded into a relatively coherent world view by the proponents and adherents of fascism. This is not a simple task. As Paul Hayes (1973: 19) has observed, 'fascist theory is not a tightly knit bundle of ideas. It is, in fact, rather untidy and inchoate . . . composed of a large number of diverse ideas, drawn from different cultures'.

These ideas were unscrupulously pillaged from other traditions, cultures and doctrines. Moreover, there is no *locus classicus* – akin, say, to the *Communist Manifesto* – which supplied the inspiration of fascist leaders and thinkers. Its tributaries flowed from a variety of sources, creating eddies of thought that surged into the mainstreams of Italian fascism and German National Socialism.

To lend some order to the task of plotting the course of the evolution of fascism the chapter provides a set of organising themes that recur in the writings of its precursors, exponents and followers. There are five such themes: statism, racialism, imperialism, elitism and National Socialism. These interact and overlap and vary in their significance across the various fascist parties and movements, each of which was influenced by its own national history, traditions, cultures and prejudices. Thus, while acknowledging that there were distinct national variations, the argument of this chapter is that fascism can be apprehended by focusing upon its intellectual heritage. The exploration of these origins thereby provides a framework within which each of the variations can be accommodated. What the chapter offers is not, therefore, an unambiguous definition of fascism but rather an exploration of its key themes.

Besides the difficulties of tracing these themes to their sources, there is another problem confronting the examination of fascism. The heavy and fatal emphasis upon racialism by Nazism that paved the way to the death camps does, in the view of some scholars, set it apart from other fascist movements. According to such writers the systematic practice of mass genocide renders National Socialism as unique, not just an exaggerated variation of fascism. While in no way diminishing this argument, the purpose here is to identify the ideas that supplied the pretext for the 'final solution', whereby the manufacture of death became a (self-financing) way of life. Moreover, to imply that other fascist regimes were not implicated in the Holocaust is to turn a blind eye to their complicity in transporting Jews and others to certain death in Auschwitz and elsewhere.

While the exponents of fascism sought to celebrate its modernity, none of the various elements that they fashioned into a body of doctrine were new in themselves. It was, however, the assiduity with which those elements were implemented – mass mobilisation, mass propaganda and mass murder – that leant fascism its modernising claim. The novelty lay in the execution of ideas – and of people – rather than the ideas themselves. Fascism owed much to an intellectually pillaged past. Most immediately, the fascist movements and regimes of the inter-war period inherited their ideas from a mood of revolt that was current in Europe towards the end of the nineteenth century and which had developed throughout its course. This mood is, then, our starting point, not least because it embodied the oppositional or antithetical nature of fascist doctrine.

Origins and derivations

The temptation to label historical periods in terms of a prevailing mood or climate is a risky undertaking, invariably concealing as much as it reveals. Nevertheless, one can characterise the European intellectual climate towards the end of the nineteenth century as one of revolt. Just as the regimes of Mussolini and Hitler emerged from economic and political crises, the embryonic ideology of fascism was one outcome of an intellectual upheaval that became more apparent as the nineteenth century drew to a close. Initially this upheaval took the form of an assault upon liberal doctrine.

The birth of liberalism, as Robert Eccleshall indicates (Chapter 2), was associated with Enlightenment optimism, its proponents stressing the importance of individual judgement as the guide to action. Enlightenment thinkers demanded a new political system that would liberate individuals from the shackles of feudalism. Their portrayal of society as an aggregate of rational individuals, possessed of natural rights, challenged conservatism's pessimistic view of human nature. The liberal belief that individuals in interaction would produce a natural harmony of interests was opposed to the conservative belief in the necessity for order imposed by a natural hierarchy. Whereas conservatives espoused a paternalistic conception of society, emphasising duty and deference, liberals stressed individual rights and belief in self-government.

However, the advance of liberalism in Europe was uneven. At first, opposition to it tended to be rather sporadic, yet, by the 1880s and 1890s, a generation of thinkers had appeared whose works constituted a challenge to what they perceived as the outmoded character of liberal ideas. It is within the context of this revolt against liberalism that the more immediate precursors of fascism can be located.

The rational individualism of the liberal doctrine, its belief in diversity, pluralism and tolerance, led, so these critics argued, to insecurity, instability and mediocrity. The focus of analysis for the architects of this intellectual revolt was not the individual but the wider community, commonly represented as a self-regarding, organic whole. Collectivism and conformity, rather than individualism and choice, were the preferred social order. Moreover, the liberal emphasis on reason as the guide to action was supplanted by a preference for non-rational motives – instinct, descent, heredity and race – which were acclaimed as the primary engines driving human behaviour.

Such thinkers, some of whom owed their inspiration to a perverse reading of Charles Darwin's (1809–82) *Origin of Species* (1859) and who have been dubbed 'Social Darwinists', portrayed individuals as unreflective, amoral creatures, spurred by the instinctive fight for survival. Darwin himself did not draw any normative lessons from the theory of natural selection in order to apply them to human society. Indeed, the very phrase 'the survival of the fittest' – not Darwin's, but coined by the British philosopher Herbert Spencer (1820–1903) – was seized upon eagerly by proto-fascist thinkers because it imparted a simplifying gloss to the theory of evolution.

Such contorted thinking provided a radical alternative to liberalism's emphasis upon deliberate, rational choice as the basis of human action. While Spencer was an arch-defender of *laissez-faire* his belief, shared by other Social Darwinists, that society progresses through a harsh struggle for survival and that the weak suffer from their own incompetence, contributed to the assault upon liberalism's values. Moreover, the muscular philosophy of Social Darwinism fostered an (anti-) intellectual climate within which racialist 'theories' flourished.

Race and state

Pseudo-scientific 'theories' of racialism, partly inspired by a wilful misreading of Darwin's ideas, were but one manifestation of a much longer current of thought. For instance, during the late eighteenth and early nineteenth centuries the theme of racial superiority surfaced in Germany with the popularisation of the *Volk*. At a literal level this concept translates as 'the people', but it also has a more abstract meaning: it represents a system of absolute values, an immutable metaphysical ideal of peoplehood. As George Mosse puts it: 'Just as individual men had a soul, so there existed a *Volk* soul which, like man's soul, gave the *Volk* its unique and unchanging character.' The task for Germans was to recover and liberate their collective soul, which was 'wild and dynamic, based on emotions rather than on a tortured intellectualizing' (1971: 8).

An early exponent of this abstract interpretation of the *Volk* was Johann Fichte (1762–1814), who, like his contemporary Johann Herder (1744–1803), depicted the German nation as a natural whole united by descent, language and culture. At the beginning of the nineteenth century Fichte propagated the belief that Germany, though disunited and militarily humiliated by France, would eventually prevail because of the natural superiority of its people. In his *Addresses to the German Nation* (1807–8) he portrayed the Germans as an archetypal *Volk*, in whom was invested a special mission on behalf of mankind: that of leading a cultural struggle against 'Western', primarily French, influence.

Such beliefs, allied to a sense of mission, provided a source of brooding consolation for nascent Germans – one that was also fed by Herder. He purported to trace the origins of the *Volk* to medieval Germany, envisaged as a close-knit rural society wherein the *volkisch* 'spirit' or 'soul' had been freely expressed. In the writings of both thinkers, the *Volk* was presented in romantic terms: it connoted a happy, rural idyll, an organically whole national community in which the interests of the individual were subordinated to the national 'spirit'. Moreover, both asserted that the German 'spirit' was superior to that of other peoples.

This emphasis upon the organic nature of the state was also characteristic of Georg Hegel (1770–1831). Unlike Fichte, however, Hegel did not equate the state with an ethnic or natural conception of the *Volk*, although he did address the issue of German unification. In *The German Constitution* (1803) he lamented the disintegration of the nation into a hotch-potch of rival petty princedoms, thereby depriving it of the collective sentiment he believed to be the foundation of statehood. He elaborated these and other ideas in *Philosophy of Right* (1821) in which history was presented as a dynamic process whose engine was the conflict or dialectic of ideas. In his view the state was the ultimate idea, the realisation of spirit or reason in history. Unlike Fichte and Herder, Hegel was preoccupied not by the search for German statehood but rather by the 'Idea' of the state which he believed to be based upon 'the power of reason actualising itself as will'.

Thus, while conceptualising the state as an integrated community, he argued that its basis was rational freedom: within it individuality and collectivity, the particular and the universal, coexisted on the basis of reason. Such a state was to be neither absolutist nor founded upon arbitrary force. It would secure many of the legal rights championed by liberals: the rights, for instance, to acquire private property and of free expression. In this way plurality and diversity would be preserved. His intention was not to subordinate the individual to the whole, but to illustrate how the state supplied its inhabitants with a common focus: a set of institutions and values with which all could freely associate. It was through their common membership of the state that individuals could move beyond their own private interests and identify with the common good. Yet Hegel's ideas, like those of Darwin later in the nineteenth century, were to fall prey to the fascists' search for an intellectual tradition.

Hegel's portrayal of the state as the culmination of history was to infatuate Mussolini and his leading ideologue and arbiter of cultural policy, Giovanni Gentile (1875–1944). But, whereas Hegel recognised the relationship between civil society and the state to be one of mutual dependence, in fascist Italy state and society were conflated: 'Everything for the State, nothing outside the State.' The quest for a renewed Roman empire required a cloak of philosophical respectability and this Mussolini and Gentile purported to find in Hegel's idea of the state as an end in itself. This, however, was a perversion of Hegel's thought: he became another casualty in the search for an intellectual tradition that could fuel national regeneration. By contrast, as we shall see, German National Socialism did not require even a distorted interpretation of Hegel. Unlike Mussolini, Hitler regarded the state not as an end in itself but as a means to assure racial superiority. It was Fichte who had laid the basis of the *volkisch* ideology that was to become a central organising principle of Nazism.

The belief in a superior German culture charged with a mission to overcome 'Western' influences, coupled with the growth of intellectual support for the primacy of the state, gathered pace throughout the nineteenth century.

In Germany, Friedrich Jahn (1778–1852) furthered the idea of a natural organic community and extolled the superiority of an anti-liberal, authoritarian Germanic political tradition. In *German Nationhood* (1810) Jahn defined the basis of nationhood as racial purity and asserted the uniqueness and superiority of all Germans. His goal was a greater German 'people's democracy', encompassing Austria, Holland, Switzerland and Denmark, from which all foreign influences would be banished.

Jahn prized national sentiment and nationhood above both individual rights and universalism and as such supplied a motive for a struggle against 'the West', i.e. against liberal precepts. It was a message that became increasingly strident at the end of the nineteenth century as intellectuals from different national backgrounds sought a 'third way' between Enlightenment values and the growing challenge of socialism.

By the mid-nineteenth century the concept of racial superiority was firmly established in European thought and was by no means confined to the works of German thinkers. One of the earliest expositions of racial 'theory' was provided by a French diplomat, Count Arthur Gobineau (1816–62), whose *Essay on the Inequality of Races of Man* (1853–5), proclaimed both the superiority of white 'races' over non-whites and Jews as well as the primacy of 'race' above individual and nation. Furthermore, he purported to identify degrees of racial purity among whites: those possessing the highest levels of purity carried the potential to advance civilisation, whereas those less richly endowed transmitted racial decay. In the former category lay the Teutons, whereas Slavs and Celts were consigned to the latter group.

The attempt to invent a racial hierarchy within which Jews occupied the lowliest position can be placed within a tradition of antisemitism that long pre-dates Gobineau. Stereotypes of Jews were commonplace throughout much of European history that, during the later eighteenth and the first half of the nineteenth centuries, expressed itself primarily in the form of religious antagonism towards Judaism. This cultural prejudice, widely propagated in contemporary popular literature, supplied a spurious rationale for antisemitism and assisted in creating a receptive climate for the ideas of Gobineau and certain of the Social Darwinists.

It had earlier been contended that the 'Jewish problem' could be solved by resocialising Jews, encouraging them to shed their religious beliefs, which served to set them apart from the dominant cultures of their 'host' societies. By engaging in 'honest toil', moreover, Jews would acquire new roots and thus become deserving of assimilation into their adopted countries. However, as the essentially irrational *volkisch* nationalism began to take root, Jews came to be regarded not merely as non-assimilable but as constituting a *racial* rather than a cultural threat to the German nation.

This transformation from cultural to biological antisemitism was stimulated by Social Darwinism. One English thinker who contributed to this metamorphosis was Houston Stewart Chamberlain (1855–1927), son-in-law of the German composer, Richard Wagner. Asserting that the fittest were those who were racially pure, Chamberlain developed the notion of the 'Aryan folk nation' which, he believed, was 'destined to triumph because of its superior genetic gifts' (Hayes, 1973: 23ff.). On this basis, interracial marriage (miscegenation) was scorned as an unnatural evil, since it diluted the purity of the blood. Moreover, egalitarianism, internationalism and pacifism were dismissed by Chamberlain on the ground that they offended the natural order of things, i.e. the struggle for ascendancy. In their place, war and the struggle for survival by the fittest were extolled as evidence of a race's vitality. Destiny belonged to those confident of their inherent superiority, a pre-eminence bestowed by racial purity.

National imperialism

During much of the nineteenth century, nationalism, through its association with the French revolution, was understood by many as an agent of emancipation and freedom. However, under the impact of a racially defined conception of statehood, a new European nationalism began to develop, nourished by the conviction that the unification of both Italy and Germany was the outcome of an intoxicating mixture of 'blood and iron'. The growing belief in a racial state spanning generations and existing frontiers, together with the advocacy of struggle by Social Darwinists of the Spencerite persuasion, merged to provide a rationale for imperialism. This found expression in the principle of *Machtpolitik*. Loosely translated, it means power politics but, more to the point, it was the belief that might was right.

The creed of *Machtpolitik* was expressed by the German general Friedrich von Bernhardi (1843–1930):

> might gives the right to occupy or conquer. It is at once the supreme right and the dispute as to what is right is decided by the arbitrariment of war. War gives a biologically just decision, since its decisions rest on the very nature of things.
>
> (Bernhardi, 1914)

Here lay the pretext for national expansion: racial superiority and the naturalness of conflict provided a perverse normative guide. In this world view, power and morality were fused: the interests of the nation took priority over the rule of international law and rejected any belief in the universal rights of man.

The interlacing of power politics with nationalism and racialism is equally explicit in the works of Chamberlain and his fellow Englishman, Karl Pearson (1857–1936). Pearson regarded the exercise of might as a moral injunction: 'when wars cease there will be nothing to check the fertility of the inferior stock' (1905: 27). Chamberlain shared this grotesque view. Presenting the process of history as a 'race struggle', and arguing that only the 'Aryans' were capable of creating culture, he declaimed: 'the power of might is the destiny of selected races . . . it is their duty to conquer and destroy the impure and inferior' (Hayes, 1973: 115).

This, in effect, meant that the advocacy of war and suppression was a 'moral' duty. Support for both the equation of race with statehood and the primacy of national as opposed to individual interests began to converge in the later nineteenth century. A 'natural' national greatness, imbued with a spiritual mission, was harnessed in order to supply the motive for imperialism.

Elitism and leadership

The growing emphasis upon race, coupled with the idea of an imperial mission, required leadership of a special character: a figure who embodied the claimed virtues of the race. The disdain for egalitarian principles shared by Social Darwinists led them to mock democratic forms of government. Not only did they postulate a natural hierarchy among 'races', they also asserted the existence of naturally superior individuals within racial groups. Here lay the justification for leadership by an elite.

One exponent of elitism was Friedrich Nietzsche (1844–1900). Some of his ideas and much of his rhetoric were to be appropriated by fascists, and yet he too fell foul of their greedy search for a philosophical tradition. Nietzsche affirmed the irrational 'will to power' as the mainspring of personality, and the value of life to be measured by perpetual struggle: 'Life itself is essentially appropriation, infringement, the overpowering of the alien and the weaker, oppression, hardness, the imposition of one's own form, assimilation and, at the least and mildest, exploitation' (Hayes, 1973: 34). This virile prescription demanded an elite of the tough and the strong that would lead the 'lower orders', whose instincts were slavishly to defer to their natural leaders and betters.

His portrayal of the leader figure took on heroic proportions: a 'Superman', a 'magnificent blond beast', who would trounce the weak, the decadent and the mediocre. Equality had no place in this vision, in its stead was a conception of hierarchy, at the top of which strode the naturally superior. This credo was to prove irresistible to later fascist leaders. In Nazi Germany this image of individual leadership was enshrined as the *Fuhrerprinzip*, and in Italy it was personified in the cult of *Il Duce*: in short, dictatorship.

Yet, as already implied, Nietzsche's albeit equivocal reputation was sullied by fascism. Although a proponent of the irrational he did not advocate the organic society favoured by proto-fascists, but instead celebrated rugged individualism. Nor did he embrace nationalism and, far from decrying miscegenation, he considered it to be the crucible in which great culture was forged. He was, however, opposed to the Judaeo-Christian tradition, labelling Christianity a 'slave religion' that, along with its secular successors, humanism and socialism, 'encouraged a false sense of universalism, tending to promote pity for the weak rather than respect for the strong' (Eatwell, 1995: 8). It was the appeal of his wilder rhetorical flourishes – the imagery of blond beasts animated by the will to power – that proved compelling to the would-be 'Supermen' of Nazi Germany and fascist Italy. As with Hegel and Darwin, the appropriation of Nietzsche as a progenitor of fascism was testimony to the selective looting of ideas engaged in by its ideologues.

The advocacy of elitism was shared by many of Nietzsche's contemporaries. At a time when the fitful movement towards mass suffrage was occurring, the fear of the implications of democracy encouraged numerous thinkers to devise arguments for the maintenance of leadership by the few. The Italian academic Vilfredo Pareto (1848–1923), for instance, in a number of works extolled the virtues of elite leadership (*Les Systèmes socialistes*, 1902, and *The Mind and Society*, 1916–19). He likened society to a pyramid, at the apex of which stood a gifted minority fitted to govern, below whom sprawled an acquiescent, pliant and mediocre mass. Such ideas bore the hallmark of Social Darwinism, as did Pareto's theory of history, which he understood as the story of conflict between warring elites. So popular were his views in Italy that in 1922 Mussolini made him a member of the Italian Senate.

Similar ideas were expressed by the German intellectual, Robert Michels (1876–1936). In *Political Parties* (1911) he argued the need for a dominant social group to ensure the well-being of social and political life. Like Pareto he feared popular participation and democratic control and was convinced of the unfitness of the people – the 'mass' – to govern themselves. Significantly, each represented his ideas not as theoretical or ideological formulations but as natural laws, thereby seeking to legitimise anti-liberal and anti-democratic beliefs by cloaking them in pseudo-scientific garb.

Disdain for 'the masses' was shared by another French theorist, Gustave Le Bon (1841–1931). His *Psychology of Crowds* (1865), later cited with approval by Mussolini, offered a justification for elitism and authoritarianism. In Germany, Julius Langbehn's (1851–1907) *Rembrandt as Educator* (1891) echoed Le Bon's contempt for mass democracy. Langbehn postulated race as the determining factor in history: the 'power of blood' was, he claimed, supreme and transcended the nation. His preferred elite was the hereditary aristocracy, which he urged to mobilise the masses in order to crush those he considered guilty of propounding liberal, democratic and socialist ideas: the bourgeoisie and assimilated Jews.

Though their precise roles as progenitors of fascism differed, Nietzsche, Pareto, Michels, Le Bon and Langbehn did help to foster the 'baleful creed' of permanent struggle, elitism and unreason. In that respect each contributed to the climate of irrationalism that characterised Europe in the later nineteenth century. The cult of elitism, the emphasis on power, struggle and authoritarianism, the stress on feeling and instinct, were pitted against the rational individualism of the liberal world. In the developing mass societies of late nineteenth-century Europe, the portrayal of the individual as an integral part of an organic whole, valued only inasmuch as s/he served that whole, was a direct challenge to liberalism. Moreover, the defiant critique of Enlightenment values supplied by Social Darwinists led them to prize inegalitarianism. The celebrants of unreason regarded the people as an unthinking, irrational mass, responsive to the appeals of emotion and feeling orchestrated by those Nietzsche had characterised as 'the highest specimens'.

National Socialism

The appeal of the prophets of unreason was not restricted to the realm of ideas, but was enhanced by their explanation of worsening material conditions confronting Europe. The experience of a severe economic depression in the last quarter of the nineteenth century weakened the grip of belief in both *laissez-faire* economics and free trade: as such liberalism's claim to be the guarantor of economic progress came under increasing strain. Furthermore, the Prussian rise to ascendancy in Germany, the Piedmont ascendancy in Italy and the defeat of France in 1870 by the Prussian army, all appeared to demonstrate the law of the strong advocated by some Social Darwinists. The conjunction of these economic and political events underpinned the threat to liberal values. But the shock troops of the doctrinal assault against Enlightenment values, armed with their irrational remedies for national renewal, also had to confront the growth of socialism.

Socialism sought to divide nations on the basis of class interests and to promote international workers' solidarity, ideas that were anathema to proponents of elite-led *Machtpolitik* intent on imperial conquest and expansion. In order to confront both liberalism and socialism a 'third way' needed to be fashioned between these competing ideologies. Part of the answer lay in extolling national solidarity and promoting economic self-sufficiency (autarky).

In German thought, the idea that all national resources should be marshalled for the national purpose was well established. Fichte, for instance, had advocated a planned economy, reduced reliance on imports and the restriction of external trade, as the means to cohere the state. His prescriptions amounted to a highly regulated economy that was wholly at odds with the tenets of economic liberalism advanced by his contemporary, Adam Smith (1732–90). Moreover, Fichte proposed the expansion of the German state to its 'natural boundaries', as did another apostle of autarky, Friedrich List (1789–1846). List advanced imperial expansion and the regulation of capital and labour by the state: in short, a planned economy founded upon a Germany that incorporated both neighbouring states and overseas territories.

In Germany during the nineteenth century economic self-sufficiency came increasingly to be seen as necessary for the development of state power, and that goal entailed imperial expansion. In an atmosphere suffused with *Machtpolitik*, the espousal of internationalism by socialists was equated with cowardice, whereas the exercise of power politics demanded the appropriation of resources. In domestic terms, autarky was deemed to require loyalty, obedience and service in the national interest, not the rights of liberty, equality and fraternity. Liberal political economy was rejected because of its opposition to state intervention and its advocacy of free trade, while socialism was spurned because it was seen to weaken the nation by advocating class conflict, championing egalitarianism and promoting internationalism.

In Britain the case for autarky was voiced both by Joseph Chamberlain (1836–1914) during the tariff reform campaign and the *fin-de-siècle* advocates of social imperialism, including George Bernard Shaw (1856–1950). What they shared in common was, as Robert Skidelsky notes, a belief in 'the national community as a value to be defended against free-trade internationalism on the one side and working-class internationalism on the other' (1975: 57). The themes of protectionism, imperial preference and belief in a technocratically managed economy that Shaw and Chamberlain rehearsed were later to be taken up by Oswald Mosley (1896–1974), the leading British fascist of the inter-war period.

While autarky did not take root in Britain, it flourished in Germany and Italy. In each case economic self-sufficiency was intimately related to the corporate state. Corporatism asserted that the array of social institutions, whether the family, region or, above all, the nation, enjoy a higher value than the individual. Its exponents claimed that the development and security of the individual depended upon the well-being of these institutions and their ability to foster social, economic, emotional and spiritual solidarity. As such their interests transcended those of the individual. From this perspective the health of the wider community, commonly represented as a living and dynamic organism, was paramount. All its constituent parts were required to serve this higher purpose.

It was no accident that Mussolini chose an organic metaphor to characterise Italy under fascism: 'A society working with the harmony and precision of the human body. Every interest and every individual is subordinated to the overriding purpose of the nation' (Walker, 1977: 17). Here lay the third way between liberal capitalism and socialism. 'Liberalism,' wrote Mussolini, 'denies the state in the interests of the individual' while 'socialism . . . ignores the unity of classes established in one economic and moral reality in the state' (Lyttelton, 1973: 42). Through the imposition of workplace organisations purporting to represent the interests of workers and employers, the wider national interest would be served.

Keenly aware of the mobilising appeal of nationalism, and persuaded of the necessity for conflict to secure change, Mussolini (a former socialist) attempted to fuse nationalism and socialism. The means lay through corporatism, which exhorted all classes to collaborate in building the fascist state. Instead of fighting among themselves on the basis of class interests, or of according primacy to the pursuit of individual interests, Italians were urged to engage in a common external struggle: that between proletarian and bourgeois nations. This would rescue Italy from its status as the poor relation of Europe, secure social cohesion and thereby restore national greatness.

In devising this corporatist formula, Mussolini appropriated and perverted syndicalist ideas (Roberts, 1979; Gregor, 1979a). Originating in France, syndicalism had advocated the creation of autonomous worker organisations (syndicates) as the basis of proletarian revolution. Syndicalists believed that through direct action at the workplace the revolutionary transformation of capitalism could be achieved. An ex-socialist – he had edited the socialist journal *Avanti!* – Mussolini was familiar with the syndicalist vision. When he came to power, and especially after 1925 when he consolidated his dictatorship, he began to install a system of corporations modelled loosely on these ideas. But, whereas revolutionary syndicalists had envisaged their organisations as worker monopolies, Mussolini's corporations encompassed both workers and employers. Moreover, though notionally equal, the spokesmen of capitalist interests in Italy were to be relatively unfettered while labour representatives were mere puppets of his regime: the authentic voices of the working class were stifled by imprisonment, exile or death.

The exertion of central control over these corporations signals a crucial distinction between the syndicalist vision and Mussolini's. The syndicalists were profoundly anti-statist whereas he elevated the state to a position of dominance:

> The keystone of Fascist doctrine is the conception of the State, of its essence, of its tasks, of its ends. For Fascism the State is an absolute before which individuals and groups are relative. Individuals and groups are 'thinkable' only in so far as they are within the State . . . when one says Fascism one says the State.
>
> (Lyttelton, 1973: 53, 55)

Here lay the crude attempt to fuse nationalism with socialism. Italian fascism emphasised duty, sacrifice and obedience in the service of the nation state. The compelling interest was that of the nation, served by the rigidly organised and hierarchically controlled corporations that were bereft of autonomy. The merger of nationalism with socialism was served by a brutally simplistic formula: the nation is the community to which all belong, thus all classes must serve the interests of the nation.

The pursuit of autarky also led to the imposition of a centralised and planned economy in Germany. While corporatism was less fully developed than in Italy, the crushing of independent trade unions and their replacement in 1933 by the 'Labour Front' was couched in organic terms. Workers and employers were exhorted to serve, in Hitler's words, 'only one interest, the interest of the nation; only one view, the bringing of Germany to the point of political and economic self-sufficiency' (Noakes and Pridham, 1974: 405)

In Nazi Germany, as in Italy, the claim to socialist credentials was baseless. Belief in the common ownership of the means of production or the abolition of wage slavery, for instance, held no place in Hitler's world view. In *Mein Kampf* (1925–6) Hitler purported to define the 'socialist' aspects of Nazism in quite vacuous terms such as 'nationalising the masses' or 'giving the broad masses back to their nation'. To be 'social' was to share in a sense of 'feeling and destiny' in the national community.

As Robert Cecil observes, in Hitler's view the only acceptable form of socialism was that of the 'front line' which had developed in the trenches of the First World War. This was characterised by Alfred Rosenberg (1893–1946), a leading ideologue of Nazism's racial 'theory', in the following terms: 'Out of the battlefield, the men in grey brought back something new: a feeling for the social and national cohesiveness of the different classes' (Cecil, 1972: 57). The camaraderie of soldiers – Mussolini coined the word 'trenchocracy' to convey the same sentiment (Griffin, 1995: 28–9) – and the common bonds forged in battle became the spurious metaphor for socialism.

The 'Twenty-five Point Programme' of the Nationalist Socialist German Workers' Party published in 1920 (Noakes and Pridham, 1974: 405) included such ostensibly impeccable socialist goals as the nationalisation of large corporations, the abolition of unearned incomes, the confiscation of war profits and the prohibition of land speculation. But the commitment to such an agenda wore increasingly thin, albeit that Hitler was keenly aware of the need to counter the growth of support among workers for socialism, which was portrayed as a 'Jewish Marxist conspiracy'.

By the later 1920s the relative failure of the Nazi party to secure mass support among the working classes led it to reorientate its appeal to capitalists, small businessmen, farmers and white-collar workers. While there were those in the Nazi party, like the Strasser brothers, Gregor and Otto, and the leader of the SA (the Brownshirts), Ernst Rohm, who sought to promote more tangible material benefits for the working class, they were progressively marginalised. The persistence of Gregor Strasser and of Rohm in seeking to sustain and develop gains for workers led, ultimately, to their murders in 1934. Their 'purge', during the 'night of the long knives', on the pretext that they were engaged in a plot against Hitler, also effectively purged the Nazi party of an already threadbare socialist programme.

Consistent with his unwavering belief in racial hierarchy, egalitarianism was anathema to Hitler, whether within or among peoples. What mattered was the moulding of a common unity among Germans as nationalists, thereby transcending the alternative appeals of class or individual interest. Like Mussolini, Hitler subscribed to an organic conception of society. Individuals mattered only in so far as they served the whole: 'If we consider the question, what in reality are the state-forming or even state-preserving forces, we can sum them up under one single head: the ability and will of the individual to sacrifice himself for the totality' (1969: 140).

A mode of economic organisation, fascist corporatism, also supplied the means to mobilise and control the working population: it served the purpose of integrating the working class into a national organic whole. The encouragement of improved working conditions through the 'Beauty of Labour' scheme; the organisation of leisure activities by the 'Strength through Joy' movement; and the reduction in high levels of unemployment achieved by a massive programme of rearmament – all were deployed to win over industrial workers.

Yet, while expressing socialist pretensions, corporatism in inspiration and practice was nothing more than state capitalism. Individuals were perceived as expendable means to be used in pursuit of a regenerated national community. The grotesque simplicity of the National Socialist dimension of fascism was epitomised by the British fascist, Oswald Mosley: 'If you love our country you are national and if you love our people you are socialist.'

Interim summary

The disparate elements of a nascent fascist world view were apparent in Europe by the later nineteenth century. The emphasis which each of them received – statism, racialism, elitism, imperialism and National Socialism – varied in accordance with the diverse traditions of those nations which produced fascist regimes, movements or parties. In Italy, Mussolini stressed statism. It was not until 1938, for instance, that racialism in the form of antisemitic laws were introduced. Five years earlier he had praised Italian Jews for their military service in the First World War and their exemplary roles in society and the economy (Fermi, 1961: 290–1). The abrupt about-turn was a cynical move by Mussolini: from being celebrated as 'good citizens', Jews of Italian birth became pawns unscrupulously used as a means of consolidating the axis with Nazi Germany. There was, though, far less rigour in implementing antisemitism in Italy and much opposition to the implementation of the 'final solution' so that, according to Eatwèll (1995: 68), four out of five Italian Jews survived the regime and the war, most in hiding.

Though Mussolini was to adopt biological racialism, proclaiming Italians to be 'Aryans of Mediterranean type', his key preoccupation was the renewal of the Italian state. The introduction of corporatism provided the means of instilling the will and of securing the resources to embark on the imperial regeneration of the fascist state, through for instance the invasion of Abyssinia in 1935–6. Portraying Italy as a living organism supplied the rationale for imperialism: just as healthy, individual organisms develop and grow, so too must the state. War and conquest were symptoms of its health: 'For Fascism the tendency to Empire . . . is a manifestation of its [the state's] vitality: its opposite, staying at home, is a sign of decadence . . . War alone puts the stamp of nobility upon the peoples' (Lyttelton, 1973: 53, 56). The renewal of empire was testimony to the fitness of the state.

In Nazi Germany the goal was racial supremacy. Hitler was a racial nationalist, obsessed by a fanatical belief in the redemptive power of blood. For him history was the record of the rise and fall of biologically determined racial groups. Humankind, he asserted, fell into three categories: creators of culture; bearers of culture; and destroyers of culture. The Aryans comprised the first group, Chinese and Japanese the second and Jews the last. To re-establish the primacy of the Aryans their blood had to be repurified – and this required the elimination of 'the Jewish threat'.

Hitler explained the German collapse at the end of the First World War as the outcome of the progressive degeneration of its people's blood, which had eroded national resolve and purpose. The responsibility for this degeneracy lay with the Jews. By promoting doctrines – liberalism and Marxism – that celebrated individualism, egalitarianism or internationalism, they had engineered the cultural acceptability of miscegenation and subverted the national solidarity of Germans. The resulting dilution of the racially pure blood stock not only left Germany enfeebled, but by proscribing mixed marriages 'International

Jewry' had kept its own blood pure and was therefore poised to achieve world domination.

In Nazi Germany, racial policy was twofold. First, Aryan blood had to be repurified and, secondly, those who threatened its purity had to be eradicated: 'There is no making pacts with Jews: there can only be the hard "either–or".' The introduction of racial laws in 1933 and their acceleration thereafter was an early indication of the path destined to lead to mass genocide. The laws were accompanied by an unrelenting propaganda campaign that depicted Jews as the enemy within. In *Mein Kampf* Hitler had portrayed Jews in terms which resonated with the conception of Germany as a 'national organism': 'virus', 'bacillus', 'parasite', 'vampire' were his preferred metaphors. Such imagery was recycled, whether in official proclamations or popular literature, presenting Jews as carriers of disease. Without the removal of 'the Jewish menace . . . all attempts at German reawakening and resurrection are . . . absolutely senseless and impossible'.

The representation of Jews as the embodiment of evil was one side of the racial policy equation: the other was an array of measures designed to promote 'racial hygiene'. Thus, while Jews and other 'lesser races' were to be exterminated and the 'hereditarily ill' (the mentally and physically handicapped) and the 'asocial' (certain criminal offenders and homosexuals) either compulsorily sterilised or killed,[1] 'positive' measures were introduced to improve and purify German blood.

Selective breeding programmes were introduced favouring those who personified 'Aryanism', the SS (*Schützstaffel* or guard squadron). Its members were ordered to 'produce children of good blood' through a union with racially pure women, whether within or outside marriage. Children from countries occupied by Germany who were deemed to exhibit Aryan characteristics were abducted and returned to 'the Fatherland' where they were to be 'Germanised' within 'racially acceptable families'. Such were the means that were adopted to create 'a community of physically and psychically homogeneous creatures'. This task was, moreover, invested with divine mission by Hitler: 'I believe that I am acting in the sense of the Almighty Creator: by warding off the Jews, I am fighting for the Lord's work.'

Such policies were also said to be consistent with what Hitler styled 'the aristocratic principle of Nature' – that the fittest, the strongest, the most racially pure would always prevail. This 'principle' was also employed to justify dictatorship: 'leadership and the highest influence . . . fall to the best minds [and] build not upon the idea of the majority, but upon the idea of the personality.' On this basis Hitler erected the *Führerprinzip*: 'absolute responsibility unconditionally combined with absolute authority . . . the one man alone may possess the authority and right to command.' Democracy was rejected as a 'sin' against the 'aristocratic principle – the authority of the individual'.

Whereas in fascist Italy imperialism was the test of the vitality of the state, in Nazi Germany it was a measure of racial superiority. The conquest and occupation of neighbouring countries designed to procure resources and living space (*Lebensraum*) symbolised the restoration of the 'natural order'. 'Nature,' declared Hitler, 'knows no political boundaries . . . soil exists for the people which have the force to take it.' In this respect, the two dictators subscribed to opposed theories of the state. Mussolini, as we have seen, regarded the state as an end in itself. By contrast, in *Mein Kampf* Hitler portrayed it as a means to the end of racial supremacy: 'the state must regard as its highest task the preservation and intensification of the race . . . We, as Aryans, can conceive of the state only as the living organism of a nationality . . . We must distinguish between the state as a vessel and the race as its content.'

The heavy and fatal emphasis on biological racialism within Nazism does perhaps set it apart from Italian fascism. But rather than trying to draw a contestable distinction between them on the basis of their ideological priorities, the preferred approach here is to represent the doctrine in fluid rather than solid terms. The argument of this chapter is that while its national varieties may have stressed differing elements, each fascist movement drew upon a common set of ideas that had long been current in European political thought. One such idea exemplifying the inegalitarian core of fascism was its treatment and representation of women.

Fascism and women

In Chapter 8 we note the pervasive dualism that has underpinned Western political thought. This assigned women to a different realm from that inhabited by men and elevated the activities and attributes of men. The distinction between the private, female 'world' and the public, male sphere was not just implicit in fascism: it was openly promoted. On this issue there was nothing to distinguish the beliefs of Hitler from those of Mussolini.

Both exemplified patriarchal attitudes, asserting that the natural sphere for women was that of home and family. Hitler distinguished between the 'greater world', monopolised by men, in which affairs of state, politics and war were conducted and the 'smaller world' which was the domain of women: 'her world is her husband, her family, her children and her home.' The enfranchisement of women, which had occurred in Weimar Germany, was an 'invention of Jewish intellectuals' that distracted women from 'the duties nature imposes'. Such 'duties' were summarised by Hitler's propaganda chief, Joseph Goebbels (1897–1945): 'The mission of woman is to be beautiful and to bring children into the world . . . the female prettifies herself for her mate and hatches the eggs for him' (Noakes and Pridham, 1974: 363).

The natural superiority of men was axiomatic within fascist ideology. This was conveyed in the popular Nazi slogan *Kinder, Kirche, Küche*. Respectively, this confined women to bearing children, attending church and working in the kitchen. The clear boundary drawn between the public and private worlds was founded upon the assertion of intrinsic, if complementary, differences between the sexes: 'Man and Woman represent two quite different characteristics: in Man understanding is dominant [which] is more stable than emotion which is the mark of Woman' (Baynes, 1969: 531).

The recurring view peddled by Hitler was of the naturally dependent and submissive woman, prone to passion and outbursts of jealousy. Preserving the public realm for men was represented as a chivalrous act preventing women from making an exhibition of themselves:

> I detest women who dabble in politics . . . There she is, ready to pull her hair out, with all her claws showing. In short, gallantry forbids one to give women an opportunity of putting themselves in situations that do not suit them. Everything that entails combat is exclusively men's business. There are so many other fields in which one must rely upon women. Organising a house, for instance.
>
> (1973: 251–2)

In Italy, Mussolini retailed similar attitudes, yet his views on women followed a more serpentine course than those of Hitler. In 1919 the fascist programme advocated female suffrage and three years later endorsed equal rights for women. Mussolini's own support for female enfranchisement seems, though, to have been less than principled. His ambition to institute corporatism led him to favour occupational suffrage rather than the enfranchisement of individuals electing representatives to a democratic assembly. Moreover, from the early 1920s the party's support for female suffrage waned and, increasingly, patriarchal policies prevailed.

As in Nazi Germany legislation was introduced barring women from certain occupations and exhorting them to produce children. Echoing Hitler's gendered perception of 'greater' and 'smaller worlds', Mussolini asserted that 'war is the most important thing in a man's life as maternity is in a woman's'. From the mid-1920s, under the slogan 'Woman into the home', measures were introduced that encouraged women back into the domestic realm where they would be prized as the pillars of the family. Such measures were utterly consistent with the views of the Vatican. In 1930 Pius XI issued his encyclical *Casti Connubi* which urged women to perform their natural roles as wives and mothers, closeted within the hearth and home (Cannistraro, 1982: 203).

Mussolini's stated opinions on women were disdainful. He regarded them as a 'charming pastime, when a man has time to pass, a means of changing one's trend of thought . . . but they should never be taken seriously, for they themselves are rarely serious'. In *Talks with Mussolini* (1933) Emil Ludwig reports that the dictator expressed his opposition to feminism, articulated his belief that women should obey men and stated that 'while a woman must not be a slave . . . in our state women must not count' (Gregor, 1979a: 287).

In one essential respect, of course, women – or, rather, acceptable women – did count in both Nazi Germany and fascist Italy: as bearers of children. Women's reproductive role was vital to both regimes. In Hitler's design Aryan women were to be the bearers of the master race, while Mussolini needed a growing population to people his planned renewed empire. Incentives were introduced in both countries to increase the birth rate (e.g. Frevert, 1990: 205; Burleigh and Wipperman, 1991: 249ff.; Stephenson, 1996: 173ff.; Durham, 1998), reducing acceptable women to little more than nationalist wombs in the service of the state. In Germany the laws governing marriage and fitness to reproduce were minutely governed by racialism; in Italy the preoccupation was with the sheer necessity of population growth, itself a signal of the vitality of the state. In 1933 Paula Siber, the acting head of the Nazi party's Association of German Women, set out the role for the 'new German woman':

> To be a woman means to be a mother . . . a woman belongs at the side of man, not just as a person who brings children into the world, not just as an adornment to delight the eye, not just as a cook and cleaner. Instead woman has the holy duty to be a life-companion, which means being a comrade who pursues her vocation as a woman with clarity of vision and spiritual warmth. To be a woman in the deepest and most beautiful sense of the word is the best preparation for being a mother . . . the highest calling of the National Socialist woman is not just to bear children, but . . . to raise children for her people.
>
> (Griffin, 1995: 138–9)

The message, although embellished in somewhat mystical terms, was clear. Acceptable women were valued only in so far as they submitted to a subordinate role within their lesser domain: having children, socialising them into the brave new fascist world, and meekly supporting their menfolk. The sexing of both Italy and Germany as the 'Fatherland' symbolised the patriarchal thinking that lay at the heart of the doctrine.

British fascism in the inter-war years

We have already noted the contribution of two English thinkers – Pearson and Chamberlain – to the evolution of fascist ideas, but the development of the doctrine in Britain is most closely associated with Oswald Mosley.

In 1932 Mosley founded the British Union of Fascists (BUF), having previously been a Conservative, an Independent Conservative, an Independent and a Labour MP. His transition from the Labour party – from which he was expelled in 1931 – to fascism was by way of the 'New Party', a short-lived parliamentary-based all-party group that was launched primarily to advance protectionist economic policies.

Mosley's political career had convinced him of the need for the pursuit of autarky via corporatism, which, he believed, had ushered in a new era. On his return from a visit to Italy in 1932 he declared: 'Italy has produced not only a new system of government but a new type of man who differs from politicians of the old world just as men from another planet' (Walker, 1977: 287). Like Hitler and Mussolini, he presented fascism as a youthful, vigorous movement propounding novel ideas for a New Age. Yet, like those he sought to emulate, there was little that was original in his thought. Mosley merely packaged fascist themes into a form he believed acceptable to 'the British character'.

Racialism

Initially Mosley denied that the BUF subscribed to racialist ideas or harboured antisemitic beliefs, yet both were to become increasingly prominent throughout the 1930s. Indeed, antisemitic sentiments were evident from the first, albeit they were expressed in coded terms. Thus: 'we have within the nation a power, largely controlled by alien elements, which arrogates to itself a power above the State' (Nugent, 1977: 149). In 1933, though claiming that antisemitism had been Hitler's 'greatest mistake', he banned Jews from joining the BUF. In the same year the Irishman William Joyce, one of Mosley's chief aides – later to achieve notoriety as 'Lord Haw Haw' – wrote in the movement's journal, *Blackshirt*: 'the low type of foreign Jew together with other aliens who are debasing the life of the nation will be run out of the country in double-quick time under fascism.'

From the mid-1930s the strain of antisemitism became more pronounced. The Jews were presented as a subversive 'state within the state' seeking to engineer war with Germany. A signal of the growing virulence of these beliefs was the change in 1936 of the name of his movement to the British Union of Fascists and National Socialists. Antisemitism, though couched in oblique terms ('the money power' or 'international finance'), bulked ever larger in Mosley's speeches. Allegations that Jews were manipulating the established political parties became routine. Only his movement could root out 'alien influences', since it alone was free of their 'money power'.

His rhetoric recalls that of Hitler. In musing on his preferred 'final solution' to 'the Jewish problem' Mosley proposed the creation of an artificial homeland 'in one of the many waste places of the world' where Jews could languish 'and cease to be the parasite of humanity'. Such a ghettoising option had been contemplated by Mussolini but, as we noted above, the introduction of racial laws in Italy did lead to the deaths of Italian Jews in Europe's concentration camps. It is not implausible to suggest that Mosley, who shifted his allegiance to Hitler in 1936, would have followed the same genocidal route had a fascist regime secured power in Britain.

Corporatism

Mosley's infatuation with the corporate state in his earlier writings deepened following his Italian excursions. His advocacy of this model of economic and political organisation dovetailed the themes of statism and National Socialism. In 1932 he argued that Britain's economic crisis was the result of the stubborn attachment of the 'old gangs' of politicians to *laissez-faire* at home and free trade abroad: an attachment which reflected the influence and power of 'international finance'. The remedy was the modernisation or 'rationalisation' of the economy through the imposition of the corporate state.

In the place of minimal government and a free-market economy he prescribed planning and protectionism. In advancing such measures his remarks were virtually indistinguishable from those of Mussolini. Urging the need to introduce corporatism so as to reconcile 'individual initiative with the wider interests of the nation' he verged on plagiarism: 'it means a nation organised as the human body, with each organ performing its individual function but working in harmony with the whole' (n.d.: 25). The national organism was paramount, its interests superseding the individualism celebrated by liberals and the class interests prized by socialists. Here lay the attempt to mesh nationalism and socialism. Yet, of course, his scheme for a 'third way' between competing doctrines extinguished autonomy and freedom and quashed democratic politics. 'There will,' he stated ominously, 'be no room in Britain for those who do not accept the principle "All for the State and the State for All".'

Internally, Britain would be run on authoritarian lines, with pride of place given to the virtues of obedience, order and discipline: all would be bent to 'the national purpose'. To ensure self-sufficiency he proposed 'insulation'. This entailed a ban on the importation of all goods that could be produced in Britain and a closed imperial economy wherein the colonies would supply resources and markets for British products. Here there are echoes of social imperialism's autarkic design, amplified by a racially inspired argument. The colonies were to be denied independence because they would be susceptible to 'alien influences' and also because Mosley considered the colonial 'races' to be unfitted for the task of economic development.

Elitism and leadership

Mosley's apocalyptic vision of impending economic collapse, allied to his conviction that the 'old gangs' had succumbed to the machinations of 'the money power', led him to justify the need for political authoritarianism. In the first edition of *The Greater Britain* (1934) he appeared to favour collective leadership, since it was better suited to 'the British character'. Two years later his view had changed: 'Leadership in fascism may be an individual or a team, but single leadership in practice proves the most effective instrument. The leader must be prepared to shoulder absolute responsibility for the functions clearly allocated to him.'

Mosley's dictatorial ambitions were clear from his plans to 'reform' Parliament, which he portrayed as an assembly of 'do-nothing committees'. The first fascist Parliament would invest the government with the power to impose the corporate state by order, leaving the executive free from scrutiny. While Parliament would, at this stage, possess the authority to dismiss the government through a vote of censure, thereafter that power would be denied. Political parties would be expunged, an occupational franchise introduced, the House of Lords abolished and replaced by a new second chamber composed of a technocratic elite charged to assist in the implementation of the corporate state.

To supplement the occupational franchise Mosley proposed to introduce a series of plebiscites or referendums. The population would be invited to express their support for the fascist programme through this populist device. Party-based democratic politics would cease:

> In such a system there is no place for parties and politicians. We shall ask the people for a mandate to bring to an end the Party system and the Parties. We invite them to enter a new civilisation. Parties and the party game belong to the old civilisation which has failed.
>
> (Skidelsky, 1975: 315)

Mosley's blighted vision, his readiness to employ force to realise it – 'by one road or another we are determined that Fascism will come to Britain' – and his parroting of themes common to Hitler and Mussolini place him squarely in the fascist retinue. His initial enthusiasm for corporatism, though it never waned, was complemented by his later alignment with Hitler: 'the principles of National Socialism are necessary to the solution of Britain.'

Contemporary British fascism

The election of a member of the neo-Nazi British National Party (BNP) to the local council in Tower Hamlets, London, in 1993 and the level of support accrued by its parliamentary candidates in Oldham's two constituencies in 2001 are a disturbing reminder of the resilience of fascist ideas. The East End of London, including Tower Hamlets, was a favoured stamping ground of Mosley and his erstwhile storm troopers, the Blackshirts. In the 1930s these uniformed thugs engaged in street fights with the area's Jewish population and others, notably communists and socialists, in the attempt to inflame prejudice against 'outsiders' and 'alien influences'. Mosley's efforts to rekindle fascism in the area following his release from wartime internment proved to be singularly unsuccessful. In his wake other groups emerged to promote fascist ideas, seeking to exploit ill founded concern over non-white immigration. One such group was the National Front.

The National Front was created in 1967, though it was to split in 1982, one faction – led initially by John Tyndall – forming the British National Party, itself flanked by a number of other neo-fascist organisations including 'Third Way', 'Blood and Honour' and the paramilitaristic organisations 'Combat 18' and 'White Wolves'. The latter two, among others, claimed responsibility for the three bomb attacks in London (Brixton, Brick Lane and Soho) in the summer of 1999 which left three dead and more than 100 injured. Each seeks to garner support by fomenting anti-immigrant feeling directed against black and brown Britons and, more recently, asylum seekers from Eastern Europe and, in the wake of 11 September 2001, Muslims everywhere. Irrespective of ethnic differences all are lumped together as 'them', an amorphous mass said to represent a fundamental threat to 'the British way of life'.

It is no coincidence that such groups seem to secure support at times of political and economic insecurity. Pressure on economic resources, coupled with atavistic feelings of British – more usually, English – supremacy, are mixed into a potent formula which lays the blame for all social ills on a culturally or physically distinctive community, be it Jewish, Black, Asian or Eastern European. The construction of 'them' as folk devils, responsible for perceived social decline, is a simplistic, populist and opportunistic response to material insecurity and political uncertainty. The experience of high unemployment in Western Europe, the advent of globalisation and the accompanying porosity of national borders has contributed to the revival of electoral support for neo-fascist parties. Their arousal of anti-immigrant feeling has been the stock-in-trade of Tyndall, whose career in fascism leaves little doubt about the lineage of the BNP.

Prior to founding the BNP, Tyndall had been involved with a number of neo-Nazi groups. In 1961 he co-founded the World Union of National Socialists, which acknowledged the 'spiritual leadership of Hitler' and included among its objectives 'the promotion of Aryanism'. A year later he joined the National Socialist Movement, whose journal, asserting 'the correctness of Nazi ideology', exhorted its readers to 'join a movement which could ideologically and . . . physically smash the Red Front and Jewry' (Walker, 1977: 45). *En route* to the NF and the BNP, Tyndall co-founded the Greater Britain Movement that advocated racial laws prohibiting marriage between Britons and 'non-Aryans' and the compulsory sterilisation of the physically and mentally handicapped. Both measures would guarantee the country's future – 'a pure, strong, healthy race'.

Biological racialism has been a consistent feature of Tyndall's beliefs. The recycling of Hitler's ideas concerning 'racial hygiene' and antisemitism have marked all the groups with which he has been associated. Though the antisemitic character of these ideas tends, as with the BUF, to be expressed in euphemistic terms – 'money power', 'loan capitalism' or 'finance capitalism' – it lies at the core of fascist groups in Britain. While they are associated primarily in the public mind with attacks on Black British communities, below the surface the ideologues of fascism also peddle racially inspired attacks on Jews.

As with Hitler, what grips their fevered imagination is the belief that Jews are engaged in a global conspiracy whose aim is to establish a world tyranny. By exercising their 'money power' so as to subvert Britain's economic independence, fostering internationalism through their support for Marxist ideas and the European Union, and 'polluting' the 'race' by promoting both inward migration and miscegenation, 'the British will to resist' will be eroded and Jewish world domination achieved. The remedies, like the analysis, are wearyingly familiar: autarky, corporatism, elite leadership, racialism, the primacy of the nation and the submissiveness of the individual to the state. Naturally, men will monopolise the public realm while women will, in Tyndall's terms, be consigned to 'the feminine role – wife, mother, homemaker': if not barefoot then certainly pregnant in the fascist kitchen.

In 1999 Tyndall was dumped as the BNP's leader and replaced by Nick Griffin, its general election candidate in Oldham West in 2001. Griffin, much younger than his predecessor, appears in the guise of the moderniser, the new man for the new millennium, an alternative to the explicit neo-Nazism of the party's past. Hence the BNP's *public* adoption of a policy of voluntary rather than compulsory repatriation for non-whites, and the formation of its 'ethnic liaison committee' ostensibly created to forge links with members of ethnic minority groups, including those opposed to Islam. But this is just window dressing: to mix metaphors, a case of old fascist wine in a redesigned fascist bottle. In 1998 Griffin was tried and found guilty of distributing material likely to incite racial hatred and routinely refers to the Holocaust as 'the Holohoax' or 'the Hoax of the twentieth century'. A former editor of the BNP's publication *Spearhead*, until sacked by Tyndall, he is reported to have told supporters in 1996 that the party 'needs to be perceived as a strong disciplined organisation with the ability to back up its slogan "Defend Rights for Whites" with well directed boots and fists'. He continued, in a phrase worthy of Hitler or Mussolini: 'When the crunch comes, power is the product of force and will, not of rational debate.'[2]

Conclusion

Proponents of fascism have proved adept at rummaging around in intellectual history in order to fashion their doctrine. In this undertaking they have been able to draw upon themes and ideas whose longevity is, I hope, evident. Such ideas began to become palpable in the later eighteenth century as a reaction against the Enlightenment. Fascism's explicit intolerance of difference and its corresponding preference for monolithic unity, whether defined in national or racial terms, represented a counter-revolution against Enlightenment values. Latterly its precursors drew upon the same or related sources when faced by the ideological challenge from socialism in the later nineteenth century.

The antithetical character of the doctrine is clear from the following remarks of, respectively, Mussolini and Goebbels. Referring to the values of liberty, equality and fraternity bestowed by the French revolution, their target was clear: 'We stand,' stated the Italian dictator, 'for a new principle in the world . . . sheer categorical definitive antithesis to the world which still abides by the fundamental principles laid down in 1789.' In a 1933 radio broadcast Goebbels was more succinct: 'The year 1789 is hereby eradicated from history.' The sheer arrogance and hubris of such remarks are breathtaking. With one rhetorical gesture, the inspiration for – and the legacy of – the French revolution were to be swept from the stage of history.

While fascists asserted the novelty of their ideas, the mainsprings of their beliefs were pre-modern. Lamenting a lost past, whether it was the Roman empire, the agrarian society of medieval Germany, or some other imagined community, fascism proposes a 'barbarous utopia' from which all diversity, individualism and pluralism would be extinguished. Now, as in the past, fascists seek to exploit the emotive simplicities of a national or a racial myth and to impose a numbing conformity upon all. Mussolini set this tone and approach in 1922:

> We have created our myth. The myth is a faith, a passion. It is not necessary for it to be a reality. It is a reality in the sense that it is a stimulus, is hope, is faith, is courage. Our myth is the nation, our myth is the greatness of the nation! And to this myth, this greatness, which we want to translate into a total reality, we subordinate everything else.
>
> (Griffin, 1995: 44)

However its exponents fashion the doctrine, whether in the past or in the contemporary world, at root fascism was, and is, profoundly non-rational. Despite, or indeed because of, this feature of its thought, it should not be lightly dismissed. The arousal of emotion, fostered by the massed marches of troops, flag-bearing youth or torch-bearing girls, was epitomised by the Nuremberg rallies. A mass, moving in unison, from which all individuality was expunged, save that of the leader, aloft on a monstrous dais, orchestrating all in pursuit of national redemption. At one level, such events appear as little more than street theatre: but it was drama with a sinister purpose. Deaden the intellect, crush the critical spirit, demand blind obedience and eliminate any moral uncertainty. As the Italian author and Auschwitz survivor Primo Levi cautioned: 'the memory of what happened in the heart of Europe, not very long ago, can serve as a warning' (1987: 397).

Notes

1   On the 'euthanasia' programme see Noakes and Pridham (1988: 997–1048).
2   See the web site of Searchlight, the anti-fascist monitoring organisation: www.searchlightmagazine.com.

Further reading

Both during the period when the previous edition was being written, and since, a clutch of texts have appeared that deal with fascist ideology. Of these, three in particular I found to be of real use. Roger Eatwell and Anthony Wright (eds), *Contemporary Political Ideologies* (1993), Andrew Vincent, *Modern Political Ideologies* (2nd edn, 1995) and Roger Eatwell, *Fascism: A History* (1995). Roger Griffin's reader, *Fascism* (1995) provides a compelling collection of documents written by fascist ideologues, critics and analysts, including more contemporary writings. Neil Gregor (ed.), *Nazism* (2001), is the equally impressive companion reader.

As someone who is not primarily a political theorist I had to plot my way through a large number of books in order to gain a purchase on the evolution of fascist ideas. Revisiting the chapter for the new edition confirmed my debt to the following authors, whose works seem to me to stand the test of time. Zeev Sternhell, 'Fascist ideology' in Walter Laqueur (ed.), *Fascism: A Reader's Guide* (1979); Karl Dietrich Bracher, *The German Dictatorship* (1973); Arno Mayer, *The Persistence of the Old Regime* (1981); George Mosse, *Crisis of German Ideology* (1964); and Eugen Weber, *Varieties of Fascism* (1964). Also recommended are Zeev Sternhell's *The Birth of Fascist Ideology* (1995) and George Mosse's *Towards the Final Solution* (1978).

More recently I have discovered a canon of work on Nazi Germany by Michael Burleigh that marries scholarship and accessibility in an enviable way. His magisterial *The Third Reich* (2001) provides a gripping account of the implementation of fascist ideas in the Nazi state. His co-authored work, with Wolfgang Wippermann, *The Racial State* (1991), is good on the prehistory of fascism and contains much primary material written by the executors of the Nazi project. Burleigh has also edited *Confronting the Nazi Past* (1996). It was stimulated by the 'historians' dispute' (*Historikerstreit*) that raged in Germany during the 1980s and which sought, as Burleigh puts it in his introduction, 'to relativize Nazi barbarities'. The text brings together writers on a variety of topics, including the precursors of racism, women, 'euthanasia' and the 'final solution'. Although the emphasis is on Nazi practice, the contributors all contextualise their material – including primary sources – in the appropriate intellectual framework. Burleigh has also written on the genocide in Nazi Germany and 'euthanasia'. See, respectively, *Ethics and Extermination* (1997) and *Death and Deliverance* (1994). Fellow historian Ian Kershaw's *The Nazi Dictatorship* (2000) is also recommended.

On Italy see Adrian Lyttelton's 'Italian Fascism' in Laqueur (ed.), *Fascism* (1979), David Roberts's *The Syndicalist Tradition and Italian Fascism* (1979) and A. James Gregor's *Italian Fascism and Developmental Dictatorship* (1979a). Gregor also authored *Young Mussolini and the Intellectual Origins of Fascism* (1979b). *The Historical Dictionary of Fascist Italy* (1982), edited by Philip Cannistraro, remains a useful source of reference on both the major figures and institutions of Mussolini's regime. Ray Moseley's *Mussolini's Shadow* (2000) is a biography of Mussolini's Foreign Minister – and son-in-law – Ciano, based upon his diaries.

Paul Hayes's *Fascism* (1973) is especially informative on the role of British thinkers in the doctrine's development and supplies brief notes on key figures. Roger Griffin's *The Nature of Fascism* (1993) is a recommended study, as is his edited reader mentioned above. On the varieties of Social Darwinism see Greta Jones, *Social Darwinism and English Thought* (1980).

There are a host of texts that convey the nature and diversity of fascism. These include three books edited by Stuart Woolf, *European Fascism* (1968a), *The Nature of Fascism* (1968b) and *Fascism in Europe* (1981); George Mosse (ed.), *International Fascism* (1979), and Ernst Nolte, *Three Faces of Fascism* (1969).

On British fascism see Robert Skidelsky's biography, *Oswald Mosley* (1975); Neil Nugent and Roger King (eds), *The British Right* (1977) and Robert Benewick's *The Fascist Movement in Britain* (1972). Two studies of the National Front are Martin Walker's *The National Front* (1977), and Stan Taylor's *The National Front in British Politics* (1982). See also Kenneth Lunn and Richard Thurlow (eds), *British Fascism* (1980). The London-based organisation Searchlight maintains a watching brief on British and other neo-fascist groups and is a helpful source of information. Its web site – www. searchlightmagazine.com – includes articles from its journal and has extensive links to other monitoring groups in Europe and elsewhere. It is especially good on tracking the activities of the BNP and more paramilitary-style neo-Nazi groups.

Hitler's *Mein Kampf* (1969), with an introduction by D. C. Watt, is a key primary source, although it is a debilitating read. See also W. Maser's *Mein Kampf: An Analysis* (1970). The one-volume *Documents on Nazism, 1919–1945* (1974), edited by Jeremy Noakes and Geoffrey Pridham, is a compelling selection with commentaries by the editors. The same authors have also edited an indispensable four-volume series on Nazism published under the aegis of Exeter University Press's Exeter Studies in History. *Hitler's Table Talk, 1941–1944* (1973), with an introduction by Hugh Trevor-Roper, provides numerous glimpses into the dictator's obsessions. Norman Baynes has translated and edited *The Speeches of Adolf Hitler, April 1922–August 1939* (1969). See also Max Domarus, *Hitler: Speeches and Proclamations, 1932–1945* (1990) for extended coverage. Mussolini's own works are more expansive. Shorter works include *Fascism: Doctrine and Institutions* (1935) and *The Political and Social Doctrine of Fascism* (1933). His autobiography is imaginatively entitled *My Autobiography* (1939). *My Rise and Fall* (1988) is worth inspecting. Key biographies of the dictators are Alan Bullock's *Hitler: A Study in Tyranny* (1973), Joachim Fest's *Hitler* (2002) and Denis Mack Smith's *Mussolini* (1981). Mosley's ideas can be found in *The Greater Britain* (1934) and *Fascism: 100 Questions Asked and Answered* (1936). His autobiography is *My Life* (1968).

The final works I would like to cite are by Primo Levi. His canon includes works dedicated to an attempt to understand the mentality of those who ran the death camps of Europe. He is an apt choice: an Italian Jew, a chemist by profession, and a partisan, he was captured and sent to Auschwitz, where he was incarcerated for a year and which, in one sense, he managed to survive. His *If this is a Man* (1987) and *The Truce* (1995) are accounts of, respectively, his period in the camp and liberation, made all the more moving by the controlled passion of their tone. Other works, *The Drowned and the Saved* (1988) and *Moments of Reprieve* (1989), recount the resilience of the inmates of Auschwitz and demonstrate that even in the most dire of circumstances common humanity could not be wholly eclipsed. In 1987 Levi took his own life. His works are a poignant and accessible reminder of the horrors that fascism visited upon so many.

References

Baynes, Norman, ed. (1969) *The Speeches of Adolf Hitler, April 1922–August 1939*, New York: Fertig.

Benewick, Robert (1972) *The Fascist Movement in Britain*, London: Allen Lane.

Bernhardi, Friedrich von (1914) *Germany and the Next War*, London: Arnold.

Bracher, Karl Dietrich (1973) *The German Dictatorship*, Harmondsworth: Penguin.

Bullock, Alan (1973) *Hitler: A Study in Tyranny*, London: Hamlyn.

Burleigh, Michael (1994) *Death and Deliverance: 'Euthanasia' in Germany, 1900–1945*, Cambridge: Cambridge University Press.

Burleigh, Michael, ed. (1996) *Confronting the Nazi Past: New Debates on Modern German History*, London: Collins & Brown.

Burleigh, Michael (1997) *Ethics and Extermination: Reflections on Nazi Genocide*, Cambridge: Cambridge University Press.

Burleigh, Michael (2001) *The Third Reich: A New History*, London: Pan Books.

Burleigh, Michael and Wipperman, Wolfgang (1991) *The Racial State: Germany, 1933–1945*, Cambridge: Cambridge University Press.

Cannistraro, Philip, ed. (1982) *Historical Dictionary of Fascist Italy*, London: Greenwood Press.

Cecil, Robert (1972) *The Myth of the Master Race*, London: Batsford.

Domarus, Max (1990) *Hitler: Speeches and Proclamations, 1932–1945: The Chronicle of a Dictatorship*, London: Tauris.

Durham, Martin (1998) *Women and Fascism*, London: Routledge.

Eatwell, Roger (1995) *Fascism: A History*, London: Chatto & Windus.

Eatwell, Roger and Wright, Anthony, eds (1993) *Contemporary Political Ideologies*, London: Pinter.

Evans, Richard (2001) *Lying about Hitler: History, Holocaust and the David Irving Trial*, New York: Basic Books.

Fermi, Laura (1961) *Mussolini*, Chicago: University of Chicago Press.

Fest, Joachim (2002) *Hitler*, London: Penguin.

Frevert, Ute (1990) *Women in German History: From Bourgeois Emancipation to Sexual Liberation*, Oxford: Berg.

Gregor, A. James (1979a) *Italian Fascism and Developmental Dictatorship*, Princeton NJ: Princeton University Press.

Gregor, A. James (1979b) *Young Mussolini and the Intellectual Origins of Fascism*, Berkeley CA: University of California Press.

Gregor, Neil, ed. (2001) *Nazism*, Oxford: Oxford University Press.

Griffin, Roger (1993) *The Nature of Fascism*, London: Routledge.

Griffin, Roger, ed. (1995) *Fascism*, Oxford: Oxford University Press.

Hayes, Paul (1973) *Fascism*, London: Allen & Unwin.

Hitler, Adolf (1969) *Mein Kampf*, trans. Ralph Mannheim, London: Hutchinson.

Hitler, Adolf (1973) *Hitler's Table Talk, 1941–1944: His Private Conversations*, intr. Hugh Trevor-Roper, trans. Norman Cameron and R. H. Stevens, London: Weidenfeld & Nicolson; repr. London: Enigma Books, 2000.

Jones, Greta (1980) *Social Darwinism and English Thought: The Interaction between Biological and Social Theory*, Brighton: Harvester.

Kershaw, Ian (2000) *The Nazi Dictatorship: Problems and Perspectives of Interpretation*, London: Arnold.

Levi, Primo (1987) *If this is a Man*, London: Sphere Books.

Levi, Primo (1988) *The Drowned and the Saved*, London: Joseph.

Levi, Primo (1989) *Moments of Reprieve*, London: Abacus.

Levi, Primo (1995) *The Truce*, London: Abacus.

Lunn, Kenneth and Thurlow, Richard, eds (1980) *British Fascism*, London: Croom Helm.

Lyttelton, Adrian, ed. (1973) *Roots of the Right: Italian Fascism from Pareto to Gentile*, London: Cape.

Lyttelton, Adrian (1979) 'Italian Fascism' in Walter Laqueur (ed.) *Fascism: A Reader's Guide*, Harmondsworth: Penguin.

Maser, W. (1970) *Mein Kampf: An Analysis*, London: Faber.

Mayer, Arno (1981) *The Persistence of the Old Regime*, London: Croom Helm.

Moseley, Ray (2000) *Mussolini's Shadow: The Double Life of Count Galeazzo Ciano*, New Haven CT: Yale University Press.

Mosley, Oswald (1934) *The Greater Britain*, London: BUF

Mosley, Oswald (1936) *Fascism: 100 Questions Asked and Answered*, London: BUF.

Mosley, Oswald (1968) *My Life*, London: Nelson.

Mosley, Oswald (n.d.) *Blackshirt Policy*, London: BUF.

Mosse, George (1964) *Crisis of German Ideology*, New York: Grosset & Dunlap.

Mosse, George (1971) *Germans and Jews*, London: Orbach & Chambers.

Mosse, George (1978) *Towards the Final Solution: A History of European Racism*, London: Dent.

Mosee, George, ed. (1979) *International Fascism: New Thoughts and Approaches*, London: Sage.

Mussolini, Benito (1933) *The Political and Social Doctrine of Fascism*, London: Leonard and Virginia Woolf.

Mussolini, Benito (1935) *Fascism: Doctrine and Institutions*, Rome: Ardita

Mussolini, Benito (1939) *My Autobiography*, London: Hutchinson.

Mussolini, Benito (1988) *My Rise and Fall*, ed. Max Ascoli, Cambridge MA: Da Capo Press.

Noakes, Jeremy and Pridham, Geoffrey, eds (1974) *Documents on Nazism, 1919–1945*, London: Cape.

Noakes, Jeremy and Pridham, Geoffrey, eds (1988) *Nazism, 1919–1945*, III *Foreign Policy, War and Racial Extermination*, Exeter: University of Exeter Press.

Nolte, Ernst (1969) *Three Faces of Fascism*, New York: Mentor.

Nugent, Neil (1977) 'The ideas of the BUF' in Neil Nugent and Roger King (eds) *The British Right*, Farnborough: Saxon House.

Nugent, Neil and King,Roger, eds (1977) *The British Right*, Farnborough: Saxon House.

Pearson, Karl (1905) *National Life from the Standpoint of Science*, London: Black.

Roberts, David (1979) *The Syndicalist Tradition and Italian Fascism*, Manchester: Manchester University Press.

Skidelsky, Robert (1975) *Oswald Mosley*, London: Macmillan.

Smith, Denis Mack (1981) *Mussolini*, London: Weidenfeld & Nicolson.

Stephenson, Jill (1996) 'Women, motherhood and the family in the Third Reich' in Michael Burleigh (ed.) *Confronting the Nazi Past: New Debates on Modern German History*, London: Collins.

Sternhell, Zeev (1979) 'Fascist ideology' in Walter Laqueur (ed.) *Fascism: A Reader's Guide*, Harmondsworth: Penguin.

Sternhell, Zeev (1995) *The Birth of Fascist Ideology*, Princeton NJ: Princeton University Press.

Taylor, Stan (1982) *The National Front in British Politics*, London: Macmillan.

Vincent, Andrew (1995) *Modern Political Ideologies*, 2nd edn, Oxford: Blackwell.

Walker, Martin (1977) *The National Front*, London: Fontana.

Weber, Eugen (1964) *Varieties of Fascism*, New York: Van Nostrand Reinhold.

Woolf, Stuart, ed. (1968a) *European Fascism*, London: Weidenfeld & Nicolson.

Woolf, Stuart, ed. (1968b) *The Nature of Fascism*, London: Weidenfeld & Nicolson.

Woolf, Stuart, ed. (1981) *Fascism in Europe*, London: Methuen.

Ecologism

Michael Kenny

Though a relative newcomer to the political scene, the ideology of ecologism has become one of the most important sources of political opposition and ethical challenge in contemporary political life. Yet in public discussion of environmentalism and politics, the very notion that a distinct green ideology exists appears only rarely. It is the contention of this chapter that a green ideological family (encompassing a number of different but related members) came into view in the early 1980s and is now an established source of independent political thought and action in a number of democratic states. The lack of public recognition afforded to ecologism, despite the growing awareness of environmental issues, reflects some of the difficulties that its proponents have encountered in finding political, institutional and cultural space for this perspective.

Greens are themselves uneasy about proclaiming the birth of a new ideological perspective. Principally this is because of a lingering hostility to the very notion of ideology. The term is often regarded in these circles as signifying rigid and unyielding intellectual structures. This is not, however, the only way to think about ideology. Political ideologies do not have to be regarded as inevitably distorting, partisan perspectives which are imposed on a more complex 'real world'. Nor are they invariably doctrinaire belief systems that require slavish adherence to a rigid value set. Some academic analysis of ideology suggests a more fertile set of interpretative possibilities – offering accounts which stress the fluidity, complexity and mutability of the concepts at the heart of an ideological system, and encouraging us to think of ideologies as 'families' containing a variety of related but independent members (Vincent, 1993; Freeden, 1996). Given the recurrence of certain conceptual patterns linking the public statements of green political actors, civil society groups, campaigning networks, academic sympathisers and radical journalists, I argue that the necessary conditions are in place for us to recognise the emergence of a distinctive green ideology. This I term *ecologism*.[1]

The core of ecologism

Are there core commitments that underpin and give shape to this fledgling ideology? In historical terms three conceptual features are recurrent within this ideological lineage, at least as it has developed in Britain and the United States. It is these that define its uniqueness *vis-à-vis* its ideological rivals.

1 *The critique of industrialism*

Perhaps the key distinguishing feature of ecologism is the hostility towards, and sometimes rejection of, aspects of modern industrialised society. The critique of industrialism as a socio-economic paradigm is a recurrent theme within modern ecological discourse. Many of the practices, values and cultures associated with modern societies are loudly criticised by ecologists, both for their adverse environmental consequences and because they reinforce an essentially alienated relationship between humans and non-human nature. Greens have pointed to the ways in which the industrial system, of necessity rather than by accident, consumes natural resources in a relentlessly harmful fashion (for instance, through the destruction of many of the world's rain forests). They point to the tremendous damage caused as it releases a frightening array of pollutants into the earth's atmosphere. Greens also highlight and explain the proliferation of crises associated with the environment in which we live – over the modern farming system, the use of pesticides in agriculture or the emergence of genetically modified food, for example – as inevitable outcomes of the industrialisation and commercialisation of practices like food production, distribution and transportation.

Greens believe that the exploitation of non-renewable resources is endemic within the industrial systems that have come into being over the last two centuries. The model of economic development, which since the Second World War has been reproduced across the globe, involves the relentless extraction of natural resources to feed an increasingly greedy manufacturing system. Underpinning this critique of modern society as an uncontrollable juggernaut (Giddens, 1991) is an appreciation of the damage to the biosphere generated by some of the side effects of industrialised living, a sentiment sometimes expressed through apocalyptic warnings of impending disaster. Greens nowadays typically adopt a longer-term and more scientifically informed perspective upon the realities of environmental degradation than eco-radicals in the 1970s, who stressed the imminence of planetary catastrophe. And they also offer a variety of explanations of the linkages between environmental impact and integral features of modern society, such as consumerism, the use of pesticides and industrial pollutants. It is the establishment of causal chains between these apparently disparate phenomena, and the location of their significance in terms of the fundamental drives of modernity, that give shape and urgency to green political agitation.

The modern industrial economy, greens argue, is sustained by the creation of artificial desires which are satisfied only through wasteful and unnecessary levels of human consumption. On a host of issues affecting our lives – such as the quality of life in cities as well as the wasteful by-products of the commercialisation of food – political ecologists suggest that we look beyond immediate causes to grasp the orgins and explanations of these phenomena. The green critique of industrial society rests upon *a particular set of social explanations* as well as an *urgent rejection of the moral priorities and values* underpinning the modern industrial order.

In their account of the discrete but interconnected processes at the heart of this system, a central place is accorded to the pursuit of economic growth. This, greens observe, has become an apparently uncontentious 'good' that all political actors endorse (Talshir, 1998). Yet it is, they argue, a source of many of our environmental problems because it legitimises the relentless depletion of natural resources to support rising levels of consumption and allots moral priority to activities which generate profits. In all strands of ecologism we find a challenge to the belief that economic growth is an essential goal. For radical greens, a 'steady-state' economy should be ordered around essential human needs and would remain subordinated to the collective interests of the community. This would use 'the lowest possible levels of materials and energy in the production phase and emit the least possible amount of pollution in the consumption phase' (Merchant, 1992: 37). For more mainstream greens, on the other hand, the principle of 'green growth' has provided a powerful way of articulating the need for economic growth to be set against the requirements of the eco-sphere in respect of non-renewable resources and a range of environmental impacts caused, for instance, by emissions into the atmosphere (Pearce *et al.*, 1989; Jacobs, 1996).

Aside from hostility to economic growth, the other idea which ecologism highlights in its accounts of the industrial system is the claim that non-renewable planetary resources are being used up at a perilous rate. Raising awareness of both the scale and the implications of the depletion of an array of natural goods, such as coal, oil and gas, is a central concern for those engaged in green politics. Activists lament these losses as both intrinsically harmful, as some important natural entities like rain forests and wilderness areas are eroded, and liable to produce highly damaging consequences for future generations.

2 *The ecosphere*

The second distinguishing feature of political ecological beliefs is the ethical and philosophical commitment to the vision of humans as an integral element within a vast, complex entity which dwarfs humanity – the ecosphere. Though the philosophical basis of this relationship has been variously presented within green circles, the claim that human capacities and identity are shaped in part by the relationship with the environments in which we emerge and develop is common to all the members of this ideological family. A familiar framework within which this claim is developed is through the notion of holism, the belief that all life develops in relation to external entities – a commitment which many greens borrow from the biological sciences (Goodin, 1992).

This ethical commitment also serves to ground the critique of modernity. The dominant cultural and intellectual traditions in the West have been subjected to a powerful critique by greens who find in its leading cultural and philosophical traditions the justification of the domineering and exploitative attitude towards the natural world (Barry, 1999). Such commitments also enable green thinkers and actors to augment the Marxist notion that modern capitalist economies produce alienated and subordinated social groups with the suggestion that any socio-economic system which reproduces a purely utilitarian relationship to the natural world is premised upon a denial of fundamental aspects of human capacity and nature. Equally, the idea of reordering humanity's relationship with its various environments gives distinctive shape to the conception of the good society which fires many adherents of ecologism.

3   The good society

Ecologism is given power and meaning by its accounts of 'the good society' as well as the questions that the different variants of political ecology raise about what is required for individuals to live a meaningful and virtuous life in modern settings. Though greens are frequently ridiculed by their rivals for their propensity to utopian speculation, it is through the proliferation of ideas about what a good human life requires, and what a sustainable society would be like, that ecologism expresses its distinctive character (Hayward, 1995: 7). The pictures of various social futures that recur within green theorising are inspirational for activists and supporters. These utopian speculations also provide an outlet for the expression of a radical set of ethical priorities that offer one of the few developed alternatives to the values vaunted within the modern social order, especially to the acquisitive model of individualism spawned by consumer capitalism (Eckersley, 1992).

There is no doubt that some parts of the green movement resort to nostalgic yearning for pre-modern living patterns when they propound the virtues of small-scale agrarian communalism as the form in which ecological values will be realised. Green discourse is indeed saturated with romantic, neo-medievalist yearning for a time when humanity supposedly developed a more harmonious relationship with the natural world, and humans enjoyed more authentic and meaningful relations with each other. But the utopianism of ecologism is not solely expressed through the conjuring of mythical Golden Ages. Such imagery and speculation generate powerful contrasts with and questions about the value set propounded by liberal individualism. The exploration of a reasonably extensive moral alternative to the largely unchallenged consumerist model of the self represents a valuable input from the political margins into the public spheres of contemporary society.

Sustainability

In particular, the emphasis upon a sustainable future as *the* socio-economic paradigm towards which contemporary society must be directed has raised some large ethical and political questions. Is an alternative socio-economic paradigm to the current one desirable or indeed plausible? And how might current practices, institutions and cultures be reoriented so that some of the values encompassed in sustainability are realised? Answers to such questions depend greatly on which principles sustainability is intended to project. Quite typically sustainability is used to advocate a mode of social development which is driven by a broader set of criteria than economic growth. The aim here is to establish a development framework which will alleviate the most damaging features of the current socio-economic paradigm. In the idiom favoured by economists, a sustainable development paradigm challenges the conventional idea that environmental damage is an 'externality' for which no agent is responsible.

But the idea of development that is *sustainable* carries a broader social sense, as well as a challenge to conventional free-market economics. The idea of 'sustainable economic development' in green discourse has come to mean that we attend to a range of interests and costs affected by a given socio-economic paradigm and consider the longer-term implications of depleting natural resources. Though greens sometimes talk of 'the sustainable society' as if earthly ecological paradise lies at the end of history, we should regard sustainability as a principle guiding our moral and economic evaluations, an injunction to think carefully about the trade-offs that socio-economic development inevitably involves – such as that between levels of consumption and the need to decrease the use of non-renewables. Sustainability is a normative device which also requires us to consider the interests of an array of (hidden) stakeholders, including non-human natural entities as well as future human generations, affected by our current decisions and priorities (Jacobs, 1996; Baxter, 1999; Hayward, 1998).

From the principles of constrained growth and consideration of non-human nature, and ethical recognition of the putative interests of future generations, political ecologists unfold chains of argument about the social and political implications of these ideas. In the translation of these ethical commitments into social and political programmes, the diversity at the heart of political ecology becomes readily apparent. At the radical ends of the green movement, we encounter declarations that the industrial system will have to be dismantled and replaced by a smaller-scale system of manufacture which is sustained by a number of self-governing, local communities (Sale, 1980; Dobson, 1990, 1995; Eckersley, 1992; Carter, 1999). The advocacy of social and political decentralisation is so frequent in green political discourse that some commentators are tempted to locate it as a core principle of ecologism. Certainly it is an important preference, and has given a distinctive shape to much green thinking about the social forms through which the ecological 'good' can be realised. Yet the virtue of decentralisation is mitigated for others in the green movement by the normative imperatives that flow from the core principles of ecology. The latter may well require that the project of devolving power be sometimes set aside if the particular environmental hazard being faced is of a sufficiently serious character. Equally there are some important practical considerations arising from the recognition of the significant role that national public authorities and agencies play in relation to the management and co-ordination of environmentalist interventions (Kenny and Meadowcroft, 2000).

Ecologism does provide fertile ground for the formulation of redistributive economic programmes, given the significance allotted to the principle of need, as well as the centrality of the public good in green thinking. Notions of sustainability are often combined with the call for a more just distribution of resources, though whether this should be regarded as a necessary feature of environmental justice is a moot point. But greens tend to be economic radicals. In the contemporary context, ecologism has also provided an important source of critical thinking about the dangers of rapid financial and economic globalisation which generates a drive towards cheap, and not necessarily environmentally benign, technologies, and provides opportunities for multi-national corporations to relocate operations to countries where less is demanded in the way of environmental regulation (Paterson, 2000). Yet, importantly, ecologism is in many ways a distinctively international perspective, and very much a product of a globalising age. Ideas are disseminated rapidly within the international community of environmental activism, particularly as greens have been at the forefront in using new information technologies, whilst networking and co-operation on an international scale are a typical feature of green political activism. In many ways ecologism is as much an accompaniment to globalisation as the source of a counter-attack upon it.

Principles beyond the core of ecologism

Are there other principles that we ought to regard as foundational for ecologism? Does green ideology require its adherents to hold to particular views of some of the central terms of Western political discourse such as democracy or liberty? These questions have given rise to some important debates among interpreters and adherents of this ideology (Dobson and Lucardie, 1993; Doherty and De Geus, 1996; Lafferty and Meadowcroft, 1996). Certainly many greens regard these as foundational values and some claim that they are revealed in nature itself. Thus we find in some works of 'eco-philosophy' the suggestion that the principle of (inter-human) equality ought to be founded upon the shared capacity of all living organisms to develop themselves. This common feature of human life should, it is sometimes suggested, undergird a principle of universal mutual respect (Baxter, 1999).

The attempt to ground ethical principles on observations about nature is especially tempting for ecologism's adherents, and reveals the importance of the lineage of romanticism for this ideology. The problem, as different critics have observed, is that such representations of the natural – for instance when the underlying harmony of the natural world is celebrated, or when ecologists personify nature as an autonomous actor obeying universal laws – are tendentious. Critics point out that such thinking obscures the sense in which our (human) understanding and knowledge of nature arise through our deployment of established traditions and categories of thinking. Our encounter with the natural is never as direct and unproblematic as ethical naturalism suggests (Soper, 1995; Hayward, 1998). More generally, offering a justification of, say, equality as grounded in nature is a self-defeating enterprise, leaving proponents vulnerable to counter-arguments which claim to detect conflicting values, like hierarchy, in nature. Green theorists, however, tend to downplay the potency of these mediations between us and nature, sometimes suggesting that we can easily and swiftly remove such 'barriers' and get closer to the natural world. There is another message in green naturalism that has proved powerful. This is the argument that we might 'learn' in a variety of ways by observing the natural world more carefully (Soper, 1995). Such a proposition tallies with the increasing popularity of biological accounts of the human self, and especially our cognitive and emotional make-up.

But naturalism offers a dubious way of incorporating values such as democracy into the core of ecologism. Moreover the instrumental fashion in which notions such as equality and democracy are frequently invoked in green discourse generates difficulties too. The reigning assumption among greens is that these are ultimately conducive to the creation of ecological good. But what if they are not? In his striking interpretation of green ideas, Robert Goodin suggests that democracy, because of its procedural qualities, and ecology, with its focus upon desirable outcomes, cannot be placed on the same moral level for ecologists (1992). Michael Saward suggests that there is no logical reason why democratic principles and practices should trump the values that greens hold dear, leading to the possibility that the green society might actually prove to be one in which some of the central rights and liberties of liberal democracy are set aside (1996).

In terms of logic alone, these critics make some telling points. But the concepts central to ideologies are related to one another not only according to logic. As Freeden shows, part of the function of ideologies is to offer particular interpretations of common political values, such as democracy (1996). This function is frequently performed through the endeavours of ideological 'entrepreneurs' (whether these are thinkers, party elites or campaigning groups) to place such a concept in a relationship with others, thereby generating new meanings for established terms. Logical compatibility is less important here than the particular, contingent configuration of values that an ideology secures, and the persuasiveness or otherwise of the intellectual and political actors who develop these ideas, knock them into shape and seek to communicate them with others. For our purposes, it is revealing that so many greens see a more democratic polity, as well as a more socially just order, as indicative of a sustainable society. It is significant that greens have frequently been at the forefront of efforts to democratise politics, campaigning for such rights as freedom of information and the involvement of local communities in planning decisions that affect them.

Philosophical criticism should not necessarily put us off taking green claims in this area seriously. But it is apparent that we should be wary of the claim that greens are required to be proponents of democracy and justice. Some thinkers have offered developed and influential accounts of political ecological beliefs and experienced little problem in avoiding such commitments (Ophuls, 1977; Hardin, 1968: Bahro, 1994). It is certainly hard to rule out these thinkers from the lexicon of ecology. Indeed, the formulation of ecologism that they offer is highly revealing, suggesting that the core beliefs of this ideology may actually be compatible with different kinds of political arrangement and a variety of socio-economic paradigms. From the point of view of a strictly ecological interpretation of sustainability, both democratic and non-democratic political communities might be permissible. The further point that arises here, and undermines confident claims about the integrity of justice or democracy for greens, is that it is dangerous to presume that a particular version of democracy or social justice programme is required for sustainability. If democracy and justice are reduced to the status of *instrumental values*, rather than independent and intrinsically valuable ones, it may well be that greens come to regard them as dispensable if it is found they do not produce the (green) outcomes required of them.

The leading adherents of ecologism have developed a web of beliefs which seek to make us regard various ethical goals, like sustainability, as imperative. Their core beliefs are one step removed from the conventional world of political action and debate, though they have plenty of implications for both. Rather than denying the significance of values such as democracy or justice for many contemporary greens, and rather than presuming that there are insuperable logical incompatibilities between ecology and these values, we should think about a range of concepts which greens actively seek to connect with ecological imperatives. They have done this in a variety of political and intellectual ways: by allying themselves with campaigns for human rights and civil liberties, for instance, as well as through the work of philosophers who seek to develop connections between the exploitation of subordinated groups and the natural environment.

Another way of conceiving the relationship between green ideology and wider libertarian goals is highly revealing about aspects of ecologism. Some theorists have interpreted the emergence of the green movement as one manifestation of a much larger phenomenon – the appearance of new wave of social movements in the 1970s and 1980s, united by their promulgation of a 'new politics' around issues of gender, racial and sexual identity (Scott, 1990). Ecology, many claim, is a natural part of this milieu. A related theory presents green politics as an important force for and expression of the shift to a post-materialist consciousness – the mind set of generations who grew up in the context of developed welfare systems and without the experience of warfare. According to Ronald Inglehart (1977), we can understand contemporary politics as increasingly oriented around conflicts over values and issues arising from the quality of life, rather than locked into the distributional questions that shaped political conflict and allegiance prior to the 1950s. These arguments can be supplemented with the observations of scholars studying contemporary radical movements who point to the overlapping networks which interweave environ-mental protest with other kinds of radical activity – such as human rights campaigning, peace activism or animal rights militancy (Melucci, 1996). In sociological terms, there are clear overlaps between the politics of the green movement and other left-libertarian currents. Within this alliance one can see the themes of democracy, political activism from below and of a pluralist civil society as central.

Sources of ecologism

Perceptions of the natural world

To understand better the ways in which the web of ecological beliefs has taken shape, at least in Britain and the United States, we need to examine some of the historical sources of current ideas. The intellectual sources of contemporary political ecology are scattered far and wide throughout the histories of different cultural systems. Science has contributed tremendously to ecological under-standing, and, in the late nineteenth and early twentieth centuries, provided a rich store of metaphors for considering social development. The permeation of Darwinist notions of evolution, as well as the impact of the science of ecology itself, are vital backdrops to the development of modern environmentalist awareness (Vincent, 1993). One of the legacies of the growth of ecology and the spread of 'organicist' conceptions of the social world from the nineteenth century was the belief that nature could be deployed as a model for human relations. Indeed, key principles that were seen as reigning supreme in nature, including pluralism, interrelatedness and harmony, were regarded as immanent within or frustrated by the development of modern society.

Such views stood in stark opposition to the hostile and domineering attitude towards (non-human) nature that emerged as a by-product of the growth of mechanistic science from the sixteenth century. Francis Bacon, writing in England at the beginning of the seventeenth century, interpreted nature as dead matter, to be appropriated for human benefit. The thinking at the heart of the emerging scientific disciplines of the nineteenth century reproduced such a view, and worked to legitimate the processes of industrialisation and urbanisation that swept across nineteenth-century Europe and the United States. Some powerful forces reshaped society in these contexts, and the imperative to perpetuate the rapid accumulation of capital dominated economic life. Such trends were propelled by technological invention, the increasingly widespread use of machines in the production process, the commercialisation of agricultural production and the sheer pace of urbanisation – all of which removed large parts of the population from direct contact with the land. Accompanying the massive growth of human productive capacity that these trends enabled was the dissemination of highly rationalist philosophies across a range of intellectual disciplines. In the work of some of the leading exponents of scientific rationalism, nature was viewed as the site of irrational and uncontrollable forces that needed to be 'tamed'. According to the seventeenth-century philosopher René Descartes, humans should 'render themselves the masters and possessors of nature' (cited in Merchant, 1992: 47). Some contemporary writers locate the origins of the domineering attitude humans have tended to adopt towards nature even further back in time, pinpointing the emergence of the Judaeo-Christian religious traditions. Lynn White, in an influential interpretation of the Christian tradition, has read the Old Testament as a justification of human exploitation of nature (1967). Robin Attfield has challenged White's interpretation of the Christian tradition, highlighting the importance of human 'stewardship' over nature as an alternative to outright domination in the Old Testament (1983; Passmore, 1983).

Attending to the different ways in which the natural world has been presented in intellectual and moral discourse should lead us to recognise that nature has played a myriad of roles, in historical terms, within the human imagination. It emerges sometimes as the untamable 'other' which human society needs to master and against which the latter develops its civilising impulse. Alternatively there is the lineage which stretches back, at least, to ancient Greece, which presents nature as a 'mirror' upon which humans ought to gaze, as a source of wonders, of sublimity, which indicates a higher purpose and vast entity against which human endeavours pale. And nature is invoked too, notably in the modern period, as a realm in which an untouched authentic aesthetic prevails, a reminder of a spontaneous and unbroken spirit with which humans were once infused, but with which they have lost touch.

This brief exegesis of the uses to which nature has been put in human thought indicates the ambivalence etched within human culture towards the non-human natural world. Ecologists have drawn deeply upon the last two of these traditions, and are especially open to currents in the nineteenth century which articulated a powerful critique of the worlds of industrial production and commercial exchange. Concern for the external world of natural beauty, as well as the nature of the human self, figured prominently in protests against the practices and values of industrial society in Britain, Germany and the United States. In these cultures the romantic movement of artists, intellectuals and critics, which emerged in the early nineteenth century, lamented the disappearance of traditional, rural communities (Bramwell, 1989). Romantic figures highlighted the disruption of customary relations between humans and the disappearance of a proximity with the natural world for many who now lived in cities and worked in factories. Many of these ideas drew strength both from an idealisation of nature and from expressive nostalgia for the harmony and integrated character of pre-modern life.

The nineteenth-century liberal philosopher John Stuart Mill reflected these sentiments in his discussion of the 'stationary state', a society without economic growth, as a counterpoint to the relentlessly acquisitive and competitive drive at the heart of entrepreneurial capitalism. His critique of this system was argued in terms of its effects upon nature and alienation of humans from the natural world, and anticipated later green thinking:

> Nor is there much satisfaction in contemplating the world with nothing left to the spontaneous activity of nature; with every rood of land brought into cultivation, which is capable of growing food for human beings; every flower waste or natural pasture ploughed up, all quadrupeds or birds which are not domesticated for man's use exterminated as his rivals for food, every hedgerow or superfluous tree rooted out, and scarcely a place left where a wild shrub or flower could grow without being eradicated as a weed in the name of improved agriculture. If the earth must lose that great

portion of its pleasantness which it owes to things that the unlimited increase of wealth and population would extirpate from it, for the mere purpose of enabling it to support a larger, but not a better or a happier population, I sincerely hope, for the sake of posterity, that they will be content to be stationary, long before necessity compels them to it.

(1986: 118)

Ideological precursors of ecologism

This critique was echoed by many conservative opponents of the changes associated with industrial development. The first decades of the twentieth century, for example, witnessed the emergence of a number of 'back to the land' movements in Britain and Germany. Such associations have encouraged critics to wonder whether ecologism remains an essentially conservative, or even reactionary, creed, one most comfortably located on the right of the political spectrum (Bramwell, 1989).

Yet others have argued that the left can also stake a claim to be the 'natural' home of ecological awareness. Examples abound of socialist concern for the impact of capitalist industrialisation upon the urban environment in the late nineteenth century, for instance in the ideas of Robert Owen in nineteenth-century Britain. Additionally, the alienated relationship between humans and the natural environment, engendered by capitalism, was rigorously denounced by Karl Marx. For socialists such as William Morris, writing in late nineteenth-century England, the re-establishment of a system of self-governing communities in which humans lived in harmony with nature, not as parasites upon it, was imperative (Thompson, 1977).

The rise of political ecology

Though ecological themes were given voice by elements to the right and left of the ideological spectrum in the early twentieth century, it is a mistake to presume that either of those traditions can lay claim to be the authentic voice of political ecology. Ecologism emerged from these and other sources as an independent set of beliefs in the early 1980s. It did so, principally, owing to the impact of two associated developments. First, the profile of environmental issues, and the perception of a crisis engendered by the practices of modern industrial society, rose to the point where the environment enjoyed independent status as an issue in a number of political systems, and several green parties began to enjoy a degree of electoral success. There emerged a distinct political 'identity' around ecological questions in the 1980s. It was this identity that provided an impulse for ecologism and to which it gives voice. The second 'trigger' was the impact of a succession of crisis events and health scares in the 1970s upon public opinion and the party elites of various liberal states. In response there appeared a set of writings enunciating concern about the impact of industrial practices upon social life which caught public attention. The publication of Rachel Carson's *Silent Spring* (1963) and Paul Ehrlich's *Population Bomb* (1968) marked the arrival of environmental concern at a popular level in post-war North America. Another important moment in the transformation of disparate anxiety about environmental problems into more focused discussion of an alternative to present-day society came with the publication of *Limits to Growth* (Meadows *et al.* 1972), a computer-simulated assessment of the dangers to human survival resulting from present levels of resource extraction, population growth and use of non-renewable resources. Despite the melodramatic nature of its claims and its dubious methodology, this study had a major impact in terms of public awareness. The development of the broadcast media was a significant background force in this regard, rapidly disseminating news of the leak from the nuclear power station on Five Mile Island, the fall-out from the disaster at the Chernobyl reactor, as well as striking images of oil tanker spillages, such as the *Exxon Valdez*, and other man-made disasters, for instance the major chemical spillage at Bhopal in India. A variety of broadcast and print outlets provided an important medium whereby concern about such issues could be vented, visualised and, increasingly, discussed.

In the early 1980s a small number of green parties began to make steady, and sometimes impressive, gains at local, European and national elections. In Europe, the German greens (*Die Grünen*), generated considerable interest for their innovative blend of red and green perspectives, and subsequently for the divisive battle between political radicals ('fundis') and reformists ('realos') over tactics and strategy (Doherty, 1992). Such internal divisions were reproduced, with national variations, across Central and Western Europe, culminating in the tentative participation in coalition administrations of several green parties (most famously in Germany) and splits in other cases, for instance among French greens (Richardson and Rootes, 1995). At the same time, some of the established environmental lobbying and campaigning groups, such as Friends of the Earth and Greenpeace, reported an upsurge in membership and interest through the decade. Simultaneously, mainstream political parties which had been hitherto indifferent to matters environmental began to include these issues in their programmes.

Ecologism has therefore emerged only recently, brought into being by these different developments. We may think of it as a web of ideas positioned at the political margins. Significantly, it has come to prominence at a moment when established ideological systems and associated allegiances appear to be in decline. The crisis of socialist thought, and the recasting of social democratic politics in the 1980s and 1990s, are a highly significant backdrop to its appearance. To some degree, the lack of consensus among interpreters about the status and character of ecologism as an ideology reflects its own necessarily ambivalent position in regard to established patterns of ideological thinking. Ecologism reproduces some of the features of other established ideologies, yet it also serves as an expression of deepening hostility to the world of conventional politics – one of the sources of scepticism about the capacity of politics to produce meaningful change. On the other hand, this ambivalence is a typical hallmark of radical ideological challengers – torn as these often are between holding to a fundamental critique of the system which excludes them, yet of necessity forced to engage with the realm of politics if they are to prosper beyond their initial minority base.

In the case of ecologism, it is important to recognise and understand the agencies and vehicles through which its constitutent ideas have been disseminated. The writings of intellectual radicals, including philosophers, biologists, radical economists and social theorists, have been particularly important; their work has been received with greater enthusiasm, for instance among students, since the mid-1980s. In more recent times ecological concerns have moved into non-scientific parts of the academy, with increasing numbers of scholars committed to engaging political ideas, philosophy, law and public policy in relation to these issues. Though not all are ardent advocates of ecologism, there is no doubt that the literature devoted to these subjects has refined some of the conceptual chains within this ideology and some of these more abstract debates have filtered into the activist-oriented 'green public sphere' (Torgerson, 1999). In terms of the latter, the experiences and perspectives of a host of groups, campaigns and organisations which have increasingly combined to form networks of activism on the fringes of the political system are significant. These networks range from those campaigns committed to radical forms of direct action and protest against, for instance, road-building schemes to bodies committed to conventional lobbying tactics. These forms of activism are poles apart and lead some commentators to wonder whether it is possible that a single ideology unites these practitioners. But this is not the only dimension along which ecologism is stretched out. Equally potent are the differences between those who are uninterested in political protest and more committed to forms of social activism which reflect ecological values – including organic farmers, ecological communities and businesses – on the one hand, and those who 'practise' their environmental commitment through more mainstream and conventional forms of social action – buying green products or supporting Greenpeace by signing a direct debit form. A further divide ought to be pin-pointed here too – between those who are committed to developing ecological practices and politics within civil society on the one hand, and those intellectuals, party actors and campaigning organisations that seek to penetrate established political and policy networks around the state. Whilst these dimensions do not reduce neatly into each other, a bipolar trend is apparent across the green movement. This has undoubtedly helped shape the preponderant tension within the family of ecological thinking – between 'light' greens seeking to gain a voice within the existing political system and 'deep' or 'dark' greens contemptuous of the values of this system and its associated methods.

The 'fundamentalist' perspectives associated with these latter forms of radical ecological politics have tended to draw upon traditions of thought like anarchism. In so doing, they connect ecological concerns with a celebration of spontaneous, direct action 'from below', in opposition to the complex political systems of liberal democracy. On the other hand, some green 'public intellectuals' (in Britain Jonathan Porritt and George Monbiot are examples, as is Ralph Nader in the United States) and leading party figures have articulated a project which involves the transformation of liberal democratic politics. These emphases are mirrored in the work of theorists keen to connect the imperatives of ecology with considerations of state capacity, the possibilities of ecological citizenship and the prospects of a fusion of social justice and environmental advance (Barry, 1999). There are many positions between these poles, yet the pull of one or the other – as other radical ideologies have found – is very hard for individuals and groups to resist. That this is so is one of the paradoxical consequences of modern politics, with its tendency to produce simultaneously powerful impulses to rejection and accommodation in the minds of its critics.

Ecologism as philosophy?

The notion that ecologism has developed unevenly with the slow growth of webs of activism which have transmuted into a green civil society (Torgerson, 1999) is not the same story as that told in a group of influential academic writings that appeared in the English-speaking world during the early 1990s. Though writers such as Robyn Eckersley (1992) and Robert Goodin (1992) disagreed about the exact content of the political theory that ecology implies, they shared the presumption that a logical reordering of ethical or philosophical precepts was required for this ideology to develop its potential. Linking these writings is the shared belief that increased philosophical rigour can translate readily into more appropriate policy programmes. A rather different conception of ecological political theory was produced around the same time by Andrew Dobson (1990, 1995). He argued that ecologism was the preserve of the most radical segments of the green movement, and could be understood only through their struggles, experiences and consciousness:

> Ecologism makes the Earth as physical object the very foundation-stone of its intellectual edifice, arguing that its finitude is the basis reason why infinite population and economic growth are impossible and why, consequently, profound changes in our social and political behaviour need to take place.
>
> (1990: 15)

The natural world, according to Dobson, is regarded uniquely by ecologism 'not just as the source of utility for humans, but as a model of the human world' (p. 24). An array of principles – diversity, toleration, interdependence, equality, tradition and the idea of nature as 'female' – could thus be deduced from the philosophical cornerstone of ecologism. So too were a distinct set of political approaches and methodologies, required to propel a break from the industrial present and enable the emergence of the sustainable future. This conception of green ideological thinking is presented as operative within a tight boundary and is strictly distinguished from 'environmentalism' – a narrowly focused concern with improving the environment for human benefit. Underneath the heading of environmentalism are placed such trends as environmental consumerism, the approaches of lobbying groups (such as Greenpeace and Friends of the Earth) and the education of the public about the dangers for humans that arise from harming our natural environment, as opposed to the fostering of a truly ecological consciousness. However important these goals may be, environmentalist commitments do not fundamentally challenge existing ideologies. Ecologism, in this view, means that care for the environment must signal fundamental changes in human relations with it, and indeed with social and political arrangements.

Dobson offers a rather prescriptive account of green ideology in which radicals are its authentic voices and 'reformists' are excluded from consideration. We should be wary of the analytical neatness of such a view, with its tendency to reduce rather complicated differences of attitude and style to two entirely separated blocs. But Dobson's argument is helpful in pointing to the clustering of a particular set of arguments which gave shape to ecologism during the 1980s. More generally, all these studies have been important in generating interest in and giving shape to emergent debates for students and scholars alike. Perhaps inevitably they have now become the objects of criticism for later interpreters (Torgerson, 1999; Barry, 1999). The study of political ideas, collective action and public policy in this field has deepened and broadened so that a wider variety of approaches and traditions have been brought to bear upon the issues. These are the signs of healthy maturation within an emerging discipline. And they provide an accompaniment to the refinement of ecologism itself, as the debates between radicals and reformists of the 1980s have given way to political thinking of increasing strategic sophistication and breadth, and a new focus upon concrete policy proposals.

Ecological variants and hybrids

Ecologism has generated an unusual number of internal variations, and has also been the partial source of a number of hybrid ideological developments. The character and significance of some of these variants and two influential hybrids involving ecology are considered below.

Radical forms of political ecology

Some commentators adopt a rather loaded vocabulary to capture the differences that exist within ecologism, delineating 'deep' or 'dark' greens, as opposed to 'shallow' or 'light' rivals (Barry, 1993). Whether these camps are so obviously separate is questionable. But there is no doubt that some very divergent conceptual pathways have emerged within ecologism and there are some important radical variants of this perspective. One of the main philosophical foundations of radical ecological politics is described by Grover Foley:

> Deep Ecology goes beyond the transformation of technology and politics to a transformation of humanity. Taking a holistic, total-field view, it denies any boundaries between man and nature.
>
> (1988: 119)

For deep ecologists this perspective involves a break from all traditions of thought that view human welfare as morally superior to the fate of other species and organisms. These established traditions which elevate humans above other species (a perspective labelled anthropocentrism) need to be challenged by an ethic which regards humans as one element within a larger biosphere made up of all sorts of morally valuable entities. The moral decentring of humanity (frequently labelled ecocentrism) lies at the heart of the work of the most renowned and influential deep ecological thinker, the Norwegian philosopher Arne Naess (1990). Since the 1970s he has argued that concern for the environment ultimately requires a novel philosophical outlook, incorporating a number of principles eschewed by anthropocentric analyses. An ecocentric perspective, Naess proposes, involves the recognition that life on earth is shared by a number of different species and organisms, all of which possess the potential for self-development. Humans are therefore merely one element of a larger biospherical community and need to rethink their position less as masters of the natural world than as willing partners within this larger entity. This principle, biospherical egalitarianism, carries a number of ethical implications. Most obviously it commits humans to as little intervention as possible within the non-human world, except in cases where the survival of the human species may be at stake. More generally, this ethic involves the contentious notion that it is possible to apply moral arguments not just to humans and animals but also to the non-sentient world, such as forests or natural habitats. Here deep ecology has generated its own internal divisions. While some ecologists welcome the opportunity to extend notions such as 'rights' to non-human nature, others reject such arguments as misleadingly anthropocentric. According to a second group of thinkers, we need to move beyond the application of human norms to nature and build into our outlook a recognition of the limits of human knowledge and thought in comprehending the complexity of the biospherical world of which we are only a small part. This has led some eco-philosophers to formulate a different defence of ecological consciousness – around the notion of the *intrinsic value* of all living entities. In other words, the value of an entity lies beyond the reach of human valuation. Intrinsic value theory represents one important way of establishing an ecocentric conception of value, though it has attracted as many critics as supporters (Dobson, 1989; Attfield, 1990; Sylvan, 1985). It offers policy makers a robust ethical reminder of the need to recognise the interests of a much greater variety of entities in human decisions.

Radical ecology also possesses a significant political wing, one which has come to much greater public attention in recent years. It has provided inspiration for groupings committed to radical protests against manifestations of the industrial system, including the once infamous Earth First! These deploy direct action tactics in a variety of campaigns. In Britain a number of protest actions – against genetically modified test crops, road-building programmes and animal exports most famously – have brought radical green groups and their unique brand of 'DiY' activism to public attention (McKay, 1998). Increasingly such activists operate through international networks, and green radicals play an important role in the fledgling 'anti-globalisation' coalition.

Social ecology

One of the most important rivals to radical ecology has emerged from the tradition known as 'social ecology'. Social ecologists reject the emphasis in green circles upon the unique character of exploitation of the natural environment. The latter arises from processes which simultaneously afflict and oppress human groups. Inspired by the American writer Murray Bookchin, social ecology recognises the significance of environmental issues within the modern world (1986, 1987, 1990). Freedom, according to Bookchin, will be achieved when intellectual and cultural progress is harnessed to environmental awareness and used to abolish human inequalities. This will mean the reconciliation of humanity with nature. In this scenario all organisms must be allowed to develop spontaneously so that they can contribute in diverse ways to the greater unity of human and natural freedom. Unity in diversity is a key principle for Bookchin and his fellow social ecologists, embodying their commitment to the inter-dependence of human life and nature. Humans may play the role of 'managers' of natural processes as long as they act only to enable the natural and diverse evolution of organisms within the biospherical community.

Not every social ecologist draws inspiration from Bookchin's thought, but the emphasis on the significance of abolishing forms of social inequality, as well as preventing the exploitation of natural resources, is indicative of the dual priorities of one strand within the green movement (Light, 1998). Both radical and social ecological variants include their own internal spectrum of views and political styles; both are important members of the family of ecologism. Equally noteworthy about this ideology is the way in which it has spawned some hybrid ideological perspectives – as green themes are yoked together with other radical traditions to form an entity that stands semi-independently of any existing ideology. Two examples are considered here.

Eco-feminism. Some feminists have been concerned to connect their ideas with an environmentalist outlook, developing the perspective of eco-feminism. (For a more complete account of the various schools within eco-feminism, see Barry, 1999.) These thinkers, and associated activist groupings, argue that the domination of nature is the product of the same masculine drives that result also in the subordination of women. The presentation of nature as embodying feminine traits that require male guidance is certainly a familiar element within contemporary culture. Some eco-feminists embrace the notion of women as beings who, for biological reasons, are closer to the rhythms and ways of the natural world, and celebrate the ideal of the earth mother (Warren, 1994; Collard and Contrucci, 1988). Within academic feminism, eco-feminism has led to the reconfiguration of the concept of patriarchal control, so that it incorporates too the impulse to exploit the natural environment. Whilst eco-feminism is a relatively unusual position within the women's movement, it does draw attention to several intellectual and political overlaps between feminism and ecologism. Both remain suspicious about the processes and institutions of the conventional political world, and the social movements which have given rise to these ideologies have developed an ethos of grass-roots, peaceful and spontaneous protest. On the other hand, some feminists believe that eco-feminism is problematic because they suspect that the ideal of the earth mother is a variant of patriarchal views of women.

Eco-socialism. Eco-socialism originated in the 1980s in the efforts of a number of socialist intellectuals to fuse socialist beliefs with an ecological outlook (Pepper, 1993). Pertinent to this project are the writings of figures such as André Gorz (1983), Rudolf Bahro (1984) and the British writers Raymond Williams (1983) and Ted Benton (1996). There are substantial variations within this outlook, yet eco-socialists agree that socialism cannot provide sufficient ideological vision for a post-capitalist society. Drawing upon many of the insights of the environmentalist movement, eco-socialism points to the interdependent character of the goals of abolishing inequality and ending human exploitation of nature. Both are achievable once capitalism is targeted and defeated by progressive forces. These writers have tended to analyse contemporary society through the lens supplied by Marxist as well as ecological categories. They have accordingly raised the awareness of greens about specific features of contemporary society such as the operation of the labour process in advanced capitalism. Gorz, for instance, has influenced the thinking of several green parties through his advocacy of the abolition of work and the need to liberate the time of individuals in a post-industrial world for the pursuit of their own self-expression and development.

As with eco-feminism, these ideas have proved relatively controversial. Eco-socialists have encountered hostility from the socialist camp for jettisoning Marxist and socialist ideas too readily in their shift to ecology. They have been criticised from green positions too for appearing to put red and green goals on a par while perpetuating the socialist belief that the liberation of nature is secondary to the prior goal of human freedom. Though eco-socialism has receded in intellectual terms since the 1980s, it has bequeathed a number of red–green networks and alliances which continue to sustain this tradition at the margins of political life.

169

The political character of ecologism

Much of the distinctiveness of ecologism stems from the ethical centrality it accords to the relationship between humans and the non-human world, an emphasis which generates a number of pressing moral questions. These include: on what grounds can we extend our categories of moral concern to include entities that make up the non-human world? How do we weigh our moral duties to our fellow human beings against ecology's injunction to repair our relationship with 'nature'? Which tradition(s) of ethical thought represents the best guide to reordering our relationship with the natural order? These questions have been central to the emerging discipline of moral philosophy that is directed at environmental issues and themes. But they also present significant *political* dilemmas for adherents of ecological ideas and have elicited varying answers in the last twenty years. Some of the political implications of these ethical imperatives have been addressed with the emergence of a fledgling body of green political thought. To gain an understanding of the present character and future directions of political ecology, it is to these issues that we will now turn.

An ideology apart?

An important question that arises for critics and supporters of green ideology is whether its political impact arises through the pursuit of an essentially left-wing trajectory. Or is it the case that political ecology represents an aspect of contemporary conservatism, one of the few mainstream political voices to celebrate tradition at a time when market-led capitalism has enshrined the values of modernity, fashion and rapid change? Greens reject the notion that their ideas can be reduced to either of these positions on the ideological spectrum, claiming to be 'neither right nor left, but out in front'. As interpreters of ecologism, should we accept this claim? With some qualification, I think that we should. And this is so despite the initial plausibility of both leftist and rightist interpretations of ecologism. The study of the networks in which green activists move, as well as assessment of green party membership profiles, lend credence to the claims of those who regard ecologism as a left libertarian ideology, part of the family of new social movements that rose to prominence in a number of democratic systems in the 1970s. In particular, it makes sense to interpret ecologism as a radical challenger to the existing pattern of debate and policy, one that is, to some degree, fulfilling the role and occupying the space once held by different varieties of socialism and, to a lesser degree, anarchism. On the other hand, there is no doubt that an overlap of sorts exists between ecologism and conservatism (Gray, 1993: 124–77). Partly this is due to some shared cultural heritage, notably the romantic tradition, which has proved a vital source of sentiment and imagery for both. More generally, there are some aspects of green thinking and culture which carry strongly conservative resonances. The emphasis upon the virtues of local traditions, as well as the scepticism about the rationalistic impulses within modern culture, give some credence to these claims. And the libertarian elements within this movement's culture rub up against the authoritarian overtones of some schemes for environmental salvation in the green movement.

Whilst ecologism undoubtedly possesses roots in and overlaps with both these traditions, it is significant that green actors have always sought to present political ecology as different from them. The independent profile of environmental issues and human relations with non-human nature that are at the heart of ecologism *require* greens to seek some degree of autonomy from the established ideological spectrum, which does not align according to the kinds of issues that greens want to highlight. In this sense greens are challengers to the established spectrum, and their claim to be neither straightforwardly right nor left is somewhat justified. Yet the paradox that afflicts radical ideological challengers affects greens too. The more they are drawn into established political systems, policy networks and electoral competitions the more they are required to respond to issues and themes which have only a loose or indirect environmentalist bearing. Adopting positions on these, which green parties have been required to do, means a necessary process of adaptation to the political alignments behind these issues. Thus greens simultaneously position themselves at particular points along more familiar party and ideological spectrums. And on the whole green parties find themselves natural, if critical, allies of social democratic and other parties of the left, for instance the significant coalition forged in German politics between the Greens and the SPD.

There is therefore an irreducible tension underlying ecologism's relationship to established ideological systems. And this tension is played out in green responses to the ethical imperatives at the heart of ecologism. On the one hand, environmentalist parties have been pulled into, and in some systems achieved some remarkable results in, established party systems. Yet the policy impact of these efforts has rarely repaid the efforts involved, leaving some wondering whether the existing political system can be 'greened' at all, or whether the strategy will simply take too long (Barry, 1999). In more radical quarters within this movement, on the other hand, little sustained thinking has taken place about how to construct a consensus around ecological values beyond rather vague assertions of the need to transform the collective consciousness of whole nations. Also lacking is much sense of the need for strategic interventions in relation to some of the major shifts taking place within patterns of international governance on environmental questions, as opposed to simply ignoring or opposing these important changes. In the wake of the Rio earth summit of 1992, as well as the proliferation of environmental plans drawn up by public authorities at national, regional and local level, new spaces have been opened up for imaginative and constructive green interventions. The adoption of the rhetoric of sustainable development by international authorities, national governments and regional bodies such as the European Union, as well as the formulation of some important policy programmes around the goals of sustainability in the wake of the Rio summit, have opened up an important dilemma for ecologism. Many green groups, campaigns and networks have deployed these opportunities in highly effective ways and raised their own profile as a consequence. But in so doing they are drawn ever further into a system which is premised on values very different from their own.

Towards a green state?

A further intellectual dilemma has begun to emerge for political ecologists, one also deepened by these developments. Does sustainability require the creation of a green state, or rather the 'greening' of existing state institutions and powers? The question is central to future green aspirations and strategies. The ethics of ecologism lend themselves to either orientation. On the one hand, many radical ecologists envisage a shift to a different kind of political order and novel systems of administrative co-ordination in which as many functions and powers as possible are devolved to appropriate scales. Yet most greens simultaneously imagine that sustainability requires central co-ordinating powers – implementing, overseeing and regulating policies appropriate to a sustainable development trajectory. The presumption of radical ecological thinking is that the state that will steer the transition to sustainability will be designed so that it responds directly to the dictates of ecology. But some important questions need to be addressed here. What kinds of institutional restructuring are required for a 'green' state to come into being? How will ecological goals be rendered central to the ethos of this state? What will be the constitutional and legal framework governing the relations between this level of authority and regional and local powers?

On the other hand, those more attuned to the rhythms, routines and ethos of liberal democracy believe in the 'greening' of existing state institutions and priorities. Though this remains a longer-term project which will encounter numerous political and institutional obstacles, it is one that is pitched within the realms of political possibility, requiring the radicalisation of some existing trends rather than wholesale institutional reinvention. The dilemmas attendant upon this programme involve such questions as: how to ensure that environmental goals and targets are incorporated into the programmes of different, sometimes rival, government departments; how to ensure that particularly obdurate problems are tackled in ways that are not short-term fixes but involve the harnessing of different kinds of social experience and expertise; and how to relegitimate some of the apparatus, language and methods of 'planning' that sustainability undoubtedly requires (Kenny and Meadowcroft, 2000; Meadowcroft, 1997). A particularly pressing issue faces those who advocate the merits of 'greening' existing state machinery and structures: is it sufficient to advance sustainability at the level of the state, or do ecological imperatives simultaneously require co-ordinated action and education within civil society to ensure popular legitimacy for, as well as participation in, environmentally benign policy? There is certainly evidence to suggest that paying heed to the latter is a vital part of a successful and sustainable environmental policy programme (Jänicke and Weidner, 1997).

Given the relative brevity of the life of this ideology, it should be no surprise to discover areas of neglect and underdevelopment. Ideologies are entities always in motion; their webs of belief are refined as new problems emerge. There are signs that such strategic issues are surfacing in political discourse in and around green circles. Equally there are indications that, despite its radical challenger/outsider status, ecologism has exerted some influence upon the agendas and debates circulating in the public spheres of different liberal states. Had ecologism and green politics not come into being, some of the central themes of contemporary public debate and concern would either be absent or only weakly articulated.

Green discourses in the public sphere

Three examples illustrate the diffuse impact of green discourse on public debate. The first concerns our sense of tradition and conceptions of time. Greens overlap with conservatives in regarding the social present as integrally connected with, and made meaningful by, what came before us and what will come after. This is as true for individual identities as for social collectivities. Ecologists not only demand that we consider our relations with much larger entities than ourselves but also connect us with future generations through the enhancement of our sense of individual environmental responsibility. It is through the exercise of our ecological consciences, as well as changing the pattern of our own life-styles, that we recognise aspects of our identity and the importance of our social past and future, in ways currently eclipsed by the rapidity and evanescence of our consumption-dominated lives. Ecologism offers us narratives about our roots and horizons, and it seeks to position us within the 'great chain of being'. Though few citizens currently buy wholesale into these narratives, it is clear that ecologism is fulfilling some important functions in propelling such arguments. In the wake of the uncertainty and insecurities that economic globalisation has brought in its wake, some commentators talk of the quest for 'identity' that characterises the fleeting and fragmented social worlds that we inhabit. Ecologism may find fertile soil for some of its principal claims, therefore, because it offers a unique but resonant account of our crisis and a story about how to regain control over our lives and reground our very selves.

A related idea with which ecologism is associated is that of risk, and it is through the diffusion of risk talk that a second contribution is discernible (Beck, 1995). Ecologism requires us to face up to the cataclysmic possibilities caused by human development models, and it offers a vocabulary through which we can discuss and calibrate 'risks'. Through a variety of media we are now inundated with panics and scares about aspects of our social experience – from what we consume as individuals to the very possibility of collective human life being finite. Environmentalists and greens have played a central role in raising questions of risk, and generating both a more conscious and informed but also more anxiety-ridden culture about modern living. The notion of 'risk' is perhaps a rather loaded one; certainly some critics call on us to resist the permeation of risk talk into different aspects of our lives (Furedi, 1997). Yet the discourse of risk is not necessarily disabling for individuals, turning us into paranoid and helpless dupes of the nanny state. It produces a heightening of citizen awareness about processes and practices (factory farming and the genetic modification of food are examples) that we once regarded as distant and irrelevant to our personal concerns. The notion of risk that greens project is not purely about personal safety and protection, though this is undoubtedly part of the appeal of environmentalist discourse. Risk represents a way of rendering questions such as food consumption and farming practice *ethical* – matters over which individuals are encouraged to exercise moral choice and be responsible. It also points to one of the fundamental questions arising from the tension between modern social life, where we increasingly view ourselves as consumers, and modern political life, in which the virtue of citizenship is paraded. Awareness and understanding of risks and the willingness to devise collective solutions to them is one way in which the ethos of citizenship might be revalidated within our frequently uncivil and egotistical society.

The third impact that ecologism has exerted on public discourse concerns the efforts of its ideologues to effect subtle transformations of the meanings of some of the key terms in our political vocabulary. Greens have, for example, been especially keen to revive the virtues of 'community'. Whilst community is often invoked in such rhetoric to stress the values of small-scale living, close personal relations and an ethos of social solidarity and mutual reponsibility that has been hollowed out by consumer capitalism, the term is given new meaning in an ecological setting (Kenny, 1996; Torgerson, 1999). The green emphasis on community serves to remind us of the moral significance of non-human entities within any spatial context that we inhabit, and ecological communitarianism requires us to consider what kinds of relationship we have with the locality we inhabit: do we eat local produce, support local businesses, recycle our waste, ensure that our town or city does not exploit or damage the locale in which it is located? Something similar has happened in the case of the term 'justice'. Through the notion of sustainability, greens have refined conventional notions of social justice in a way that requires us to attend also to the interests of those yet to be born: can we call a society 'just' if it destroys the heritage of future generations (Dobson, 1998)? This is not to suggest that these concepts now carry irreducibly ecological meanings. Yet in the struggle over their use within political discourse, these alternative meanings are current and have made an impact upon political argument in general and, occasionally, the calculations of opinion formers and policy makers.

Conclusion

Ecologism is an ideology in the early stages of construction and dissemination. Rather than viewing it as a set of internally consistent beliefs that are grounded on logically ordered philosophical foundations, it is better to think of it as a family of ideological beliefs which contains some quarrelsome members. Some of its interpreters are confident that green ideology offers a fully fledged alternative philosophy that necessitates an entirely new take on all the major concepts and ideas that govern modern politics. Others regard it as an ideology, but of a different kind from liberalism, conservatism or socialism – one that is at present oriented around an unusually thin conceptual core. This means that when ecologism strays from its central focus upon the relationship between humans and the natural world, it is likely to draw upon other traditions for political insight. Still others doubt whether we can see any kind of distinct ideology arising from environmentalist concerns.

The account offered in this chapter is closest to the second of these three views. Ecologism is a recognisable ideological entity, shaped by a set of pressing ethical questions and imperatives. Yet as a *political ideology* its status is somewhat ambiguous. These ethical commitments can be translated into a variety of political programmes, strategic orientations and ideas. Against those who think that green political thought and practice need to be secured by philosophical or ethical argument, I would suggest that greens are in the process of discovering the need for independent political reflection and understanding as well. They are facing a variety of dilemmas generated by developments which provide some limited grounds for optimism, notably the emergence of a loose but significant pattern of environmental governance at the international level, the construction of government agencies to oversee environmental affairs, and the formulation of sustainability plans by many governments. Set against these trends are some of the continuing and apparently ineradicable processes producing adverse ecological outcomes and storing up the possibility of future disasters: deepening inequity between the rich 'North' and poorer 'South' in the global economy; rising levels of consumption *per capita* in the most 'developed' economies; and countries' unwillingness to accept responsibility for adverse environmental effects. Green politics and political theory have to understand, interpret and construct engagement with these contradictory and beguiling trends. In so doing, green ideology has a vital part to play if it is to mature into an established presence within democratic political systems. A key role for a distinctively green ideology is to provide a language which can be deployed and refined by various green political and intellectual actors, and from which will be fashioned more accessible and hard-hitting ideas for the wider public audience that greens have to address.

Acknowledgement

I am indebted to John Barry, Bob Eccleshall and Nick Stevenson for their thoughts and advice on a draft of this chapter.

Note

1   Readers will notice a variety of labels applied to this ideology. Some authors label this 'green ideology', or interpret it as a distinctive, 'modular' kind of ideology (Talshir, 1998), whilst others prefer the broader label 'environmentalism'.

Further reading

Scholarly accounts of green political ideology have proliferated in recent years. I would particularly recommend: J. Barry, 'The limits of the shallow and the deep' (1993), M. Freeden, *Ideologies and Political Theory* (1996), pp. 526–50, J. Meadowcroft, 'Green political perspectives at the dawn of the twenty-first century' (2001), Y. Stavrakis, 'Green ideology' (1997), M. Smith, *Ecologism* (1999), G. Talshir, 'Modular ideology' (1998), and A. Vincent, 'The character of ecology' (1993). There are a number of books on green political theory which include valuable discussion of the ethical and political character of ecologism, including: J. Barry, *Rethinking Green Politics* (1999), B. Baxter, *Ecologism* (1999), A. Dobson, *Green Political Thought: An Introduction* (1990) and *Green Political Thought* (1995), and T. Hayward, *Ecological Thought* (1995). The approaches of R. Goodin, *Green Political Theory* (1992), and R. Eckersley, *Environmentalism and Political Theory* (1992), are particularly stimulating. In-depth analysis of the meaning of central political values like democracy and justice in relation to political ecology can be found in B. Doherty and M. De Geus (eds), *Democracy and Green Political Thought* (1996), A. Dobson and P. Lucardie (eds), *The Politics of Nature* (1993), W. Lafferty and J. Meadowcroft (eds), *Democracy and the Environment* (1996), and A. Dobson, *Justice and the Environment* (1998). Selections from many green figures and theorists can be found in A. Dobson (ed.), *The Green Reader* (1991). With the salience of ecological arguments there has developed a genre of anti-green writing. See especially M. Lewis, *Green Delusions* (1992) and the controversial history of ecological thinking offered by A. Bramwell, *Ecology in the Twentieth Century* (1989).

References

Attfield, R. (1983) *The Ethics of Environmental Concern*, Oxford: Blackwell.
Attfield, R. (1990) 'Deep ecology and intrinsic value: a reply to Andrew Dobson', *Cogito*, 4 (1), pp. 61–6.

Bahro, R. (1984) *From Red to Green: Interviews with* New Left Review, Verso, London.

Bahro, R. (1994) *Avoiding Social and Ecological Disaster: The Politics of World Transformation: an inquiry into the foundations of spiritual and ecological politics*, Bath: Gateway.

Barry, J. (1993) 'The limits of the shallow and the deep: green politics, philosophy and praxis', *Environmental Politics*, 3, pp. 369–94.

Barry, J. (1999) *Rethinking Green Politics*, London: Sage.

Baxter, B. (1999) *Ecologism*, Edinburgh: Edinburgh University Press.

Beck, U. (1995) *Ecological Politics in an Age of Risk*, Cambridge: Polity Press.

Benton, T., ed. (1996) *The Greening of Marxism*, New York: Guilford Press.

Bookchin, M. (1986) *Post-scarcity Anarchism*, Montreal: Black Rose.

Bookchin, M. (1987) *The Rise of Urbanization and the Decline of Citizenship*, San Francisco: Sierra Club.

Bookchin, M. (1990) *The Philosophy of Deep Ecology: Essays on Dialectical Naturalism*, Montreal: Black Rose.

Bramwell, A. (1989) *Ecology in the Twentieth Century: A History*, New Haven CT and London: Yale University Press.

Carson, R. (1963) *Silent Spring*, London: Hamish Hamilton.

Carter, A. (1999) *A Radical Green Political Theory*, London: Routledge.

Collard, A. and Contrucci, J. (1988) *Rape of the Wild*, London: Women's Press.

Dobson, A. (1989) 'Deep ecology', *Cogito*, 3 (1), pp. 41–6.

Dobson, A. (1990) *Green Political Thought: An Introduction*, London: Unwin Hyman.

Dobson, A., ed. (1991) *The Green Reader*, London: Deutsch.

Dobson, A. (1995) *Green Political Thought*, 2nd edn, London: Routledge.

Dobson, A. (1998) *Justice and the Environment*, Oxford: Clarendon Press.

Dobson, A. and Lucardie, P. eds (1993) *The Politics of Nature*, London: Routledge.

Doherty, B. (1992) 'The fundi–realo controversy: an analysis of four European green parties', *Environmental Politics*, 1 (1), pp. 95–120.

Doherty, B. and De Geus, M. eds (1996) *Democracy and Green Political Thought*, London: Routledge.

Eckersley, R. (1992) *Environmentalism and Political Theory: Toward an Ecocentric Approach*, London: UCL Press.

Ehrlich, P. (1968) *The Population Bomb*, New York: Ballantine.

Foley, G. (1988) 'Deep ecology and subjectivity', *Ecologist*, 18, pp. 4–5.

Freeden, M. (1996) *Ideologies and Political Theory*, Oxford: Clarendon Press.

Furedi, F. (1997) *Culture of Fear: Risk-taking and the Morality of low Expectation*, London: Cassell.

Giddens, A. (1991) *The Consequences of Modernity*, Cambridge: Polity Press.

Goodin, R. (1992) *Green Political Theory*, Cambridge: Polity Press.

Gorz, A. (1983) *Ecology as Politics*, London: Pluto.

Gray, J. (1993) *Beyond the New Right: Markets, Government and the Common Environment*, London: Routledge.

Hardin, G. (1968) 'The tragedy of the commons: the population problem has no technical solution, it requires a fundamental extension in morality', *Science*, 162, pp. 1243–8.

Hayward, T. (1995) *Ecological Thought*, Cambridge: Polity Press.

Hayward, T. (1998) *Political Theory and Ecological Values*, Cambridge: Polity Press.

Inglehart, R. (1977) *The Silent Revolution: Changing Values and Political Styles among Western Publics*, Princeton NJ: Princeton University Press.

Jacobs, M. (1996) *The Politics of the Real World*, London: Earthscan.

Jänicke, M. and Weidner, H., eds (1997) *National Environmental Policies*, Berlin: Springer.

Kenny, M. (1996) 'Paradoxes of community' in B. Doherty and M. De Geus (eds) *Democracy and Green Political Thought*, London: Routledge.

Kenny, M. and Meadowcroft, J., eds (2000) *Planning Sustainability*, London: Routledge.

Lafferty, W. and Meadowcroft, J., eds (1996) *Democracy and the Environment*, Aldershot: Edward Elgar.

Lewis, M. (1992) *Green Delusions: An Environmentalist Critique of Radical Environmentalism*, London: Pion Press.

Light, A. (ed.) (1998) *Social Ecology after Bookchin*, New York: Guilford Press.

McKay, G., ed. (1998) *DiY Culture: Party and Protest in Nineties Britain*, London: Verso.

Meadowcroft, J. (1997) 'Planning, democracy and the challenge of sustainable development', *International Political Science Review*, 18 (2), pp. 167–89.

Meadowcroft, J. (2001) 'Green political perspectives at the dawn of the twenty-first century' in M. Freeden (ed.) *Reassessing Political Ideologies: The Durability of Dissent*, London: Routledge.

Meadows, D., Meadows, D., Randers, J. and Behrens, W. (1972) *The Limits to Growth: A Report for the Club of Rome's Project on the Predicament of Mankind*, London: Earth Island.

Melucci, A. (1996) *Challenging Codes: Collective Action in the Information Age*, Cambridge: Cambridge University Press.

Merchant, C. (1992) *Radical Ecology: The Search for a Livable World*, London: Routledge.

Mill, J. S. (1986) 'Principles of political economy with some of their applications to social philosophy' (1848) in E. Jay and R. Jay (eds) *Critics of Capitalism: Victorian Reactions to Political Economy*, Cambridge: Cambridge University Press.

Naess, A. (1990) *Ecology, Community and Lifestyle*, Cambridge: Cambridge University Press.

Ophuls, W. (1977) *Ecology and the Politics of Scarcity: Prologue to a Political Theory of the Steady State*, San Francisco: Freeman.

Passmore, J. (1983) *Man's Responsibility for Nature*, 2nd edn, London: Duckworth.

Paterson, M. (2000) *Understanding Global Environmental Politics: Domination, Accumulation, Resistance*, New York: St Martin's Press.

Pearce, D., Markandya, A. and Barbier, E., eds (1989) *Blueprint for a Green Economy*, London: Earthscan.

Pepper, D. (1993), *Eco-socialism: From Deep Ecology to Social Justice*, London: Routledge.

Richardson, D. and Rootes, C., eds (1995) *The Green Challenge: The Development of Green Parties in Europe*, London: Routledge.

Sale, K. (1980) *Human Scale*, London: Secker & Warburg.

Saward, M. (1996) 'Must democrats be environmentalists?' in B. Doherty and M. De Geus (eds) *Democracy and Green Political Thought*, London: Routledge.

Scott, A. (1990) *Ideology and the New Social Movements*, London: Unwin Hyman.

Smith, M. (1999) *Ecologism: Towards Ecological Citizenship*, Buckingham: Open University Press.

Soper, K. (1995) *What is Nature?* Oxford: Blackwell.

Stavrakis, Y. (1997) 'Green ideology: a discursive reading', *Journal of Political Ideologies*, 2 (3), pp. 259–79.

Sylvan, R. (1985) 'A critique of deep ecology', *Radical Philosophy*, 40, pp. 2–12.

Talshir, G. (1998) 'Modular ideology: the implications of green theory for a reconceptualization of "ideology"', *Journal of Political Ideologies*, 3 (2), pp. 169–92.

Thompson, E. P. (1977) *William Morris: Romantic to Revolutionary*, London: Merlin.

Torgerson, D. (1999) *The Promise of Green Politics*, Durham NC: Duke University Press.

Vincent, A. (1993) 'The character of ecology', *Environmental Politics*, 2 (2), pp. 248–76.

Warren, K., ed. (1994) *Ecological Feminism*, London: Routledge.

White, L. (1967) 'The historical roots of our ecologic crisis', *Science*, 155 (37), pp. 1203–7.

Williams, R. (1983) *Towards 2000*, London: Chatto & Windus.

Feminism

Rick Wilford

> [A]t the very least a feminist is someone who holds that women suffer discrimination because of their sex, that they have specific needs which remain negated and unsatisfied, and that the satisfaction of these needs would require a radical change in the social, economic and political order.
>
> (Rosalind Delmar in Mitchell and Oakley, 1986)

The above quotation suggests that one should tread warily and not stray beyond a minimalist definition when discussing feminism. Indeed, in supplying her 'baseline' statement of feminism's rationale, Delmar cautions the reader that if one ventures further 'things immediately become more complicated'. The risk of courting controversy in exploring feminist ideas is underscored by Vicky Randall: 'It is hardly possible to specify a core of beliefs that would not be contested by some of those who call themselves feminists' (1991: 516). Of course, if all that is required is a brief statement of the core principles of feminism then Delmar's formulation would suffice and the chapter would be admirably brief, not to say terse. However, feminism's complexity, and the attendant disagreement among its exponents, alert us to its problematic nature.

In those respects, feminism is no different from the other doctrines discussed in this book. As each chapter demonstrates, political ideologies are relatively open-textured. This is not to imply that divisions cannot be drawn between or among doctrines: that would be an absurd proposition. Rather, it is to recognise that under the umbrella of each ideology there exist different camps, factions or tendencies, each lending its own distinctive interpretation to the core principles of the relevant doctrine. The contributors have, for instance, drawn distinctions between libertarian and organic conservatives, revolutionary and reformist socialists and between the exponents of lighter and darker green politics. Two examples from contemporary Northern Ireland can serve further to illuminate the intensity of intra-ideological dispute.

The achievement of the Belfast agreement on 10 April 1998, while subsequently endorsed by referendum on each side of the Irish border, has deepened divisions within both the unionist and the republican communities. Though a (narrow) majority of unionist voters endorsed the agreement, a significant minority were utterly opposed to its terms, accusing pro-agreement unionists of betraying the basic principles of unionism by setting in train a process that would detach Northern Ireland from the United Kingdom, rather than achieving a stable political settlement. On the other side of the communal divide, those republicans (Sinn Féin) who signed up to the agreement were accused of political heresy by some members of the republican movement. These dissidents – including the 'Real IRA' – interpreted the agreement as sustaining the partition of the island by guaranteeing a continuing role for Britain within the 'six counties'. From their perspective, Sinn Féin has succumbed to a partitionist settlement rather than initiating a process that will inexorably lead to Irish unification and, therefore, the dissidents believe that the continued waging of 'the long war' is justified.

The risk that such intra-ideological disputes can sustain and provoke violence demonstrates the potency of ideas. Disputes also surface when political parties engage in the search for a new leader. In stable democracies such contests seldom involve physical violence but they can become verbally bruising affairs as candidates vie for success, and strive for recognition as *the* truest 'blue', 'green', 'red' and so on. Competing to be perceived as the most authentic voice of a particular ideological tradition does not mean that doctrines are immutable. They do evolve, not least because they need to respond to the values, policies and choices offered by their ideological competitors. Indeed, at a particular moment a party may undergo a more radical transformation of its ideas such that its leader may be accused of transgressing core principles. In Britain, for instance, the Thatcherite 'revolution' led some to entertain the proposition that Mrs Thatcher was a neo-classic liberal rather than a conservative, while the invention of 'New' Labour has prompted many to query whether Tony Blair is a socialist.

The point of this preamble is to convey the idea that, beyond a core of beliefs, ideologies are fluid, plural and diverse rather than solid, unified and monolithic bodies of thought. This is no less true of the loosely woven doctrine, feminism – or rather, *feminisms*. Indeed, a theme of this chapter is that the plurality of feminist schools of thought while, on the one hand, rather baffling is, on the other, a sign of its growing maturity and of the increased confidence of its various adherents.

One symptom of this confidence is that the days when it was normal to articulate an unexamined notion of universal sisterhood have receded, to be replaced not just with the awareness of differences among women but their celebration. So much so that in the stead of an assumed shared female identity, the *politics of identities* has become a characteristic feature of contemporary feminist discourse. Feminists have, in effect, moved away from a singular pre-occupation with the debate over similarities and differences *between* women and men, and towards the recognition of differences *among* women. This shift signifies that feminists have become more resolved to interrogate their own assumptions – including the belief that women enjoy a transcendent common identity. Thus, rather than toeing a doctrinal line that obliterates differences among women, whether based on age, ethnicity, race, religion, class, marital status or sexuality, feminism now appears to be a much more commodious body of ideas.

Its variety, however, encourages sceptical observers to portray feminism as a house divided. Riven with diagnostic disputes over the causes of women's oppression, and associated arguments over remedies, it may appear that feminism is creaking in its foundations and threatening to collapse into disarray. It would be more accurate to portray feminism as a house within which there are now many mansions, whose occupants are engaged in a series of dialogues over the means of resolving the wrongs perceived to afflict women.

This is not to finesse the issue of what feminism is by engaging in semantic sleight of hand. There are competing schools of feminist thought, yet such competition is not new in itself. Just as some claim that there has always been a women's movement, there have always been differing interpretations of feminism. More recently, however, the analyses and prescriptions on offer have multiplied to the point where one may experience a sense of bewilderment. Such bafflement can, though, be resolved by reformulating a key question. Instead of asking oneself 'Am I a feminist?' one might pose the question 'What kind of feminist am I?' In effect, this is no different from asking 'What kind of conservative is Ian Duncan-Smith?' or 'What kind of "socialist" is Tony Blair?' Posing the question in such terms allows one the opportunity to explore feminist ideas and, perhaps, to identify with a particular style of feminist thought.

A clamour of voices

One cannot, however, sidestep the matter of feminism's diversity. As already implied, few now accept that the terms 'feminism' and 'feminist' are self-evident, so that the current orthodoxy is to employ the term *feminisms* in order to capture the wide array of views expressed by self-regarding feminists. Even within what may have been popularly (mis)understood to be unified positions, perhaps radical feminism can serve as an example, diversity is the norm (Crow, 2000). Further still, the emergence of interest in postmodernism which rejects any and all 'master narratives', including political ideologies, adds immeasurably to the proliferation of voices within feminism.

The insistence by postmodernists on peeling away the encrustations of thought bequeathed by the past, of subverting received 'truths' and 'objectivities' and, instead, relishing doubts and subjectivities has profound consequences for feminists. Postmodernism is immensely, perhaps deliberately, difficult to comprehend, both in itself and in its relation to feminist thought.[1] Put simply, in social and political theory it argues that we should reject certitude of belief in any grand doctrinal design and celebrate difference, variety and complexity. This prescription disorientates many feminists because they are, in effect, enjoined to disavow any bodies of thought that purport to reveal the 'truth' about women. Indeed, the very concept of 'woman' itself is contested by postmodernism (Gamble, 1999; Zalewski, 2000). What it means to be 'a woman' is not, insist postmodernists, revealed by recourse to any single political doctrine, including feminism(s), but rather must be explored by each individual, stripping away layers of (largely man-made) meanings through an internal journey of discovery. So, in addition to a concern with identity politics, apprehended on a collective or group basis, women are encouraged to delve into their own individual subjectivities.

While this perspective may be puzzling – if not frustrating, because of its dizzying relativism – the broader concern with identity politics within contemporary feminism has supplied a healthy corrective to unexamined assumptions about the existence of a universal sisterhood, especially when articulated by white, educated, middle-class women in the developed world. One notorious slogan of the 1960s – 'Women are the niggers of the world' – betrayed not just the ethnocentrism of Western, radical feminism, but an insensitivity to language that beggared belief. Now, however, the identities of women are understood widely to be structured by a host of interacting factors – including, for instance, age, ethnicity and class – which complicate the achievement of an integrated women's movement and challenge attempts to regiment them into a single doctrinal camp. However, this does not impede the formation of strategic coalitions of feminists who campaign for the removal of obstacles hindering the exercise of autonomy for women. Indeed, the history of the women's movement, however defined, has been the story of a succession of strategic coalitions mobilised in pursuit of a progressively expanding bundle of rights and freedoms.

The challenge posed by postmodernism, not just to feminism but to all doctrines, is a profound one. In rejecting feminist theory, postmodern thinkers are effectively abandoning projects designed to improve the material conditions of women's lives, since, they insist, no ideology can supply a reliable compass to guide political action: there is no star to steer by. In disavowing wider political campaigns and movements, one may question whether it is possible to be a 'postmodern feminist': indeed, the phrase may be regarded as a contradiction in terms.[2]

Post-feminism?

In the light of its growing complexity, hesitancy in adopting anything other than a minimal definition of feminism seems justified. But for some even this is a redundant exercise. 'Post-feminists' assert that, however defined, feminism has outlived its usefulness. Women, the argument runs, 'now have it all': put another way, 'the future is female'. Indeed, the term 'post-feminism' (see Gamble, 1999: 43–54) has been minted to express the idea that women are now the full co-equals of men, able to exercise their unfettered autonomy in making choices about their lives, both public and private. This proposition has incensed many, including Germaine Greer (1999), a leading voice during the 'second wave' of feminism in the 1960s and 1970s. More recently, and having championed multifarious styles of feminism, she was moved to write a sequel to her seminal *The Female Eunuch* (1970) by the appearance of a 'post-feminist' literature:

> [I]t was not until feminists of my own generation began to assert with apparent seriousness that feminism had gone too far that the fire flared up in my belly. When the lifestyle feminists chimed in that feminism had gone just far enough in giving them the right to 'have it all', i.e. money, sex and fashion, it would have been inexcusable to remain silent . . . It's time to get angry again.
>
> (Greer 1999: 1, 3)

For Greer, the 'rhetoric of equality' has supplanted the true task of feminism, namely the liberation of women from what she terms 'contradictory expectations'. Not knowing, for instance, whether to act like men at work, or like themselves, and uncertain about whether to perceive motherhood as either a punishment or a privilege.

Greer identifies a host of disabling disadvantages that confront women today, both at home and at work, and in the process ridicules any notion that an egalitarian, post-feminist world has been achieved in which women do 'have it all'. More – recalling those who articulated a global sisterhood thirty or more years ago – she insists that 'to be feminist is to understand that before you are of any race, nationality, religion, party or family, you are a woman' (1999: 7). This notion of an overarching (or perhaps submerged) unity does not sit comfortably with identity politics and the concern with difference that has come to the fore in contemporary feminist thinking. Greer also subscribes to the idea of female essentialism, thereby buying into the notion of a basic difference between women and men. As she puts it: 'Liberation struggles are not about assimilation but about asserting difference [between the sexes], endowing that difference with dignity and prestige and insisting on it as a condition of self-definition and self-determination' (1999: 1). This issue – of sameness versus difference between the sexes – is a source of considerable debate among feminists, and is by no means peculiar to the contemporary women's movement, as we shall see.

Wave-ing – or drowning?

Although the preceding discussion may leave one feeling dazed and confused, it should be evident that to discuss feminism is to dicuss a dynamic body of thought that has evolved into a self-critical doctrine rather than one that has become settled – and certainly not stale. In fact, the sheer volume of con- temporary feminist literature, both scholarly and popular, is daunting. This vibrancy has led some to discuss the gathering of a 'third wave' of feminism, summarised by Barbara Arneil thus:

> Third wave feminism(s) are characterised by a commitment to beginning one's analysis from women's own perspective; that is, a recognition of 'differences' in perspective, both between women and men and *among women*.
>
> (1999: 9, my emphasis)

To identify a third wave, of course, implies a first and a second wave of feminism. The adoption of the 'wave' metaphor is instructive. It indicates that at certain moments the tide of feminist ideas surges forward, while at others it appears to ebb. In turn, this suggests that there is a body – or sea – of ideas, the force of which is influenced by the prevailing intellectual, political and social climate and the capacity of women to mobilise and organise around a campaign of reform.

Histories of the evolution of feminist ideas conventionally distinguish between two waves, the first, from the late eighteenth century to the 1920s, set within a predominantly liberal tradition that sought formal equality between the sexes and which crested around the issue of women's suffrage. This tradition stressed sameness of treatment for both sexes, although not on the basis of an entirely uniform position, as we will see. The second wave gathered momentum in the shape of the women's liberation movement in the mid to later 1960s that was preoccupied with differences between women and men. By contrast, the third wave swirls around differences among and between women, reflecting the current concern with subjectivities and identity politics.[3]

The latter is motivated by the politics of recognition, seeking the validation of discrete identities – e.g. black women, Muslim women, lesbians, disabled women – although each of these collectivities can be further disaggregated, since their notional integrity conceals as much if not more than it reveals. The focus on identity politics has, though, attracted criticism because it risks frustrating the growth of a strategic, even majority, coalition among women precisely because of its emphasis upon differences. However self-defined, the critique runs, women risk either drowning in a sea of discordant voices or being channelled into self-regarding tributaries where, cut off from the mainstream, their collective political strength evaporates. Postmodernists, as might already be guessed, voice a different criticism of identity politics. They argue that the notion of *an* identity is flawed, based as it is on modernist assumptions that impart a settled, closed meaning, whereas for them identities are contingent, multi-faceted, even protean. As Alcott puts it, the task is to 'liberate one *from* identity, rather than reifying those identities' (in Code, 2000: 264).

The rejection of a unified identity has particular relevance to the relationship between feminism and nationalist movements and politics. Nationalism can be narrow and exclusive or broad and inclusive, ethnic or civic (see Chapters 5 and 6). However, nationalism as an ideology and a political movement is invariably gendered. Nations are, for instance, commonly 'sexed': one thinks of 'Mother Ireland' or 'Mother Russia' or recalls phrases such as 'mother tongue' and 'motherland'. (Although, as we saw in Chapter 6, Hitler's Germany and Mussolini's Italy were each styled as a 'fatherland': no accident, given the patriarchal character of fascist doctrine!)

The sexing of nations as female is no guarantee that women will be valued as equal citizens in them: indeed, the obverse may be the case. So, while images of women may be adopted as the symbolic form of a nation – e.g. Britannia (Britain) or Marianne (France) – men usually emerge as the beneficiaries when nations attain statehood, whereas women are invariably left holding the short end of the citizenship stick. Whether the process of state formation takes the form of a peaceful and orderly transition from an old to a new regime or, conversely, there is a sharp and violent break with the past, nation and state building tends to advantage men (e.g. Pettman, 1996; Yuval-Davis, 1997; Wilford and Miller, 1998).

The perception that nationalist movements and nation-building projects work to the disadvantage of women has led many feminists to be distrustful of nationalism *per se*. That distrust is founded largely upon the lived experience of women who have been marginalised by nationalist movements, whether in the past or the present. But it is also informed by contemporary feminism's concern with identity politics. Suspicious of the idea of *a national identity* – which may venerate women as symbols of the nation while simultaneously hobbling their rights as citizens – the celebration of *identities of nationality* is a promising alternative. It allows of plurality and difference, and enables women to be (notionally) free from male-crafted notions of their 'proper' place in the national design.

An interesting example of this expression of identity politics is the Northern Ireland Women's Coalition (NIWC). Formed in 1996, two of its candidates were elected to the devolved Assembly in 1998. Not only is it the first women's party in the United Kingdom – or Ireland, for that matter – to achieve electoral success, but it did so by refusing to identify with either of the competing national traditions in Northern Ireland, namely unionism and nationalism, neither of which has proved to be receptive to women. Indeed, when the Coalition's two elected representatives signed the members' register as required by the terms of the Belfast agreement, they chose to style themselves as 'Inclusive Other', rather than as either 'Nationalist' or 'Unionist', signifying their rejection of these mutually exclusive and seemingly monolithic national identities. The Coalition's politics are those of inclusivity, rather than of exclusivity – a difficult stance in the context of a divided society, where chronic political violence has nourished sectarian 'them' and 'us' attitudes. In fact, Northern Ireland has been characterised, aptly, as an 'armed patriarchy', with women marginalised – and divided – by male power structures, whether in the realms of conventional or paramilitary politics.

While the NIWC scored a modest but noteworthy success, women's political parties find it difficult to mobilise electoral support. In comparison with other sources of political identity, gender and sex, while ubiquitous, cannot compete effectively with parties that organise around, say, class, region, ethnicity or religion. Joining these established parties, rather than the creation of women's parties, offers a more promising means of entering the public realm of politics in order to campaign for the needs and interests of women. However, entry into existing parties is a relatively recent development, in part because many second-wave feminists, especially radical feminists, shunned main/malestream political institutions, which they perceived to be quintessentially patriarchal: designed by and for men in order to dominate women.

Historically, whether by choice or the sheer denial of opportunity to enter the formal, public realm of electoral politics, feminism has tended to operate as a social movement, mobilising women in a myriad of groups and organisations in pursuit of both general and particular demands. Of course, it is less than 100 years since women in most countries secured the right to both vote and to stand for election – in some they still do not enjoy either of these rights – and they have yet to secure equal representation in any national parliament.[4]

Suffrage: a fragile unity

Until the vote was won, albeit at different dates in different countries, movement or group politics were the only alternatives available to women, whatever style of feminism they subscribed to. But the legacy of the campaigns for suffrage, secured by women of all races, religions, the young and the old, the rich and the poor, imparted an apparent unity to feminism. Here, it seemed, was an object lesson in the ability of women to act collectively for a common purpose. Yet, while suffrage movements brought together many women (and men) in a shared pursuit, it also contained underlying tensions. The motives that impelled different women to become involved in suffrage campaigns varied, not least those harboured by, on the one hand, equal rights feminists and by welfare or evangelical feminists on the other (Banks, 1981).

What differentiated them was precisely the question of whether women should be treated the same as, or differently from, men in matters of law and public policy. Inspired by the doctrine of natural rights, equal rights feminists insisted that women should be treated as human, not sexual, beings because they were as capable as men of governing themselves through the exercise of reason. Mary Wollstonecraft's (1759–97) *A Vindication of the Rights of Woman* (1792) was the first systematic attempt to promote this idea. Inspired by Enlightenment principles, Wollstonecraft based her plea for women to be treated as free and independent individuals upon the cardinal premise that 'the mind has no sex'. Here lay the seeds of the 'sameness' argument that informed many early proponents of female enfranchisement and which continues to reverberate within feminist debate: that women must be treated by law and policy in exactly the same way as men.

The equal rights tradition of feminism thus advocated the removal of legal obstacles to the fulfilment of women's autonomy as individuals, thereby ending their dependence upon, and hence subjection by, men. The insistence upon removing legal constraints upon women took as its measure the rights accorded to men: the male citizen became the template upon which the rights of women were to be inscribed. Like treatment of women was the dominant motif of equal rights feminism, whereas evangelical – or welfare – feminists emphasised differences between the sexes, and campaigned for different treatment for women, not least in employment. For instance, they championed legislation that was intended to protect women from the physical demands involved in particular occupations on the ground that they were, or would become, wives and mothers. In effect, they sanctioned the sexual division of labour both at home and in the workplace.

Evangelical feminists were neither radical nor liberal but socially conservative. Besides championing protective legislation, they saw themselves as paragons of what they believed were characteristically womanly virtues, derived from their roles as prospective or actual wives and mothers. Women were, for instance, perceived by them as co-operative where men were competitive; pacific as opposed to aggressive; selfless rather than selfish; and, perhaps most distinctively, were believed to be morally superior to men. The assertion of such differences justified the extension of the vote to women not on the ground of equal rights, but in the belief that these natural qualities would enhance the public realm of politics by applying a moral brake to the excesses of men.

The coexistence of the ideas of equal rights and evangelical feminists throughout the nineteenth century and into the twentieth did not, however, prevent their respective advocates from combining to press for female suffrage. Yet, in the immediate aftermath of women's enfranchisement in both the United States and Britain, the tension between these variants of feminism could no longer be contained.

In America the campaign for the Equal Rights Amendment (ERA), begun in 1923 and spearheaded by the National Women's Party, split the strategic coalition that had formed in pursuit of suffrage. The ERA sought, by con-stitutional amendment, to eliminate all legal inequalities between women and men, including those laws affording special protection to women, including in the field of employment. Having fought hard for protective legislation designed to prevent the exploitation of women (and children), evangelical feminists rushed to defend, and extend, those gains, reasserting the special needs of women and the characteristics attendant upon maternity that distinguished them from men. The ERA campaign continued for six decades but, ultimately, it failed (Berry, 1988)

In Britain during the 1920s the campaign led by self-styled 'new' or welfare feminists for a state-funded family allowance payable to wives, rather than their husbands, offended equal rights or 'old' feminists because of its assumption that women's maternal role naturally anchored them to the home. Whereas equal rights feminists sought to challenge conventional beliefs about the sexual division of labour within the family, many of those who espoused state welfare for married women endorsed marriage and maternity as means of fulfilment for women. It was this latter view that prevailed in post-Second World War Britain in that the male breadwinner model became the organising principle of its new welfare state. A self-defined 'old' feminist drew the distinction thus: 'The "New Feminism" emphasizes the importance of the "women's point of view", the "Old Feminism" believes in the primary importance of the human being' (Humm, 1992: 43). That distinction between 'sameness' – the essential humanness of women – and 'difference' – the woman's point of view – which had been accommodated in pursuit of the vote now ruptured the fragile unity effected over suffrage.

Historical diversity

Gaining a purchase on the evolution of feminist ideas is an uncertain undertaking, so much so that it is impossible to identify a seminal text or a decisive moment that sparked its beginnings. Texts that discuss the issue of women's citizenship, and hence their rights and responsibilities, have existed since classical Greek political thought in, for instance, the very different treatment of women by Plato and Aristotle. One history of feminist theory identifies Christine de Pisan (1364–1430) as 'the first woman to write about the rights and duties of her sex' (Bryson, 1992: 11), while Mary Astell (1666–1731) has been identified as 'the first English feminist' (Hill, 1986). Seeking to trace the roots of feminist thinking is not just about establishing an ideological tradition, though that is important and necessary – not least because it contributes to writing women into history (Scott, 1996) or, in this case, the history of ideas. It is also important for a political reason. Identifying a de Pisan in France or an Astell in England underlines the fact that they were writing in isolation. Such women had no organised women's movement to promote their views or inform their thinking – and, of course, they would have been addressing few people, because most of their contemporaries were illiterate. Consciously feminist groups appealing to a larger audience appeared later, although their emergence does not resolve fully the question of *when* feminism as an organised body of theory appeared.

Suffice to say that writing that can be placed within the feminist canon has a lengthy ancestry, one enriched by organised activities intended to secure equal rights for women. For instance, the roots of the modern women's movement can plausibly be traced to the creation of women's clubs during the French revolution, or the activities of women involved in the movements to abolish slavery and to promote temperance during the nineteenth century. In the case of abolition, this led to the meeting at Seneca Falls NY in July 1848 and the publication of the 'Declaration of Resolutions and Sentiments'. The opening line of the declaration extended, simply but cleverly, the Declaration of Independence to include all American people: 'We hold these truths to be self-evident: that all men *and women* are created equal.' That statement may be taken as the catalyst of the emergence of the suffrage movement which came to dominate the agenda of first-wave feminists on both sides of the Atlantic.

The point here is not to insist that any one individual, event or text has a prior claim over another as the source of the first wave. Rather, it is to suggest that the emergence and progression of feminist ideas and activity was uneven rather than linear – just, in fact, like the motion of a wave! The emergence of the second wave is even more difficult to pin down because much of the early activity took place in informal settings where women engaged in 'consciousness-raising' sessions, sharing their 'herstories' and experiences in relatively unstructured ways.[5] Indeed, the lack of structure was for some an explicit choice: it signified a style of behaviour unlike that practised in male-dominated institutions, betokening the concern with differences between women and men that came to be the hallmark of the second wave. The unorganised and non-hierarchical nature of these sessions itself contributed to the diversity that has always characterised the feminist project. While it would be misleading to claim that their predecessors were concerned only with the vote, later feminists have fostered a wider agenda of discussion. In particular, the priority given to differences between the sexes and, latterly, among women, has expanded the feminist chorus.

Siting feminisms and subverting orthodoxy

If we accept that diversity is a characteristic of feminism, how can we begin to understand the doctrine? One convenient but nevertheless reliable guide is to site feminism within the context of other ideologies. This may seem a somewhat odd, if not dismissive, approach because it suggests that feminism does not have, as it were, a life of its own, but exists only in relation to other bodies of thought. Such relationism is characteristic of all doctrines to the extent that their exponents seek to distinguish their ideas from those of their competitors, but here what is implied is that feminism evolved within the context of existing (liberalism) or emerging (socialism, Marxism) ideologies. This had two pronounced effects. First, as exponents of new, women-centred and hence radical thinking feminists had to negotiate space for their ideas within each of these doctrines. Secondly, in the process of this negotiation, they became aligned with the core principles of these existing 'isms'. Thus early differences among feminists derived from their association with one or another of these ideologies. It therefore makes sense to discuss the evolution of, for instance, a distinctively liberal, socialist or Marxist feminism.

Feminist ideas are not, however, merely derivative. Early feminists of whatever persuasion not only sought to negotiate with existing ideologies, but also interrogated them. In doing so they challenged a number of key assumptions which have underpinned the development of Western political thought since the time of Plato and Aristotle, particularly its 'pervasive dualism' (Coole, 1993).

Feminists interested in the development of political ideas have observed that the history of political thought is invested with a series of 'binary oppositions', each pole of which is accorded either a positive or a negative value. Key dualities have included: culture–nature, reason–emotion, public–private and, crucially, male–female. The first of each pairing were arranged together, such that maleness was associated with cultural activity and rationality, both of which were enacted in the public sphere. By contrast, femaleness was equated with nature, that is, reproduction, and passion, which belonged in the private sphere of home and family. Moreover, such associations were not presented as equivalent or co-equal, but in terms of a simple hierarchy. Put bluntly, male characteristics or virtues were deemed superior, female ones inferior: men and women were not only different, they were also unequal. Much of the energy of the wider feminist project has been directed towards undermining these dualities, thereby lending it a distinctively subversive character.

Such subversion has, though, taken different forms. Some feminists have adopted an androcentric (male-centred) strategy, encouraging women to adopt the characteristics traditionally ascribed to men, and/or to have male rights extended to them. Others have sought not to emulate men, but rather to prescribe an androgynous (male *and* female) solution, whereby the qualities ascribed to women and men are integrated in a common and non-hierarchical human identity. Some have sought to reverse the polarities by adopting a gynocentric (female-centred) strategy which places a positive value on the attributes conventionally ascribed to women, while yet others insist that, although women and men are different, they are, nevertheless, equal and that such differences should be celebrated rather than being denied or merged.

These differing strategies are influenced by the significance attached by feminists to either *sex* or *gender* as a means of analysing and explaining in-equalities between women and men. Some insist upon the primacy of biological identity – the distinction between the female and male sexes – as the explanation for the oppression of women. Here inequality is inderstood to arise from the different reproductive roles performed by women and men. That is, women's childbearing and nurturing are used to produce and reproduce inequality between the sexes, so that unless and until these roles are transformed, women will continue to be subordinate to men. This perspective, as we shall see, has been characteristic of those generally described as 'radical feminists' who have been concerned largely, though not exclusively, with the politics of sexuality and reproduction.

Other feminists focus not upon biological identity but rather upon the ways in which societies construct gendered, that is, feminine and masculine, roles to explain differences in the life chances of women and men. Here the focus is on the cultural meanings attached to the roles learned by children of either sex and which particular societies consider appropriate for women and men. Such roles, which vary across time and space, are then social constructions rather than being determined by biological identity: there is nothing fixed or determined or universal about them. And, just as they are socially constructed, so too they can be deconstructed and reconstructed.

The significance attached to either sex or gender informs much of the debate among feminists. Those favouring the former insist that woman's social identity is determined by her sex – biology as destiny – whereas those stressing culturally created differences emphasise the gendered character of woman's identity. The relative weight attached to sex and gender, and the ways in which they are understood to interact, critically influences the question of whether women should be regarded as being essentially the same as, or fundamentally different from, men.

Patriarchy: the 'man problem'

What one might call 'the man problem' became increasingly prominent within the second wave of feminism. There were and are feminists who cast men as the unremitting enemies of women and who prescribe a separatist and autonomous route to the fulfilment of their needs: from this perspective, espoused by cultural and some radical feminists, men become wholly redundant in women's lives.

Conversely, there are feminists – including liberal and socialist feminists – who regard men as their allies in the struggle for gender equality and justice. The active support of men is sought not only for pragmatic reasons – that is, because men enjoy a virtual monopoly of political power – but because it is understood to be essential for the achievement of a genuinely just society. This perspective, unlike the former, also allows that men can lay claim to a feminist identity.

While not an entirely novel issue, the portrayal of men as either the friends or the foes of women is still a matter of intense debate among feminists. The prominence of the 'man question' was assured by the emergence of radical feminists who rejuvenated the concept of *patriarchy* to explain the subordination of women.

In its undiluted form, patriarchy is understood in ahistorical and universal terms: that men always have been, are, and always will be, motivated to dominate women and will employ both subtle and unsubtle means to exert their control. This understanding of power relations between men and women is not restricted to the 'public' worlds of politics and work: patriarchy also extends into the 'private' sphere of the family and the intimate realm of sexual relations. This notion of patriarchy's boundless reach led to the coining of the phrase 'the personal is political' as a means of conveying its pervasiveness and its deep-rootedness. In the second wave it led to a fresh assault on the conventional family, regarded anew as a site of women's oppression. It also generated campaigns in the public realm, including strict controls over pornography, changes in the law on rape and domestic violence, the creation of refuges for battered women and children, and the liberalisation of abortion laws. The rejuvenation of patriarchy as an explanation for women's oppression in effect reopened the home front, earlier assaulted by utopian socialists and Marxists (see below), in what now became dubbed the 'sex war' and consolidated interest in differences between women and men.

Patriarchy as an analytical category was/is also deployed as shorthand for describing the conditions of inequality and disadvantage experienced by women in the public and private realms, i.e. as giving rise to gender discrimination. In this more extended sense, patriarchy is understood to be socially constructed through the respective meanings imparted to masculinity and feminity. By contrast, the more radical interpretation of patriarchy – which set the agenda for the second wave – rests on the determinism of biological difference, and perceives men to be naturally driven by their need to exercise power over women. Whereas the former, gendered, interpretation allows the possibility for change to occur in relations between women and men, the essentialist construction lends an immutable character to relations between the sexes: men have no interest, perhaps even choice, in relinquishing their control over women.

The unqualified interpretation of patriarchy has not escaped criticism by other feminists.[6] One criticism is that it presents all women as enduring victims of male oppression, representing men as irredeemably 'bad' and women as quintessentially 'good', and thereby prescribes both political and sexual separatism. But, critics argue, stressing victimhood status is as, if not more, likely to disempower rather than empower women, while shunning men leads to an impoverished political (and sexual) life. (It also glosses over the fact that many women do succeed on their own terms, and that there are many caring men – and uncaring women.) Its universalism and ahistoricism – patriarchal relations are expressed as an eternal condition – are also said to lack analytical precision: it describes rather than explains and is unconvincing about the origins of patriarchy. Moreover, its universalism occludes other forms of oppression experienced by women based, for example, upon race, ethnicity and class – and/or their interaction. As such, it is criticised for ignoring differences among women, of being race, ethnic and class-'blind'. This criticism contributed in particular to the sparking of interest in the politics of identities, spearheaded by 'black' women in the developed world and Third World women who felt ignored and marginalised by the ethnocentrism of second-wave feminism in the First World.

The revitalisation of patriarchy – whether it is a constant or a variable condition of relations between the sexes – enlivened feminist debate and contributed to the diversity of feminism. But the issue of sameness/difference that it addresses has reverberated throughout its history as the following brief excursion into the evolution of feminist ideas demonstrates.

Early liberal feminism

In exploring the development of feminist ideas it is difficult to do other than take a stand on an approximation, for the reasons indicated earlier. That said, the appearance of Mary Wollstonecraft's *Vindication* was an early and considered plea for equal rights for women and supplies a convenient historical starting point.

Wollstonecraft insisted upon the capacity of women to engage in rational thought, and voiced the demand for equal educational opportunities as the means through which women could realise their independence. Having benefited from the same education, girls and boys would develop into rational individuals and be better fitted to enter marriage, where they could fulfil their respective and complementary roles within the context of a companionate relationship. Such a union would displace the common pattern of marriage – especially among the middle classes to whom Wollstonecraft directed her arguments – wherein 'emotional' women, their intellects stunted by being trained for domestic docility, sought material security and hence slavish dependence upon 'rational' men.

Here Wollstonecraft anticipates an understanding of the gendered character of the roles deemed appropriate for men and women. She rejected the representation of 'feminity' as a natural attribute, insisting that it was an artificial construct, made by men in their own interests and devised so as to deny the essential humanness of women. In debunking feminity she levelled her sights at, among others, her near contemporary, Jean-Jacques Rousseau (1712–78).

His educational tract, *Emile*, had asserted innate differences between the sexes which led him to consign women to dependence upon men. Rousseau had represented women as naturally emotional, weak and obedient, thereby lacking the attributes required for citizenship – reason, strength, autonomy – traits that he contended were naturally male. These asserted differences led Rousseau to prescribe wholly different educational philosophies for children: boys were to be educated to become rational, moral and self-governing individuals whereas girls were to be trained for domestic submission and to acquire the skills required to please and entertain their future husbands.

Wollstonecraft disdained this 'natural' distinction drawn by Rousseau, insisting upon the common ability of both sexes to engage in rational thought and action. In so doing she rejected the proposition that women were possessed of any singular qualities that were determined by their sex, albeit she did acknowledge that the 'peculiar destination' of most women was marriage and motherhood. But she envisaged women as enacting the independence gained from a common education within the domestic sphere, where they would exercise the tasks of household management rationally and efficiently: 'Make women rational creatures and free citizens, and they will quickly become good wives and mothers' (1974: 197). The astute Wollstonecraft was not shy of encouraging men to act on the basis of enlightened self-interest!

She did not, however, entertain the idea that the sexual division of labour within the family should be transformed, nor did she consider the family necessarily as the site of female oppression. This latter view was common to socialist and Marxist feminists, that is, in relation to the family in capitalist society, and was to be reinvigorated by radical feminists almost 200 years later. Moreover, Wollstonecraft restricted her understanding of working women to those who chose not to marry: the dual burden of household labour and paid employment was not contemplated by her because she addressed an audience who could rely on domestic servants to undertake the drudgery of housework.

Stressing equal rights, early liberal feminism was wedded to the achievement of formal legal equality for women and, in the work of Harriet Taylor (1807–58) and her second husband, John Stuart Mill (1806–73), was to encompass suffrage and widening opportunities for employment. A utilitarian liberal, rather than an exponent of natural rights like Wollstonecraft, Mill's advocacy was framed largely in terms of the benefits that would accrue to society from the implementation of equal rights. A wider array of talents would be available and moral progress more swiftly advanced if relations between men and women were placed upon an equal footing: in consequence, the sum total of human happiness would be increased.

Though allowing the possibility that married women might enter paid employment, Mill considered this choice the destination only of 'exceptional' women. It was more important that women were educated to the point where they could, rather than should, seek work outside the marital setting. Like Wollstonecraft, he envisaged married women as choosing to assume the roles of wife and mother. Harriet Taylor, however, held decidely different views. She actively encouraged women, single and married, to seek employment, not simply as a means of assuring financial but, more important, psychological independence. Paid employment would buttress self-respect and facilitate a genuine and equal partnership between wives and husbands.

Though Taylor's ideas on this matter were more expansive than Mill's she, like him and Wollstonecraft before, held internalised assumptions concerning the sexual division of labour. None proposed an equitable distribution of domestic tasks, blithely assuming that wives would supervise the running of the home. Even Taylor, the advocate of women's employment, presumed that the working wife and mother would juggle an occupation with domestic management. Here one encounters another problematic assumption shared by all three early liberal feminists. They took it for granted that the women they were addressing, drawn from the middle classes, would employ domestic servants, working-class women, who would wash, scrub, cook and polish.

This blinkered perspective reflected existing class divisions among women and represented a less than inclusive vision of emancipated womanhood. Moreover, none acknowledged that there might be structural causes of women's oppression rooted in the economic bases of early and developing capitalism. A more robust critique, not only of capitalism but also of the family, emerged from the utopian socialists of the late eighteenth and early nineteenth centuries.

Utopian socialist feminism

While the early liberals couched their feminist ideas in formal and rather abstract terms, and encouraged men to perceive the injustice and unhappiness caused by excluding women from the enjoyment of equal rights, the utopian socialists focused more upon the material inequalities intrinsic to a class-based society.

Historically, utopian socialism emerged between the natural rights philosophy of Wollstonecraft and the utilitarianism of Mill. However, while the early liberal feminists saw no contradiction between women achieving civil and political rights while remaining within the private sphere, utopian socialists – such as William Thompson (1775–1833), Anna Wheeler, alias 'Concordia' (1785–?) and Robert Owen (1771–1858) in Ireland and Britain, and Charles Fourier (1772–1837) and Henri Saint Simon (1760–1825) in France – understood women to be doubly oppressed: not only within the public sphere but also in the family, where they were treated as domestic slaves by their husbands. Here is an early anticipation of patriarchy's reach: the perception that women were subject to exploitation by men in both the public and private realms. Further, while liberal feminists sought to extinguish difference by adopting an androcentric perspective, some utopian socialists emphasised what they believed were the distinct qualities of women.

In general, utopian socialists understood marriage as practised in capitalist society to stunt the moral, cultural and psychological development of both women and men and to foster both selfishness and inefficiency. The solution lay in open, authentic relationships founded upon co-operation, itself nourished by the disposition to sympathy and benevolence intrinsic to human nature. For Thompson and Wheeler the achievement of civil and political equality for women was not enough: the economic dependence of women upon men had to be ended. This entailed the abolition of private property, the communal provision of those services normally provided in the home and an economy that redistributed resources on the basis of equality: such provision would contribute to the maximisation of human happiness.

The implications of this project for men and, particularly, women were profound. Freed from the economic motive for marriage, liberated from the toil of running a household, and enabled to engage in fulfilling and creative labour, men and women alike would reap the benefits of mutual support within a society where collective ownership meant none was advantaged by material possessions.

The utopian socialists differed from the early liberals in two important respects. First, they stressed the economic dimensions of equality; secondly, they drew a distinction between women's and men's natures. Here is a clear prefiguring of the sameness/difference polarity that was to be renewed in the wake of suffrage. Belief in the moral superiority of women underlay much of their writing, as did the conviction that the feminine virtues of caring, patience and fortitude endowed women with a capacity to promote benevolence and sympathy within the context of mutually supportive communities.

Besides seeking to establish the affinity between such virtues and communal socialism, utopian socialists expressed uninhibited and, for their time, controversial views about the joys of sexual fulfilment. For them in general it was not a case of sensibility triumphing over sense, but rather a harmony between physical and emotional needs and rationality that led to individual happiness and co-operative endeavour. Indeed, their advocacy of free sexual expression offered a marked alternative to the rather passionless companionate relationships preferred by Wollstonecraft and Mill.

Certain of the ideas of the utopian socialists were given practical application in the communal experiments initiated by Owen and followers of Fourier (see Chapter 4). The eradication of the sexual division of labour, the disavowal of marriage, coupled with the collective provision of child care and housework by both sexes, each demonstrated that the utopian socialists understood the rights of women to be integral and not marginal to the realisation of a genuinely egalitarian society.

Marxist feminism

The place of utopian socialism in the development of feminism is an important though rather neglected one. However, Karl Marx (1818–83) and Friedrich Engels (1820–95) dismissed its exponents and their prescriptions as 'un-scientific'. Wedded to a theory of history founded upon class conflict and a revolutionary transition to a socialist, and ultimately communist, society, they subordinated feminist ideas to the primacy of class struggle. This relegation of gender relations was to prompt non-Marxist feminists to accuse Marx and others of 'sex-blindness' and later even prompted some on the left to characterise the relationship between Marxism and feminism as 'an unhappy marriage'.

Such criticisms rest in part upon the virtual absence from Marx's own works of what socialists came to style the 'woman question'. Marx paid scant attention to relations between women and men, believing that female emancipation would be a by-product of the creation of socialism. As such the position of women, and of men, was taken for granted: the transition to communism would provide the context and the opportunity for sexual equality to prevail, just as day follows night.

While Marx understood, as did liberals and the utopians, that human nature was shaped by the social environment, he rejected the idea that it could be realised within capitalism or in the communal margins of co-operative association perched on the fringes of capitalist society. He insisted that free, self-determined human nature would flourish and sexual egalitarianism exist only with the transformation of capitalism, and that change required revolution by class-conscious workers, with all energies directed towards its achievement. All else was a mere distraction, hence women and men must engage in class politics, effectively setting aside the 'woman question' until capitalism was overthrown.

Marx's inattention to relations between the sexes was corrected by his friend and collaborator Friedrich Engels and the German Social Democrat August Bebel (1840–1913). Both exhorted women to throw in their lot with men in the common struggle to achieve a classless society, free of the exploitative relations intrinsic to capitalism. Private property would disappear and with it the materialist motive for marriage which had enslaved women. Neither Marx, Engels nor Bebel was opposed to marriage, but each contended that only in a socialist society would this relationship be based upon love and be free of male domination.

Marxists, then, viewed the subordination of women as an endemic feature of capitalist society, and one that would disappear under socialism. Of course, the 1917 Bolshevik revolution seemed to create the opportunity for the realisation of what Lenin (1870–1924) termed 'the real emancipation of women'. An exponent of equal rights for women, Lenin believed the path to emancipation lay through their full participation in economic and political life. Much energy was directed by the new regime into making public provision for tasks formerly undertaken by women in the private home: nurseries, kindergartens and public dining rooms were established as means of enabling women to play a full part in the economic and political mission to build socialism. Additionally, divorce was made easy, as was access to abortion facilities. Such provision, coupled with the mass entry of women into the work force, was seen as essential to ending domestic slavery.

The promise of revolutionary socialism was beguiling: in the event it was to be broken. After an initial flurry of activity and reform in the 1920s designed to secure 'equality of life' as well as equality of rights, the 'woman question' was to be neglected and the earlier reforms reversed with the accession to power of Stalin (1879–1953). By 1930, just thirteen years after the revolution, he was to declare the woman question 'solved'. Only with the demise of the Soviet Union has the full extent of women's subordination under communism been appreciated. Despite the advent of women into the public sphere, notably into paid employment, patriarchy, far from having withered away, was seen to have been deeply entrenched in Soviet society. Women suffered occupational segregation, just as in the West, were the object of successive pro-natalist campaigns and, like their Western counterparts, were expected to shoulder the double burden of unpaid domestic labour and low paid employment.

For later Marxist and socialist feminists the legacy of the Soviet Union has been discomfiting. While arguing that women were subject to material oppression under capitalism, being treated as a reserve army of labour, hired and fired at will and receiving only low wages, Marxists neglected the possibility that women were also vulnerable to patriarchal oppression. The premium that Marxism placed upon class solidarity thereby glossed over relations between men and women. The portrayal of them as class allies could not allow that patriarchy would endure once capitalism had been superseded.

This attempt to associate patriarchy with a particular economic system did not, however, persuade other feminists. Convinced of its universal character as a system of oppression, and underscored by the treatment of women in the Soviet Union and on the revolutionary left outside the USSR, radical feminists in particular were to accuse Marxism of sex-blindness. This charge, as we shall see, left socialist feminists in the second wave reeling and struggling to reconcile both the sex and class-based systems of women's oppression.

The 'other' woman

The achievement of female suffrage was a milestone in the evolution of feminist ideas, representing the acquisition by women of a basic political right. Yet, by the 1920s, there were alternative approaches to the means of consolidating that fundamental equality. As we have noted, in both Britain and the United States debate was joined between the exponents of the 'old' equal rights tradition of feminism and the 'new' welfare feminists, revolving around the issue of sameness and difference between women and men.

The idea of women's difference is in part explained by the association of women with nature, renewed with the advent of eco-feminism, as we shall see. Traceable to the origins of Western political thought, this association also characterised the emergence of modern science. As Coole (1993: 269–70) points out, Francis Bacon employed quite explicit sexual imagery to portray the character of scientific inquiry. Knowledge (male) was used to comprehend and control nature (female), thereby conveying a relationship of dominance and subordination between the sexes. Man became the active, inquiring, rational subject, woman the object of study, pliant and submissive. Embedded in such a view was the perception of man as 'self' and of woman as 'other', understood only in her relation to man.

The 'otherness' – if you will, subjection – of women was explored in detail by the French philosopher Simone de Beauvoir (1908–86), whose *The Second Sex* appeared in 1949, bridging the apparent gap between the first and second waves of the feminist movement. It is a vast work, informed by Marxism, psychoanalytic theories and existentialism's preoccupation with the ability of individuals to realise themselves. The work also posed the question 'What is a woman?' thereby foreshadowing the more recent concern with identity politics.

While recognising the economic subordination of women, as well as the constraints imposed upon them by the biological function of reproduction and the denial of equal civil and political rights, de Beauvoir was not entirely satisfied by structural or biological explanations of women's inferior status. Nor was she wholly convinced that either Marxist or liberal projects were sufficient to secure women's liberation. Instead, she argued that the project for woman was woman herself. Here was the influence of existentialism, a philosophy that insists upon the unique capacity that human beings enjoy for self-awareness and the ability they possess to make conscious choices to realise their existence.

Women, de Beauvoir argued, are required to understand not only that their 'otherness' has been imposed upon them by men, but that they have internalised this condition themselves. This signifies the psychoanalytic aspect of her ideas. She contested Freudian theory, which explained the female psyche in terms of penis envy – that women regard themselves as incomplete and, hence, imperfect men – and resolutely rejected the proposition that women's anatomy defined their destiny. Women, she insisted, were not fated to become submissive others whose existence was given meaning only in relation to, and by, men. Rather, they must realise their own capacity for self-awareness, make their own choices and celebrate their own needs.

This vision of women shedding their internalised sense of inferiority and overcoming their subordination did not mean that differences between the sexes would disappear. While biological distinctions would persist, the availability of contraception and abortion meant that women would be able to take control over their bodies rather than be enslaved by them: anatomy offered opportunity, not a destiny cast in marble.

In observing the social construction of womanhood – 'One is not born but rather becomes a woman' – de Beauvoir was to appeal to a subsequent generation of liberal feminists, concerned to expose and debunk gendered rationalisations of the inequalities confronting women. Equally, she was to strike a chord among later Marxist feminists because of her insistence that the material inequalities confronting women would be resolved only in a socialist society. At the same time, her encouragement of women to take control of their bodies was consistent with radical feminism's later concern with the politics of sexuality and repro-duction. In addition, her injunction that women should embark on an interior exploration of their selfhood was to commend itself to postmodern feminists more overtly concerned with the psychoanalytic aspects of women's identities. Her vision was prophetic and her legacy to feminism is rich and rewarding.

The second wave

The period between the first and second waves was not marked by feminist inactivity, although there was a certain ebbing of its tide. Following the Second World War, and within the context of the emergence, in Europe at least, of the welfare state, provision of publicly funded support for wives and mothers reflected the fact that women were being reprivatised within the home setting. In that respect, the agenda of self-styled 'new' feminists had prevailed: 'state feminism', if it can be described as such, wore a domestic hat.

But, far from generating a sense of fulfilment, the experience of being decanted back into home and family following their mobilisation during the war – into the armed forces, agriculture and industry – had merely created a sense of loss among many women. It was that sense of forfeiture that the American writer Betty Friedan (1921–) was to identify in *The Feminine Mystique* (1963), a work that many regard as a key text of second-wave feminism.

Her book was located firmly in the liberal tradition of equal rights feminism. Set within a cultural climate that prized women's domestic role, it exposed the image of the happy, contented housewife as a disabling myth. Hemmed in by fashionable theories of 'maternal deprivation', sociological works that endorsed a traditional division of sexual labour, and a popular culture which, in Friedan's words, portrayed married women as 'brainless, fluffy kittens' (and single women as dedicated to catching a husband), she argued that women had become trapped in a lifestyle that allowed them no independent identity or sense of achievement. She exhorted women to achieve educational qualifications and to re-enter employment as the means of escape from the gilded cage of domestic life.

In 1966, frustrated by the timidity of the US government in implementing the newly won equal rights for women enshrined in the 1964 Civil Rights Act, Friedan co-founded the National Organisation for Women (NOW). Its remit was 'To take action to bring women into full participation in the mainstream of American society now, exercising all the privileges and responsibilities thereof in truly equal partnership with men.' Within a year, NOW had published a bill of rights for women which endorsed the Equal Rights Amendment, urged the full enforcement of laws against sex discrimination, demanded equal educational opportunities for women, child-care centres and, most controversially, the right of women 'to control their reproductive lives'.

With the exception of the latter, which endorsed women's freedom to choose, NOW's agenda was fully consistent with mainstream American thought. It was no more, or less, than a set of liberal demands which argued for the removal of all legislative and economic barriers impeding women from participating in the full range of social, political and economic activities. It assumed no structural inequalities within society, unlike Marxist and socialist feminism, and appealed in large measure to well educated, middle-class, white, heterosexual women. Moreover, while challenging the prevailing gendered image of woman as the dutiful wife preoccupied with pleasing her man and children, it assumed that women would be enabled to pursue a career while supported by sweetly reasonable partners who were prepared to share in domestic tasks.

This reformist and rational view echoed the ideas of early liberals, although in encouraging women to enter the labour market it owed more to Harriet Taylor than to Wollstonecraft or Mill. But it was, nevertheless, reformist, believing that legislative and policy change, coupled with enhanced educational opportunities, would facilitate the entry of women into the public realm. Moreover, it accepted the family as a basic social institution, insisting that marriage could become an alliance of rational, co-equal individuals.

Friedan's renewal of liberal feminism was of course at odds with the socialist tradition of feminism that stressed the material basis of women's oppression. However, an emerging radical feminism rejected liberal and socialist feminism alike.

Radical critiques

In the United States radical feminism grew out of the campaign for black civil rights and the 'New Left' in the 1960s. While ostensibly egalitarian, these groups were discovered by women to be no less discriminatory and sexist than mainstream, or, as they became styled, 'malestream', organisations: 'We [men] make the policy, you type it up' was a common attitude confronting women. When in 1967 some 200 radical and leftist groups met in Chicago at the National Conference for a New Politics, the mainly male delegates dismissed as 'trivial' a motion to debate the problems of women (Bouchier, 1983: 52–3; Crow, 2000: 1–9).

This experience confirmed a growing belief among a number of women on the left of the necessity of developing new radical groups from which men would be excluded. Marginalised on the left, and unattracted to the liberal reformism of NOW, radical feminism began to crystallise around the issue of male power and privilege and generated a host of groups. These included the Furies, SCUM (Society for Cutting Up Men) and WITCH (Women's International Conspiracy from Hell), motivated to foment the liberation of women from patriarchy, not least on the left. An early statement of the centrality of patriarchy to radical feminism appeared in a 1969 manifesto issued by the New York group, Redstockings:

> Women are an oppressed class. Our oppression is total . . . We identify the agents of our oppression as men. Male supremacy is the most basic form of domination. . . . All men receive economic, sexual and psychological benefits from male supremacy. All men have oppressed women . . . we

will always take the side of women against their oppressors. We will not ask what is 'revolutionary' or 'reformist', only what is good for women.

(Crow, 2000: 223–35)

The representation of women as a universal 'sex-class' was developed by one of the authors of the manifesto, Shulamith Firestone (1945–), in *The Dialectic of Sex* (1970). Both the title of the book and the phrase 'sex-class' suggest something of an intellectual debt to Marxism. But, in place of the centrality of struggle between economic classes, Firestone depicted the driving force of history as the struggle between the biological classes. What was required to secure the liberation of women was, therefore, a biological, not an economic revolution, with women seizing control of the means of reproduction rather than the means of production.

Firestone, who dedicated her book to de Beauvoir, envisaged that new and developing technologies would liberate women by enabling fertilisation to take place without intercourse, embryos to come to term outside the womb and children raised outwith the context of the nuclear family. In the process, the family as a reproductive and economic unit would disappear and a society freed from sexually assigned roles would flourish. In its stead she, like her con-temporary Kate Millett (1934–), proferred a vision of an androgynous society wherein the virtues of men and women would be fused in a common identity.

Millett's *Sexual Politics* (1970) was the first second-wave text to elaborate at length upon the concept of patriarchy. According to Millett, the family is the basis of patriarchal relations, functioning to indoctrinate women to accept the power of men in both the public and the private worlds. By representing male power as intrinsic to domestic as well as public life she reinforced the idea of the personal as political. Unlike Firestone, however, Millett understood the oppression of women to be based upon the gendered construction of feminity rather than being determined by biological difference. As such, she insisted upon the necessity of a sexual revolution rather than the hi-tech solution favoured by Firestone. This entailed an end to monogamous marriage and the ideology of motherhood: the privatised family would be supplanted by collectively provided child care. But it was her endorsement of the free expression of sexual practices, whether heterosexual, bisexual, homosexual or lesbian, that distinguished her prescriptions. Only through such a transformation in consciousness and sexual activity would male supremacy be ended and both men and women evolve towards an androgynous future in which their positive qualities would be fused in a common humanity.

These visions of a society of androgynes did not appeal to radical lesbian feminists in the United States. Accepting fully the pervasiveness of undiluted patriarchy, they understood heterosexual relationships to be essentially about power: women in such relationships were accused of collaborating in their own oppression, of, in effect, sleeping with the enemy. The most explicit expres-sion of sexual politics was captured in the slogan 'Feminism is the theory, lesbianism the practice'. Lesbianism was regarded not as a matter of sexual preference, but rather as an essential political choice: one that signified the rejection of men as both sexual and political partners.

The response of Marxist and socialist feminism

The debate about the political correctness of lesbianism as a sexual practice, and of the feasibility of separatism as a political strategy, was not confined to the United States. In Britain the 'separatist' issue dominated feminist debate in the later 1970s and was to be the cause of a major split between a vocal minority of radical lesbian and liberal and socialist feminists loosely joined under the umbrella of the 'Women's Liberation Movement' (e.g. Coote and Campbell, 1987; Sebestyen, 1988; Rowbotham, 1990). While endorsing lesbianism as a freely chosen expression of sexuality, liberal and socialist feminists argued that political separatism offered nothing by way of engagement with the overwhelming majority of women who chose heterosexuality. Moreover, socialist feminists objected to the separatist strategy because it isolated women from their potential male allies, to whom they were ideologically wedded. However, the centrality of patriarchy to the renewal of feminist debate forced socialist feminists to respond to the charge that their ideological tradition rendered them sex-blind.

One such response was the Wages for Housework campaign. This and the accompanying 'domestic labour debate' of the early 1970s stressed the material contribution women made to the economy through their unpaid work within the home. The provision of state-funded domestic labour would, its proponents argued, raise the political consciousness of women (and men), and drive home the lesson that, without women's unpaid work in the home, capitalist society would collapse. It was, however, a debate that took a largely theoretical and somewhat abstract form among socialists, rather than engaging the attention of other feminists, still less women in general. Moreover, many socialist and non-socialist feminists objected to the idea of paying women for domestic work on the ground that it legitimised rather than confronted the prevailing division of labour within the family. Another response among socialists was to develop 'dual systems' theory, one version of which is associated with Heidi Hartmann. She argued that it was in the material interests of men, of whatever class, to perpetuate the sexual division of labour in both the public and the private realms (1986: 1–41).

From this perspective, men are seen to gain material advantages from the unequal division of domestic labour and from occupational segregation within the economy: horizontal segregation that divides jobs into lower-paid women's and higher-paid men's work; vertical segregation whereby women occupy only the lower-status positions within an occupation, now epitomised as 'the glass ceiling'. The combined effect, the argument ran, was to produce a mutually reinforcing system of exploitation that was termed 'patriarchal capitalism'. It was not enough to focus on the subordination of women within the economy: battle also had to be joined on the domestic front. Unless women struggled to make their partners aware of the double burden to which they were subjected, patriarchy would survive the transition to socialism.

While wedded to a material explanation of oppression, Hartmann sought to identify the functional interaction between the home and the capitalist economy in maintaining women's subordination, rather than focusing solely upon the wider economy. Without a dual strategy, tackling women's oppression in the home and economy, men would not relinquish their vested material interest in maintaining both patriarchy and capitalism. An alternative dual-systems theory sought to fuse the Marxist analysis of women's subordination with the insights offered by psychoanalysis.

Juliet Mitchell (1940–) argued (1974) that women's oppression could not be explained solely in material, but had also to be understood in psychological and cultural, terms. She focused on the family's role in transmitting to individuals their respective social identities as members of either the male or the female sex. In essence, Mitchell was seeking to accommodate patriarchal analysis by underlining the ways in which the family engendered women's and men's roles and, in the process, set a higher value on the latter. While understanding the appeal of patriarchy as a means of explaining the subordination of women, Mitchell rejected its determinism. She presented patriarchy as a socially con-structed value system, not as a fixed and universal condition based upon biological identity. From this perspective, patriarchy could be challenged and defeated.

This analysis, like that of Hartmann, marked a departure from orthodox Marxism. Rather than accepting that women were only materially oppressed in the home and the economy, Mitchell contended that they were also psychologically oppressed. The site of that oppression was the family. Visualising it as an agency that reproduced patriarchy by conditioning women to accept their subordination, she prescribed an ideological struggle within its confines. This meant that women should realise how they were subordinated in three 'structures of oppression': reproduction, the socialisation of children and the expression of sexuality. Unless these were transformed, patriarchy would not wither on the vine with the demise of capitalism, and the material oppression of women within the 'structure of production' would be sustained. A psycho-cultural revolution, led by women, was therefore crucial to the elimination of patriarchy.

Hartmann and Mitchell, in responding to the critique that Marxism is sex-blind, veered from its monocausal, class-based explanation of women's oppression. Both allowed patriarchy an independent existence, but dismissed the separatist solution preferred by some radical feminists as well as the reformist strategies of liberal feminists which, even if successful, would leave intact the structural inequalities endemic to capitalism.

The primacy of sexual politics in radical feminist analyses of women's oppression has left a profound mark upon feminist debate. By seeking to integrate patriarchy into their ideas, both liberal and socialist feminists have had to acknowlege its importance in explaining the continuing inequalities that beset women. However, rather than interpreting patriarchy in terms of biological essentialism, liberals in particular have sought to stress its gendered character by emphasising the cultural and psychological construction of women's roles. In the case of socialist feminists the experience has been rather more painful, involving some intellectually gymnastic attempts to reconcile patriarchy with the enduring attachment to materialist explanations of women's oppression.

Pro-family, eco- and pro-woman feminism

The significance attached to sexual politics by radicals has not been accepted by all feminists, notably those who perceive motherhood as a means of empowerment and fulfilment for women and who have generated a literature of pro-family feminism that has been characterised (dismissively) as 'maternal revivalism' (Segal, 1987: 145). What has united the proponents of this view – including Jean Bethke Elshtain (1981), Betty Friedan (1983), Germaine Greer (1984) and Sara Ruddick (1990) – is that motherhood is compatible with feminism: in effect, each has sought to rehabilitate maternity.

Greer's *The Female Eunuch* (1970) established her reputation as an influential (hetero)sexual radical of the formative stages of second-wave feminism. Opposed to monogomous marriage and conventional patterns of child-rearing within the nuclear family, she advocated plural child care within a transgenerational 'stem family' and, critically, the recovery of sexual energy by women. The unalloyed pursuit of sexual passion would, she believed, turn women from their pitiable feminine condition of passivity, dependence and sexlessness – engineered by the patriarchal motives of men – into dynamic, energetic and self-fulfilled individuals, especially in the bedroom. Through these means all differences, bar that of the physiological, would be eradicated.

By 1984, however, in *Sex and Destiny*, Greer came to expound a version of pro-family feminism that emphasised essential sexual differences between women and men. Continuing to reject the numbing isolationism and lovelessness of the suburban nuclear family, she identified the extended 'family' common to peasant communities as a realm within which mother–child relations and sisterhood – 'a word we constantly use without any idea of what it is' – can flourish.

Friedan followed up *The Feminine Mystique* with *The Second Stage* (1983), which represented something of a *volte-face*. In it she accused the women's movement of creating a 'feminist mystique' that 'denied the profound, complex human reality of the . . . biological relationship between woman and man . . . the reality of woman's own sexuality, her childbearing, her roots and life connection within the family' (p. 51). Sexual politics had, in her revised view, generated an adversarial relationship between the sexes and alienated women who sought fulfilment through motherhood. Having previously styled the nuclear family a 'comfortable concentration camp' for suburban women, she now presented it as one form of relationship within which women could satisfy their emotional needs.

While neither Greer nor Friedan equated the family only with its nuclear form, this is not true of Elshtain. In *Public Man, Private Woman* (1981) she assaulted the politicisation of personal life promoted by radical feminists, defended the privacy of child-centred family life and celebrated mothering as 'a complicated, rich, ambivalent, vexing, joyous activity which is biological, natural, social, symbolic and emotional' (p. 243). Embedded in these arguments is the celebration of biological difference and the dovetailing of motherhood with feminism.

A related perspective is also present in the development of 'pro-woman' feminism, one expression of which is ecological feminism. Like feminism itself, ecological feminism – or eco-feminism – embraces a variety of perspectives. It refers to the relationship between women and nature, but in terms that are entirely positive, unlike the dominant tradition in Western political thought that portrays the association between women and nature in ways that are detrimental to them both: the notion of 'otherness' referred to earlier.

Eco-feminism emphasises the connectedness of human and non-human nature, and insists upon the integrity of all living things. Its exponents equate the threat posed by the untrammelled exploitation of the earth's resources and its peoples by corporate organisations with the development of the arms industry by politico-military elites, and insist that these are feminist concerns. Both threats are seen to flow from an assumed masculine psyche, motivated to dominate and subject nature and 'others', including women. Just as patriarchy oppresses women, so too it oppresses nature, both human and non-human. The alternative is an ethic of connectedness and the creation of a sustainable, global economy, the realisation of which will reconstruct gender relations and transform the relationship between humans and nature: 'Nature has been feminised and women naturalised, so that understanding these connections is necessary to understanding their respective oppressions' (Val Plumwood in Code, 2000: 150–3).

Here we witness another challenge to the 'sameness' strategy adopted by mainstream liberal feminism. Instead of seeking to extend the concept of equal rights, as defined by a male model, the model is itself subverted because it is predicated upon a dualism – man = reason, woman = nature – that is hierarchical and oppressive: reason (male) deployed to subject nature (female).

Thus pro-womanism, including eco-feminism, stresses difference between women and men on an essentialist basis. More, it is gynocentric, tending to elevate women's qualities above those of men, thereby rejecting both andro-centrism and androgyny. Woman's attributes are seen to derive from their innate closeness to nature, to their bodies and to nurture. Hand in hand with these claims comes the rejection of rationality and instrumentality, which are seen to be characteristically male attributes. Pro-womanism asserts a biologically based, universal and established female character that transcends race, ethnicity and class. Such essentialism is most fervently expressed by eco-feminists, who equate men's rape and despoliation of the earth with their treatment of women and insist that the future of both can be assured only through the acceptance and diffusion of womanly virtues. A more radical expression of pro-womanism is found in the work of cultural feminists, including Mary Daly (1928–). She advocates (1984) withdrawal into a woman-only culture untainted by patriarchal constructions of femininity. Only in such a separate and segregated context can 'wild' and 'lusty' women express their natural and unrequited passions. At this end of the feminist spectrum one may also encounter notions of women's spiritual communion with nature, invariably caricatured by its non-feminist critics as the literature of the 'earth mother'.

The celebration of motherhood and essentialism has also provoked criticism from other feminists. In particular, pro-family feminists are regarded as having fallen headlong into a patriarchal snare by internalising a value system that has been insinuated by men into Western political thought. As such, they are accused of providing ammunition to anti-feminists who perceive women's natural place to be the home. Similarly, the advocates of cultural/lesbian separatism, retailing beliefs founded upon the essential superiority of women, have been criticised on the ground that patriarchy can be undermined only if it is confronted head-on, not avoided by a retreat into a women-only cul-de-sac.

Differences and subjectivities

The legacy of second-wave feminism was, and is, a critical discourse about patriarchy, underpinned by the insistence of radical feminists upon difference between women and men and the corresponding assertion that women share in a potential and universal sisterhood: sisters under the skin, as it were.[7] However, the demarcation of differences between the sexes, coupled with the assertion of an overarching unity among all women, entailed the neglect of the needs and agendas of ethnic minority women in the First World and of women in general in the less developed world. Western feminism, including radical feminism, thereby came to be regarded by non-white women as ethnocentric: focused upon the conditions of disadvantage affecting white women as if they had universal applicability. Mainstream feminism, from this perspective, was culpable of cultural and ideological imperialism. So disaffected were some 'black feminists' that they chose to style themselves 'womanists' as a signal expression of their rejection of their feminist 'sisters'.

bell hooks (1952–) is an eloquent critic of the colour-blindness of mainstream feminism in the United States and its complicity in perpetuating racial oppression: 'despite all the rhetoric about sisterhood and bonding, white women were not sincerely committed to bonding with black and other groups of women to fight sexism. They were primarily interested in drawing attention to their lot as white upper and middle class women' (1981: 142). She also articulates the dilemma black women face in tackling patriarchy within their own communities and white racism within the wider society: historically, the priority of the civil rights movement was, of course, to confront racism, with issues of gender (and class) relegated to a second order. This has posed particular difficulties for black women in the United States: challenging black male sexism laid them open to the charge that it would impede the struggle against racism. This disempowering accusation also consolidated black patriarchy: 'the equation of black liberation with black manhood promotes and condones black male sexism' (1996: 65). As a black feminist/womanist, hooks expresses the double-front in which she and others (Giddings, 1984) have been and are engaged: fighting against both the sexism of black males and the racism that is endemic in American society, and that has infused mainstream feminist discourse. The latter charge has also informed black feminist groups in Britain:

> The women's movement has never taken up the question of racism in any real way . . . [this] has ensured and will continue to ensure that the women's movement as a whole is irrelevant to the needs and demands of most black women.
>
> (Parmar, 1978: 55–66)

Such alienation fostered the growth of separate black feminist groups seeking to explore their own 'herstories' and identities, thereby further extending the facets of feminism and, among other things, generating a literature that essays black feminist thought (e.g. Collins, 1991; Mirza, 1997). The proliferation of such ethnically distinct groups not only challenges the presumption of universal sisterhood but also deconstructs the concept of a unified 'black womanhood'. In large measure, the emergence of such groups was to stimulate concern for identity politics.

Conclusion

The diversity of feminist thinking should by now be apparent. One reflection of this diversity is the availability of dictionaries, readers and encyclopaedias of feminist thought: their publication is testimony to the complexity of the doctrine. A taxonomy of contemporary feminism will include not just liberal, socialist and Marxist feminists but, among others, exponents of lifestyle, stand-point, cultural, ecological, postmodern, lesbian and both radical and 'black' feminisms. There is, in short, a rich menu of feminist theory on offer, with varying explanations of the causes of, and remedies for, women's oppression.

Such diversity may seem self-defeating because the complexity of feminism implies a political cost. If this body of thought is so plural, can 'feminists' – however defined – combine to press for change in the condition of women? The preoccupation with identity politics and the politics of subjectivities seems almost designed to create barriers among women. But to ask the question is to answer it. In local, regional, national and international arenas, countless numbers of women and women's groups come together to tackle both specific and more general disadvantages that qualify their life chances. Indeed, in many governments, including Britain, Ministers for Women and Women's

Departments have been established to mainstream the agendas set by feminist organisations, so much so that 'state feminism' is now a meaningful concept.

That said, the shift from margin to mainstream may come at a price. It may mean that women's groups have to abide by the rules of the political game established by men. For that reason, many feminists prefer to operate on the margins where they are free from what they perceive as state-sanctioned patriarchy rather than state feminism. But that does not prevent contemporary feminists, just like their predecessors, from combining in pursuit of their needs, rights and interests through a succession of strategic, if temporary, coalitions. Such coalitions need not be fully inclusive of all feminisms – indeed, there is something of a division of labour within the contemporary women's movement. Some, including liberal feminists, press for legislative and policy change and operate in the mainstream of politics, while others, including cultural feminists, prefer to operate on the margins of political discourse, creating their own, separate responses to the wrongs they perceive to afflict women. But this division of labour is functional: some help to set the political agenda, others see it through to legislative enactment and policy implementation.

Feminists of whatever persuasion do, however, share the status of social critic precisely because they are women-centred: women's experiences in various social and political contexts are the texts that are drawn upon to analyse and explain conditions of inequality and which supply the motive for change. It would, however, be misleading to suggest that one can reconcile the views of those who emphasise sameness with those who stress difference(s), between women and men and among women. Hence the need to reformulate the question: from 'Am I a feminist?' to 'What kind of feminist am I?'

Notes

1   For illuminating discussion of the relation between postmodernism and feminism see Bryson (1999: 36–43), Vincent (1995: 186–9) and Arneil (1999: 186–223).

2   For a contrary set of views see Butler and Scott (1992).

3   A brief summary of identity politics is provided by Linda Martin Alcott in Code (2000: 263–4).

4   See, for example, United Nations (2000). The Swiss-based Interparliamentary Union also produces periodic data on women's representation in national parliaments on a worldwide basis.

5   For a contemporary account of early second-wave feminism see Tanner (1971: 231–54).

6   For a summary of these criticisms see Bryson (1999: 28–30).

7   See Morgan (1970) for an unapologetic contemporary assertion of global sisterhood.

Further reading

Overviews of the evolution of feminist thought and the treatment of women within the canon of Western political thought abound. Among those which I found of particular use and interest were Diana Coole, *Women in Political Theory* (2nd edn, 1993), Valerie Bryson, *Feminist Political Theory* (1992), and Rosemarie Tong, *Feminist Thought* (2nd edn, 1998). Valerie Bryson's *Feminist Debates* (1999) supplies a balanced assessment of theoretical and practical questions confronting contemporary feminists. Also recommended are Judith Squires's *Gender in Political Theory* (2000), Chris Beasley's succinct *What is Feminism?* (2000) and Chris Corrin's *Feminist Perspectives on Politics* (1999), another happy blend of theoretical debate and practical politics.

Choosing among the texts that survey the evolution of feminism is a challenging undertaking. One short cut is to explore the collections included in a number of readers. Among the more eclectic collections are those edited by Mary Evans, *The Woman Question* (2nd edn, 1994), Sandra Kemp and Judith Squires (eds), *Feminisms* (1997), and Maggie Humm (ed.), *Feminisms: A Reader* (1992). More focused collections are Barbara Crow (ed.), *Radical Feminism* (2000), and Heidi Safia Mirza (ed.), *British Black Feminism* (1997). See also Miriam Schneir (ed.), *The Vintage Book of Feminism* (1995).

Histories of the women's movement abound, as do treatments of specific campaigns, including suffrage. Texts that address both suffrage and other campaigns in Britain and America include Christine Bolt, *The Women's Movement in the United States and Britain from the 1790s to the 1920s* (1993), and David Bouchier's *The Feminist Challenge* (1983). Martin Pugh's *Women and the Women's Movement in Britain, 1914–1999* (1992) is recommended for its scholarly and historical overview. On suffrage see Pugh's *The March of the Women* (2000), Ray Strachey's *The Cause* (1978), *One Hand tied behind Us* (1978) by Jill Liddington and Jill Norris, and Sylvia Pankhurst's *The Suffrage Movement* (1977). Other texts which survey the evolution of the women's movement that are worth inspecting include the five-volume Belknap series *A History of Women in the West*. The two most recent volumes are Volume IV, Genevieve Fraisse and Michelle Perrot (eds), *Emerging Feminism from Revolution to World War* (1996), and Volume V, Françoise Thebaud (ed.), *Toward a Cultural Identity in the Twentieth Century* (1996). See also the two-volume study *A History of their Own* (1990) by Bonnie Andersen and Judith Zinsser. A two-volume work more focused on feminist theory is Susan Miller Okin and Jane Mansbridge (eds), *Feminism* (1994). Dale Spender's *Women of Ideas and what Men have Done to Them* (1990) is a highly readable attempt to put women back into the history of ideas.

Debates concerning the development of feminist political thought in Britain also abound. Recommended are Juliet Mitchell and Ann Oakley's edited collection *What is Feminism?* (1986), itself a 'sequel' to the equally rewarding *The Rights and Wrongs of Women* (1979), also edited by Mitchell and Oakley. Terry Lovell's *British Feminist Thought* (1990) is a rich collection of writings by prominent second-wave feminists. On earlier first and second-wave debates see

Leslie Tanner's *Voices from Women's Liberation* (1971), a compilation of extracts by American women covering both the first and second waves of feminism. A comparable British focus on the early phase of second-wave feminism is provided by Micheline Wandor's *The Body Politic* (1972).

Classic primary sources include Mary Wollstonecraft's *The Rights of Woman* and John Stuart Mill's *The Subjection of Women*, available in one volume (1974) with an introduction by Pamela Frankau; August Bebel, *Woman under Socialism* (1971); Friedrich Engels, *The Origin of the Family, Private Property and the State* (1972); William Thompson, *Appeal of One-half of the Human Race, Women* (1983); Simone de Beauvoir, *The Second Sex* (1972); Betty Friedan, *The Feminine Mystique* (1963); and Shulamith Firestone, *The Dialectic of Sex* (1970).

On third-wave and postmodern feminism see Marysia Zalewski, *Feminism after Postmodernism* (2000), and Sarah Gamble (ed.), *The Icon Critical Dictionary of Feminism and Postfeminism* (1999). On 'Third World women' and feminist critiques of nationalism and nationalist movements see, respectively, Chandra Talpade Mohanty *et al.*, *Third World Women and the Politics of Feminism* (1991) and Nira Yuval-Davis, *Gender and Nation* (1997).

References

Andersen, Bonnie and Zinsser, Judith (1990) *A History of their Own*, London: Penguin.

Arneil, Barbara (1999) *Politics and Feminism*, Oxford: Blackwell.

Banks, Olive (1981) *Faces of Feminism*, Oxford: Martin Robertson.

Beasley, Chris (2000) *What is Feminism? An Introduction to Feminist Theory*, London: Sage.

Beauvoir, Simone de (1972) *The Second Sex*, Harmondsworth: Penguin.

Bebel, August (1971) *Woman under Socialism*, New York: Schocken.

Berry, Mary Frances (1988) *Why ERA Failed*, Bloomington IN: Indiana University, Press.

Bolt, Christine (1993) *The Women's Movement in the United States and Britain from the 1790s to the 1920s*, Hemel Hempstead: Harvester Wheatsheaf.

Bouchier, David (1983) *The Feminist Challenge: The Movement for Women's Liberation in Britain and the USA*, London: Macmillan.

Bryson, Valerie (1992) *Feminist Political Theory: An Introduction*, Basingstoke: Macmillan.

Bryson, Valerie (1999) *Feminist Debates: Issues of Theory and Political Practice*, Basingstoke: Macmillan.

Butler, Judith and Scott, Joan W., eds (1992) *Feminists Theorize the Political*, London: Routledge.

Code, Lorraine, ed. (2000) *Encyclopedia of Feminist Theories*, London: Routledge.

Collins, Patricia Hill (1991) *Black Feminist Thought: Knowledge, Consciousness and the Politics of Empowerment*, London: Routledge.

Coole, Diana (1993) *Women in Political Theory: From Ancient Misogyny to Contemporary Feminism*, 2nd edn, Hemel Hempstead: Harvester Wheatsheaf.

Coote, Anna and Campbell, Bea (1987) *Sweet Freedom*, Oxford: Blackwell.

Corrin, Chris (1999) *Feminist Perspectives on Politics*, London: Longman.

Crow Barbara, ed. (2000), *Radical Feminism: A Documentary Reader*, New York: New York University Press.

Daly, Mary (1984) *Pure Lust: Elemental Feminist Philosophy*, Boston MA: Beacon Press.

Elshtain, Jean Bethke (1981) *Public Man, Private Woman: Woman in Social and Political Thought*, Princeton NJ: Princeton University Press.

Engels, Friedrich (1972) *The Origin of the Family, Private Property and the State*, New York: Pathfinder Press.

Evans, Mary (1994) *The Woman Question*, 2nd edn, London: Sage.

Firestone, Shulamith (1970) *The Dialectic of Sex*, New York: Bantam Books.

Fraisse, Genevieve and Perrot, Michelle, eds (1996) *Emerging Feminism: From Revolution to World War*, A History of Women in the West IV, London: Belknap Press.

Friedan, Betty (1963) *The Feminine Mystique*, Harmondsworth: Penguin.

Friedan, Betty (1983) *The Second Stage*, London: Abacus.

Gamble, Sarah, ed. (1999) *The Icon Critical Dictionary of Feminism and Postfeminism*, Cambridge: Icon Books.

Giddings, Paula (1984) *When and Where I Enter: The Impact of Black Women on Race and Sex in America*, New York: Morrow.

Greer, Germaine (1984) *Sex and Destiny: The Politics of Human Fertility*, London: Secker & Warburg.

Greer, Germaine (1999) *The Whole Woman*, London: Doubleday

Hartmann, Heidi (1986) 'The unhappy marriage of Marxism and feminism: towards a more progressive union' in Lydia Sargent (ed.), *The Unhappy Marriage of Marxism and Feminism: A Debate on Class and Patriarchy*, London: Pluto.

Hill, Bridget (1986) *The First English Feminist: Reflections upon Marriage, and other Writings by Mary Astell*, Aldershot: Gower.

hooks, bell (1981) *Ain't I a Woman? Black Women and Feminism*, Boston MA: South End Press.

hooks, bell (1996) *Killing Rage: Ending Racism*, Harmondsworth: Penguin.

Humm, Maggie, ed. (1992) *Feminisms: A Reader*, Hemel Hempstead: Harvester Wheatsheaf.

Kemp, Sandra and Squires, Judith, eds (1997) *Feminisms*, Oxford: Oxford University Press.

Liddington, Jill and Norris, Jill (1978) *One Hand tied behind Us*, London: Virago.

Lovell, Terry (1990) *British Feminist Thought: A Reader*, Oxford: Blackwell.

Mill, John Stuart (1974) *The Subjection of Women*, London: Dent.

Mirza, Heidi Safia, ed. (1997) *British Black Feminism: A Reader*, London: Routledge.

Mitchell, Juliet (1974) *Psychoanalysis and Feminism*, Harmondsworth: Penguin.

Mitchell, Juliet and Oakley, Ann, eds (1979) *The Rights and Wrongs of Women*, Harmondsworth: Penguin.

Mitchell, Juliet and Oakley, Ann, eds (1986) *What is Feminism?* Oxford: Blackwell.

Mohanty, Chandra Talpade, Russo, Ann and Torres, Lourdes, eds (1991) *Third World Women and the Politics of Feminism*, Bloomington IN: Indiana University Press.

Morgan, Robin, ed. (1970) *Sisterhood is Powerful: An Anthology of Writing from the Women's Liberation Movement*, New York: Vintage Books.

Okin, Susan Miller and Mansbridge, Jane, eds (1994) *Feminism*, Aldershot: Edward Elgar.

Pankhurst, Sylvia (1977) *The Suffrage Movement*, London: Virago.

Parmar, Prathibha (1978) 'Other kinds of dreams', *Feminist Review*, 31: 55–66.

Pettman, Jan Jindy (1996) *Worlding Women: A Feminist International Politics*, London: Routledge.

Pugh, Martin (1992) *Women and the Women's Movement in Britain, 1914–1999*, London: Macmillan.

Pugh, Martin (2000) *The March of the Women: A Revisionist Analysis of the Campaign for Women's Suffrage, 1866–1914*, Oxford: Oxford University Press.

Randall, Vicky (1991) 'Feminism and political analysis', *Political Studies*, 34 (3), p. 516.

Rowbotham, Sheila (1990) *The Past is Before Us*, Harmondsworth: Penguin.

Ruddick, Sara (1990) *Maternal Thinking: Towards a Politics of Peace*, London: Women's Press.

Schneir, Miriam, ed. (1995) *The Vintage Book of Feminism*, London: Vintage Books.

Scott, Joan Wallach, ed. (1996) *Feminism and History*, Oxford: Oxford University Press.

Sebestyen, Amanda, ed. (1988) *'68, '78, '88: From Women's Liberation to Feminism*, Bridport: Prism.

Segal, Lynne (1987) *Is the Future Female? Troubled Thoughts on Contemporary Feminism*, London: Virago.

Spender, Dale (1990) *Women of Ideas and what Men have Done to Them*, London: Pandora.

Squires, Judith (2000), *Gender in Political Theory*, Cambridge: Polity Press.

Strachey, Ray (1978) *The Cause*, London: Virago.

Tanner, Leslie, ed. (1971) *Voices from Women's Liberation*, New York: Signet.

Thebaud, Françoise, ed. (1996) *Toward a Cultural Identity in the Twentieth Century*, A History of Women in the West V, London: Belknap Press.

Thompson, William (1983) *Appeal of One-half of the Human Race, Women*, London: Virago.

Tong, Rosemarie (1998) *Feminist Thought: A more Comprehensive Introduction*, 2nd edn, Sydney: Allen & Unwin.

United Nations (2000) *The World's Women: Trends and Statistics*, New York: United Nations.

Vincent, Andrew (1995) *Modern Political Ideologies*, Oxford: Blackwell.

Wandor, Micheline (1972) *The Body Politic: Writings from the Women's Liberation Movement in Britain, 1969–1970*, London: Stage 1.

Wilford, Rick and Miller, Robert, eds (1998) *Women, Ethnicity and Nationalism: The Politics of Transition*, London: Routledge.

Wollstonecraft, Mary (1792) *The Rights of Woman*, repr. London: Dent (1974).

Yuval-Davis, Nira (1997) *Gender and Nation*, London: Sage.

Zalewski, Marysia (2000) *Feminism after Postmodernism: Theorising through Practice*, London: Routledge.

The end of ideology?

Moya Lloyd

It may seem somewhat perverse at the end of a book outlining the parameters of competing political ideologies to offer a chapter entitled 'The end of ideology?' After all, the preceding chapters have contended in different ways that the work of ideology is anything but over. Each chapter has not only plotted the genesis and evolution of different ideologies, but has also assumed the continuing relevance of the ideology in question – even though the chapters on socialism and conservatism, for example, raise questions about the future shape of these ideologies in changing circumstances. Moreover, there is plenty of evidence within the field of politics to demonstrate the vitality of ideology. One has only to think about the responses of the US President, George W. Bush, to the events of 11 September 2001 when the United States was the victim of terrorist violence on its own soil, to realise the potency of, in this instance, liberal ideology. Take, for instance, the comments he made in his address to the nation on the day of the attacks: then Bush declared that 'America was targeted for attack because we are the brightest beacon for freedom and opportunity in the world' (http://www.whitehouse.gov/news/releases/2001/09/20010911-16.html). Similarly in a meeting the next day with his National Security Team, Bush proclaimed that 'Freedom and democracy are under attack' and that 'this enemy [al Qaeda] attacked not just our people, but all freedom-loving people every-where in the world' (http://www.whitehouse.gov/response/faq-what.html). His political rhetoric is thoroughly infused with liberal values and ideas, principally freedom, democracy and opportunity. Not only that, but he represents these values as symbolic of civilisation itself and, of course, presents his enemy as barbaric, immoral and lawless (see http://www.whitehouse.gov/news/releases/2002/03/20020311-1.html). What sense does it make then, in this context, to ponder the end of ideology? Surely the extracts from the speeches I have referred to exhibit clearly the power and pervasiveness of ideological thinking as a way of understanding the world, events within it and other people. So what, given all this, is the purpose of this chapter?

One look at its title should give a clue. The title does not baldly assert that ideology (or ideological thinking) has ended. The question mark suggests that our relation to the study of ideology should be interrogative. That is, we should ask questions not only about the contours of specific ideologies or about the nature of ideology as such: we should also ask questions about the continuing relevance of ideological thinking in itself. In other words, we need to consider whether ideological thinking gets us anywhere: does it actually help us to understand the world in which we live? In an era of globalisation and McDonaldisation, where differences between nations and cultures seem to have been eroded by the expansion of capitalism, the revolution in information technology and by the internationalisation (or rather 'Americanisation') of culture, are there really different ideologies competing for people's support? Or have our ideas and understanding of culture, politics and society converged to the point where we all share the same values? If such a convergence does exist, are we then all victims of 'false consciousness', that is, do we mistakenly believe that the dominant (bourgeois) ideology serves all our needs rather than merely protecting the interests of capitalists?[1] Or is a single ideology the only way that we can think of and comprehend the world around us? Moreover, if our values and ideals have converged, what sense can we make of the resurgence of national, religious and ethnic conflict across the globe? Is there something outside or beyond ideological thinking that can aid our understanding?

This injunction to question the significance of ideological thinking adds to the chart that MacKenzie outlined in the opening chapter. There he asserted that we needed first to map the ideological terrain by plotting the contours of specific ideologies. In essence, that is what this book has done. We have seen Michael Kenny consider the nature and contours of ecologism, Alan Finlayson explicate the parameters of nationalism and Robert Eccleshall account for both liberalism and conservatism as distinct ideologies with particular characteristics. MacKenzie also advocated a 'geological' investigation into the nature of ideology itself. In the introduction he excavated the ways in which thinkers as diverse as Destutt de Tracy, Karl Marx and Michael Freeden have articulated the nature of ideology. That is, he examined meta-theoretical assumptions about what ideology is. In other words, he asked questions about the underlying principles or ideas governing how ideology is theorised. (We might think of this as theory about the theory of ideology.) In this chapter I will add a third dimension to the debate: what might be loosely termed ideology critique. In the sense that I am using the term, ideology critique relates to three sometimes interrelated approaches to the study of ideology. First, it refers to the way that questions have been raised about the continuing relevance of ideology today. Second, it explores the question of whether or not the opposition laid down by some Marxists between ideology and science can be sustained. (Here it touches upon the geological approach noted by MacKenzie.) Lastly, ideology critique refers to the challenge laid down by some thinkers of a post-Marxist conception of ideology.

The question underpinning this chapter concerns the relevance of ideological thinking to our understanding of the political and social world. Importantly, this requires us to contemplate the operation of ideology in specific and determinate contexts. This specification of context for understanding ideology works in two different ways in the thinkers explored here. I begin by exploring the work of Daniel Bell. This is followed by an examination of the arguments put forward by Francis Fukuyama. Both Bell's and Fukuyama's contentions about ideology can be understood only in the light of the specific historical contexts in which they emerge and *to which they pertain*. That is, their arguments do not put forward general or universal claims about the nature and operation of ideology *per se*. They relate to ideology at a specific time and place. The second set of thinkers examined (the post-structuralist, Michel Foucault, and the post-Marxists, Ernesto Laclau and Chantal Mouffe) take a different approach. The conclusions they draw with regard to ideology may be taken to be general conclusions about the work of ideology *per se*, unlike the conclusions of Bell and Fukuyama. Their work also has to be set against the historical backdrop in which it emerged: once again the 'crisis of Marxism' is important but it has to be set alongside the emergence of post-structuralist ideas.

As the observant reader will have already noted, there is no direct mapping between the different styles of ideology critique noted above and the way that context plays out. There is, however, one theme that unites all the ideology critics examined in this final chapter: that is, they are all, in one way or another, responding to the challenges posed by the putative failure of Marxism.

The End of Ideology, or, Socialism is dead!

In 1960 the American sociologist Daniel Bell published *The End of Ideology*. Almost immediately the book produced an outcry and sparked a debate (that is still on-going) about the future of ideology. Taken by his critics to be arguing that all ideology was dead, Bell has been variously castigated for proclaiming the demise of ideals in politics and thus of political philosophy (Skinner, 1985: 3–4), for celebrating apathy and thereby endorsing the *status quo* (Mills, cited in Bell, 1988a: 142), for ignoring empirical evidence that contradicted his conclusions (Mills, 1968 126–40) and for failing to take account of the emergent radicalism of the 1960s (see also Waxman, 1968, and Rejai, 1971). Bell, it is contended, argued that ideological disputation had been replaced by 'limited technocratic disputes over problem-solving in industrial societies' (Lent, 1998: 7). Reflecting in a 1987 lecture upon the legacy of his book, Bell notes that 'There are some books that are better known for their titles than their contents. Mine is one of them' (1988a: 126). If *The End of Ideology* is not about the 'end of ideology' *per se* as critics have interpreted it, what is it about? What is the 'ideology' that Bell declares has 'ended'? To answer this, we need to look at the context of the book's composition. A clue to this is provided in the subtitle: *On the Exhaustion of Political Ideas in the Fifties*.

Throughout the late 1940s and the 1950s intellectuals in Western Europe and the United States, concerned about developments in the Soviet Union under Stalinism (the show trials, the imprisonment of millions in labour camps and the recently ended Nazi–Soviet pact), were engaged in a debate about the continued relevance of socialist ideology. Disaffection with developments in the Soviet Union translated into a general disaffection with socialist thinking. It is in this context and at this time that the idea of the end of ideology began to gain ground. The French philosopher Albert Camus, for instance, in 1946 counselled the French Socialist party to renounce Marxism 'as an absolute philosophy', as an example of the way 'our period marks the end of ideologies' (cited in Bell, 1988a: 133). In 1955 Raymond Aron, the French sociologist, ended his book *The Opiate of the Intellectuals* with a chapter entitled 'The end of the Ideological Age?' in which he contended that the conditions of ideological debate no longer existed in the advanced industrialised nations of the West. It was in this intellectual atmosphere that Bell's arguments originated. *The End of Ideology* is a book of and about a specific time and place: 1950s America. (Significantly, Bell is not the only American academic at this time to question the role of ideology in US political life: political scientist Seymour Martin Lipset included a chapter called 'The end of ideology?' in his book *Political Man*, 1963.) So what precisely is the basis of Bell's proclamation that ideology is dead and political ideas are exhausted in the United States (and by implication in Western Europe) of the 1950s? More specifically, what does Bell mean when he is talking about ideology?

An answer can be found if we turn to the epilogue of the book. Here Bell draws an important distinction between 'old' and 'new' ideologies. He describes the 'old ideologies' as those that emerged in Europe during the nineteenth century: they were 'universalistic, humanistic and fashioned by intellectuals' (Bell, 1960: 403). Their 'driving force' was social equality. Their goal was freedom. These were ideologies characterised by ideas of revolution, of action and of social transformation.[2] When Bell talks about the end of ideology, then, he means the end of these nineteenth-century ideologies that have informed politics in the West. But which ones were they? These were the ideologies of the left, or rather, of Marxism in particular. This is, of course, a much narrower, historically specific conception of ideology than one that refers in a general sense to bodies of ideas. Indeed, Bell regrets the fact that the term 'ideology' has been dehistoricised to the extent that it connotes any and all 'ideas, ideals, beliefs, creeds, passions, values, *Weltanshauungen*, religions, political philosophies, moral systems, [and] linguistic discourses' (Bell, 1988b: 321). This explosion of meanings of the term 'ideology' renders it ineffectual as a tool of analysis (specifically, for Bell, of sociological analysis). For Bell, ideology must be understood in more limited classical Marxist terms as 'an epiphenomenon' of economic developments: the 'fusion of class and politics' (Bell, 1988b: 324). It is this alone that gives it its validity or operational utility as a methodological tool.

When Bell contends, therefore, that ideology is not pertinent to the study of the United States in the 1950s, he means that this society cannot be examined in terms of ideology. The conditions that exist in the United States of the 1950s do not lend themselves to an analysis in class terms. Structurally, the United States at that time was experiencing neither deepening economic crisis nor an intensification of class conflict. Rather its industrial working class had shrunk and society was divided more along gender, age, ethnic and cultural lines than along class ones. The ideas circulating in this society were not mere outgrowths of class interest. The United States had become what he later termed a 'post-industrial society' (Bell, 1974). Methodologically, therefore, ideology understood in classical Marxist terms had no purchase in the United States of the 1950s. It was 'devitalized'; there were no longer 'easy "left" formulae for social change' and 'few issues . . . [could] be formulated any more, intellectually, in ideological terms' (Bell, 1960: 404, 405, 404).

When Bell sounded the death knell of ideology in *The End of Ideology* he did so in a very particular sense. He notified us that ideology understood in terms of class analysis had passed – it was no longer historically viable – and consequently sociology needed to rethink its analytical tools. Indeed, he reiterates this message even more forcefully in his reflections on his book almost thirty years after its composition when he questions the vitality of and viability of contemporary sociology's ability to understand *any* society affected by problems other than those relating to class (Bell, 1988b: 327–8). Ideology (in the limited classical Marxist sense) was incapable of generating significant observations about reality. It was impractical as a descriptive or analytic tool. It is because of its impracticality that Bell proclaimed his own approach to be 'anti-ideological' (1960: 16). The significance of *The End of Ideology* lies then in the gauntlet it threw down to intellectuals, particularly on the Left, to rethink the nature and extent of social change in modern societies (or, if they disputed Bell's analysis, which some did, to demonstrate the continuing viability of class analysis). This challenge became all the more pressing in the late 1980s as political certainties worldwide were shattered. Take the events of 1989.

The year 1989 was tumultuous in the political world. In the spring, students demanding democratisation occupied Tiananmen Square in Beijing, China. In June the tanks of the Chinese army ruthlessly crushed this protest. In July the trade union Solidarity was elected to govern Poland. Throughout the summer, thousands fled East Germany to the West, an exodus ultimately culminating in the fall of the Berlin Wall in December 1989. This was followed by a series of 'velvet revolutions' in Eastern Europe as one regime after another moved away from communism. Add to this the effect of Gorbachev's policies of *glasnost* and *perestroika* that led eventually if not directly to the dissolution of the Soviet Union. What sense could we make of these movements for social change? If Marxism was ideologically bankrupt as a tool of social analysis, as Bell charged, what other kinds of theories or ideologies in the non-Marxist sense were available to account for these events (especially since they seemed to demonstrate profound rejection of socialist beliefs and values and dismissal of its utopian vision of future society)? What occasioned this disillusionment, if such it was, with socialist ideology apprehended as a body of ideas? What did the 'end' of communism mean for ideology in general? In 1989 a deputy director of the State Department's policy planning staff by the name of Francis Fukuyama offered a highly contentious answer to this question in an article in a small American periodical, *The National Interest*. It signified what the title of his paper called 'The end of history?'. It is to this second version of the end of ideology thesis that we now turn.

The End of History, or, We're all liberals now!

To say that history has ended seems like a grandiose statement to make. Since 1989 there have been many historically significant political events, some reshaping the geopolitical world, others more local in their effects and orientation but no less important for that. Take the following: a post-apartheid South Africa was constructed, Northern Ireland experienced peace and an apparent end to terrorist violence, there was a war in the Gulf, Rwanda was decimated by civil war, and then on 11 September 2001 members of al Qaeda hi-jacked four US passenger planes and flew one into each of the twin towers of the World Trade Center in New York, one into the Pentagon in Washington DC, whilst the final plane crashed in Philadelphia (possibly because passengers wrested control of the plane from the hi-jackers). The result was massive loss of life. It was the first time that the continental United States had suffered foreign incursion on its territory.[3] Surely these events were historical events? What sense does it make, if any, to talk of an 'end of history' in such a context?

According to Fukuyama it means:

> not just the end of the Cold War, or the passing of a particular period of postwar history, but *the end of history as such*; that is, *the end point of mankind's ideological evolution and the universalization of Western liberal democracy as the final form of human government . . . the victory of liberalism.*

(Fukuyama, 1989: 4, emphasis added)

For Fukuyama, the end of history is not the end of political events of the order described above; it is the triumph of liberalism over other competing ideologies in the march of history towards its goal: fascism and Nazism were defeated after the Second World War; communism in the Eastern bloc was disintegrating; the fortunes of communist and socialist parties throughout Europe were waning; liberal capitalism was spreading throughout Asia, with some notable successes in South Korea, Taiwan and Japan; and the Chinese economy was becoming increasingly commercialised. Socialism, once a viable global alternative to liberalism, had been discredited. Those ideologies that persisted, such as nationalism and (religious/Islamic) fundamentalism, were merely local phenomena without the capacity for universalisation that would establish them as serious contenders to liberalism. The liberal state and capitalist economics had prevailed. Human history (in the West, at least) had reached its developmental end point.

As Fukuyama himself avers, the 'notion of an end of history is not an original one' (1989: 4). Although its most famous proponent is Marx, it derives from the work of G. W. F. Hegel. Fukuyama's own thesis is a reworking of Hegel's account, indebted to the interpretation of Hegel promulgated by Alexandre Kojève (a Russian *émigré* philosopher who gave a series of highly influential lectures on Hegel in Paris in the 1930s). According to Hegel, history is an evolutionary process moving towards a final culmination. In contrast to Marx, who focuses attention on material production and class conflict, Hegel's theory is idealist, that is, it focuses on developments in the realm of consciousness or what Hegel terms *Geist*, meaning mind or Spirit. History is thus the progress of *Geist* along a logically necessary path leading to the goal of freedom. For Hegel, history culminated with the triumph of Reason. At that moment a rationally ordered society and state would emerge. The tensions or contradictions that existed in previous historical moments (those between master and slave, for instance) would be transcended. Individual and collective interests would be harmonised within the rational state. Human freedom would be realised. With this very brief sketch of Hegel in mind, it is time to turn to Fukuyama's book, *The End of History and the Last Man* (1992) to see how these influences play out in his interpretation, for it is here that he elaborates upon the analysis he sketched in his earlier piece. (The question of whether he is faithful either to Hegel, or to Kojève for that matter, in the development of this thesis is a matter for debate elsewhere.)

Two factors lead, according to the author, to the cessation of history and to the attainment of liberalism. The first is natural science and the second, the human struggle for recognition. Let us take each in turn. Modern natural science, according to Fukuyama, alone is able to explain the 'directionality and coherence of History' (1992: xiv). It is the only activity that is progressive in direction and cumulative. Moreover, it is the only social practice that has a uniform effect on all those who experience it, because science follows the laws of nature and not of human invention. It is, in particular, the connection between natural science and the development of technology that is crucial. This guarantees human progression towards liberal democracy. How? First, nations possessed of technology are militarily superior to those without it. It guarantees their independence and thus their security. Secondly, technological advance has beneficial effects on economic development. Technology allows the continued accumulation of wealth and the satisfaction of continually expanding material desires (the so-called 'Victory of the VCR', Fukuyama, 1992: 98). What is more, this process leads to the homogenisation of societies; that is, all economically modernised societies, despite national and cultural variation, resemble one another. The logic of scientific or technological development pushes all states towards a universal consumer culture – guaranteed by the globalisation of markets (and he cites developments in Eastern Europe in support of this). Thus it is that societies will all eventually become capitalist. The emphasis on natural science, however, explains only one part of the movement of history towards liberalism (that is, the seemingly unbreakable connection of liberalism with the emergence of capitalism). In order to account for the development of liberal democracy, Fukuyama turns his attention to the other plank of his argument – the idea of the struggle for recognition.

For Hegel the essence of man is the desire to be recognised as fully human by others. (All other characteristics of his identity are culturally and historically determined.) This involves him in confrontation with others 'in which each contestant seeks to make the other "recognize" him by risking his own life' (Fukuyama, 1992: 147). Initially, this produces relations of master and slave as one conquers and the other concedes defeat in return for his life. Since a slave is not fully human, this relation is basically unsatisfactory and contradictory. The contradiction inherent in the relation is overcome by the French and, Fukuyama adds, American revolutions. These were democratic revolutions based on the principles of equality and liberty for all men. Here the inegalitarian relation between master and slave is replaced by 'universal and reciprocal recognition' embodied in the rule of law and the distribution of equal rights (Fukuyama, 1992: xviii). As Fukuyama puts it, liberal society is thus a 'reciprocal and equal agreement among citizens to mutually recognize each other'; liberalism is the 'pursuit of *rational recognition*' (1992: 200, original emphasis). Liberalism is the *only* ideology that can guarantee the universal recognition of humanity. No others can. The spread of capitalism and of liberal democracy around the globe indicates to Fukuyama the necessary logic of historical development as more and more countries move towards the End of History. The spread may be uneven (some states remain in History while others are post-historical) but in the West history has ended. There are no ideologies remaining that can compete with liberalism.

Needless to say, just as Bell's earlier book had spawned a debate, so too Fukuyama's intervention generated considerable interest, not all of it favourable. Charges of inconsistency were levelled at his argument (Ryan, 1992); critics contended that Fukuyama was simply defending the ideological *status quo* (Norris, 1991) whilst others challenged the idea that the demise of communism meant the end of socialism as such (Anderson, 1992; Hobsbawm 1995; see also Bertram and Chitty, 1994 and Kumar, 2000). Two sets of criticism are of particular interest, though. Fukuyama, as we have seen, yokes together capitalism and liberalism in his account of historical development. There is, however, a question mark hanging over the potential for continued economic expansion across the globe that challenges Fukuyama's claim that people's material desires can be endlessly sated. As many environmentalists and ecologists have pointed out, present levels of capitalist development are just not sustainable (Anderson, 1992; see also Chapter 7 in this volume). They threaten the very existence of humanity. The spate of anti-globalisation demonstrations in recent years reveals the extent to which many people have rejected capitalist values and the proliferation of desires in need of satisfaction produced by capitalism. Some of these people have already begun to embrace an ideology that rejects such materialism: environmentalism. Is environmentalism, then, a possible rival to liberal ideology as a value system that could be universalised? There is, after all, nothing parochial or local about its concerns; quite the converse. Could environmentalism itself be the end-historical ideology?

Doubt is also cast on Fukuyama's analysis from another quarter. The American political scientist Samuel Huntington accuses Fukuyama of failing to realise that developments in the West are not 'universal' developments that the rest of the world will inevitably follow (1993, 1997). Counterposing the triumph of liberalism against the decline of communism merely perpetuates Cold War thinking and ignores what is happening elsewhere in the world, where religion, in particular, is 'a, or perhaps *the*, central force that motivates and mobilizes people' (Huntington, 1997: 66–7, original emphasis, see also Kumar, 2000: 64–6). For Huntington future conflicts will be based around 'cultural' factors, that is, clashes between different civilisations over questions of ethnicity, religion, and so on. (The wars in the Gulf and in Bosnia seem to confirm this.) Significantly, for Huntington, the clash of civilisations also includes the rejection by many non-Western nations of Western values (including those of capitalism and democracy). This is a position Huntington regards as typified by Islam. In the light of 11 September this is a prescient observation. Recall that al Qaeda not only 'bombed' the 'liberal' United States but by targeting the World Trade Center, it also attacked capitalism, symbolically at least. Are liberal values as universal as Fukuyama pretends? Did the end of the Cold War and the decline of communism really signal the triumph of liberalism after all?

In the two accounts that we have considered so far we have seen two competing conceptions of ideology at work. Bell operates with a conception of ideology as a method of assessing 'conflicting claims about the reality of social structures' (MacKenzie, 1994: 12). By comparison, Fukuyama treats ideologies as competing sets of values and ideas about how one ought to live one's life. When each talks about the end of ideology, they talk therefore about different things. In the next section I return to the question raised by Bell's thesis of the capacity of ideology to assess reality by considering the work of Michel Foucault. Foucault, who famously refused to define his position (1997: 113), may nonetheless usefully be categorised as a post-structuralist thinker. (Others include Jacques Derrida, Jean-François Lyotard and Jacques Lacan.) Post-structuralism is a notoriously difficult concept to define, not least because it is used interchangeably with the term 'postmodernism'. Simplifying considerably, however, we can say that it consists in a refusal of a number of key themes that characterised modern thought from liberalism to Marxism. It thus rejects teleological or progressive accounts of history; the idea of the unified subject, that is, that the subject has a stable and defining core (such as the conception that man is, above all else, rational); overarching – or 'totalising' – explanations; and the idea of absolute truths or values. It is useful to keep this description in mind when considering Foucault's account of ideology. For, unlike either Bell or Fukuyama, for whom there are ideologies whose time has ended (the redundancy of ideological analysis in the United States of the 1950s or the disappearance of competitors to liberalism in the West at the century's end), Foucault contests the very notion of ideology itself. He does so by engaging, implicitly at least, with the ideas of one of the twentieth century's leading neo-Marxists, the French philosopher Louis Althusser.

Farewell to ideology: Foucault *contra* Althusser

Althusser set out his account of ideology and science in *For Marx* (1969), originally published in French in 1965. Ideology for Althusser is a 'system (with its own logic) of representations (images, myths, ideas or concepts, depending on the case) endowed with a historical existence and role within a given society' (1969: 231). Science, by contrast, is knowledge produced through theoretical practice.[4] The crux of the difference between ideology and science concerns the functions that each performs. Ideology is 'a matter of the *lived* relation between men and their world' (Althusser, 1969: 233). It has a 'practico-social' function, in contrast to the 'theoretical' function of science. Ideology is additionally 'an organic part . . . of every social totality', a 'structure essential to the historical life of societies' (Althusser, 1969: 232). It has an indispensable role to play in all societies (including, importantly, a future communist society).

What's more, ideology is not merely, or even mostly, conscious; it is in great part unconscious. That is, people are largely unaware that their activities and beliefs are ideological. In this ideology consists, as he puts it in a later essay, in the 'imaginary relationship of individuals to the relations of production' (Althusser, 1971: 155). This imaginary relationship is one that *'expresses a will* (conservative, conformist, reformist or revolutionary), a hope or a nostalgia' (1969: 234). It does not describe reality. So ideology determines the real historical conditions of people's lives, their beliefs and how they experience the world. Rejecting the idea that ideology implies falsity (or false consciousness, we might say), Althusser sees it as a coherent and logical way of making sense of the world. But this making sense may itself involve misrepresenting power and class relations. I may believe, as Fukuyama suggested, that capitalism allows the expression of individual freedom when the reality is that I am exploited at work every minute of every day; that far from being free I am a 'wage slave'. As Althusser remarks in *For Marx*: 'it is clear that *ideology (as a system of mass representations) is indispensable in any society if men are to be formed, transformed, and equipped to respond to the demands of their conditions of existence'* (1969: 235, original emphasis).

There is much more that could be said about Althusser's views on ideology (see Barrett, 1991). For the purposes of this chapter, however, I want to turn to the work of one of Althusser's former pupils: the French philosopher Michel Foucault. During the course of an interview Foucault offered the following critique of ideology:

> The notion of ideology appears to me to be difficult to make use of, for three reasons. The first is that, like it or not, it always stands in virtual opposition to something else which is supposed to count as truth . . . The second drawback is that the concept of ideology refers, I think necessarily, to something of the order of a subject. Thirdly, ideology stands in a secondary position relative to something which functions as its infrastructure, as its material, economic determinant, etc. For these three reasons, I think that this is a notion that cannot be used without circumspection.
>
> (Foucault, 1980: 118)

In brief, then, Foucault offers three reasons for rejecting ideology: first, because ideology is seen as the opposite of truth or science; second, because of its link with the subject; and finally, because it relies upon the base–superstructure model of Marxism. It is, of course, the first of these that is most important in respect of Althusser. Why specifically does Foucault reject the pairing of ideology and science proposed by Althusser? His answer concerns how we understand truth. For Foucault:

> the problem does not consist in drawing the line between that in a discourse which falls under the category of scientificity or truth, and that which comes under some other category [ideology, say], *but in seeing historically how*

> *effects of truth are produced within discourses which in themselves are neither true nor false.*

(1980: 118, my emphasis)

Two points are of note here: first, Foucault rejects the idea that ideology and science are of a different order in relation to truth. That is, science is no more truthful than ideology; ideological thinking no more distorted or false than scientific thinking. Second, instead of trying to discern which is more truthful, we should examine the way in which 'effects of truth' are produced. That is, we should explore what he calls 'regimes of truth' (Foucault, 1980: 131). To do this, first we need to examine discourse. Discourse, for Foucault, connects language and practices (Foucault, 1972). Discourses bring together groups of statements that combine to produce and delimit an area of knowledge (say, psychoanalysis). They operate by a set of internal rules and procedures. These rules and procedures are what then enable the psychoanalyst, in this case, to practise psychoanalysis. They determine what s/he does, says and thinks in relation to psychoanalytic practice. How then do these relate to regimes of truth?

By regimes of truth Foucault means a '"general politics" of truth: that is, the types of discourses which it [society] accepts and makes function as true' (1980: 131) together with the techniques that enable us to distinguish true from false; the methods society approves of as appropriate to the acquisition of truth; and who is charged with speaking the truth. In today's society, we generally see science as a more truthful 'discourse' than magic; experimentation as more valid than reading tea leaves; and a doctor as a more legitimate authority on the state of our health than a soothsayer. Despite the fact that we make such a differentiation, the point for Foucault is that neither science nor magic is more authentic than the other. The fact that science is perceived today as more authoritative is *political*: a matter of power. Truth for Foucault is very much 'a thing of this world' (1980: 131). It is a way of referring to the 'system of ordered procedures' (Foucault, 1980: 133) that produce, regulate, distribute and circulate the statements that we regard as 'true'. In this it is intrinsically connected with power.

Systems of power produce and reinforce the truth. Truth produces power effects; and paradoxically power produces truth effects. Power and truth are not opposites. Returning to ideology, the point for Foucault is that any opposition between ideology and science is untenable. Both are truth effects secured by, and producing, effects of power. Instead, therefore, of placing ideology and science at the heart of analysis, Foucault suggests focusing on the interconnections of truth and power (or power/knowledge, as he puts it in his later work). Concentrating on ideology merely masks what the real work of analysis should be: 'truth itself' (Foucault, 1980: 133).

What though of Foucault's second and third reasons for jettisoning ideology: its relation to the subject and its secondary status? When talking about the subject in this context, Foucault is referring to the idea of a unified subject (possibly with certain essential qualities – the capacity for creative labour, described by Marx as 'species-life'). This is the subject that is deceived by the workings of ideology; the labourer under capitalism who does not see himself as alienated but rather as a free individual who has chosen to sell his labour power to company X. His beliefs, however, are ideological rather than real in the sense that they are false; objectively he is alienated. Moreover, this is the subject who will be able to liberate himself from the deception and achieve emancipation.

Foucault offers a different account of the subject. He rejects the idea that there is anything essential to humans (reason, labour power, etc.). Instead, as we noted earlier, Foucault sees subjects as the effects of power/knowledge. There is nothing natural about us. The qualities we are ascribed (sex, rationality, compassion, emotion and so forth) are effects of particular discourses and practices. One of Foucault's famous examples is the creation of the homosexual. According to his *History of Sexuality* (1978), sexologists and psychoanalysts (including Freud) produced the category of the homosexual at end of the nineteenth century. These forms of power/knowledge created a new identity, spawning new terms and new laws of sexual behaviour. The homosexual did not exist before this point. No one, that is, would be regarded as homosexual or would recognise him or herself as such until sexology and psychoanalysis created the category. One might argue that something similar is at work in the production of 'race-d' subjects (see, for instance, Carter, 1997). Here discourses of immigration, scientific racism and imperialism, together with practices such as censuses, recording births and the use of passports, converge to form a power/knowledge nexus that creates particular categories of 'race-d' subject (say, those who see themselves as, and are seen by government as, subjects of a particular nation and thus entitled to certain benefits from that nation). In dismissing ideology Foucault is also dismissing its understanding of the subject and offering an alternative account in its place.

Foucault's final objection to ideology concerns its secondary status. Foucault rejects the idea common to many forms of Marxism of an economic base determining the cultural and political superstructure. Nothing, for Foucault, has the determinist role of the economy. That is, there is no overall logic such as capitalist logic behind the beliefs operating at any one time, the kind of subjects that exist, or the way that society as a whole is organised. Quite the contrary: discourses and practices emerge in chance and haphazard ways. Indeed, it is one of the features of Foucault's work that he stresses the importance of local 'micropractices' of power. Often it is at the margin or periphery that new technologies of power or new discourses are produced. These technologies or discourses may be appropriated or utilised later on for different purposes than those for which they were initially conceived. Psychoanalysis appropriates (and modifies) the practice of confession common to Catholicism; television shows such as *Oprah* appropriate the confession for another purpose: voyeuristic television. Alternatively, a technique such as ultrasound, used primarily for the detection of foetal abnormality (and potentially tied to abortion), gets borrowed for other purposes: for sex determination and, in some cases, sex selection; or, by showing film of a foetus gathered through ultrasound, to bolster the claims of the anti-abortion movement that the foetus is a 'separate entity – in need of protection' (Zalewski, 2000: 120). The point, for Foucault, is that there is no necessary logic linking one element with another. His is an anti-reductionist account, in the sense that he repudiates any idea that the economic base determines all other political, social and cultural phenomena. (Unsurprisingly, Foucault also abandons the teleological history of Marxism.)

In rejecting ideology, Foucault is rejecting the tenets of Marxism and in their place offering an alternative scheme of thinking. Needless to say his alternative has generated considerable interest, both critical and supportive. The advantage of his account is that it allows the consideration of aspects of identity other than class. One of the most strident criticisms of Marxism throughout the 1960s and 1970s, a period that saw the emergence of new social movements (the women's movement, the gay and lesbian movements, environmental groups and anti-racist groups, for instance), was that it tended to treat non-class aspects of identity as epiphenomenal to class. Additionally, it allows consideration of the chaotic and chance way in which particular practices develop and extend throughout the social body. Critics would argue, however, that these advantages do not compensate for the deficiencies of Foucault's approach. First, his approach is incapable of dealing with structural inequalities – that is, with the systematic nature of power. Second, by representing truth as an artefact, he undercuts any attempt to discriminate between true and false (and, by extension, between good and bad). This latter, in particular, might be taken to imply that there is utility, after all, in holding on to the idea of ideology. To explore this further, I turn now to the work of post-Marxists, Ernesto Laclau and Chantal Mouffe.

Ideology and hegemony: from Gramsci to Laclau and Mouffe

In many ways, the ideas of Laclau and Mouffe, as we will see, bear affinity with the ideas of Foucault. This is because, like Foucault, Laclau and Mouffe utilise insights drawn from post-structuralism (including the work of Foucault) in the development of their theory. Yet there are differences between them. Some of these may be traced to the fact that, unlike Foucault who abandons Marxism, Laclau and Mouffe continue to utilise certain Marxist concepts. One such is ideology. For this reason Laclau and Mouffe are taken to be exponents of post-Marxism, understood as a blending of post-structuralism with Marxism.

When Laclau and Mouffe refer to ideology they usually do so in connection with the concept of hegemony. This is a concept drawn from the work of the Italian Marxist, Antonio Gramsci. In his *Prison Notebooks* (penned between 1929 and 1935 whilst he was imprisoned under Mussolini's fascist regime) Gramsci develops the idea of hegemony to analyse culture and politics.[5] Building on the Marxist conception of ideology, captured in Marx's epithet 'The ideas of the ruling class are in every epoch the ruling ideas' (1977: 176), Gramsci offers an account of the way that ruling ideology is produced, maintained and reproduced. Hegemony, or 'political leadership' (Gramsci 1985: 104), operates not simply by coercion or the direct imposition of ruling ideas on the subordinated groups, but also crucially by winning the active 'spontaneous' consent of the dominated. Indeed, Michèle Barrett surmises that 'hegemony is best understood as *the organisation of consent*' (1991: 54). This means, of course, that hegemony can be maintained only to the degree that the ruling bloc (different factions of the ruling class and other social forces working together, albeit uneasily) is able to frame the way in which reality is defined for the majority of people, such that the power of the bloc seems to be natural and legitimate. Ideology is crucial to this. Critically, Gramsci distanced himself from those versions of Marxist ideology that imply a 'negative value judgement' of the kind that ideological thinking is 'useless, stupid, etc.,' (1971: 376). His concern was with 'historically organic ideologies', those that are historically necessary. These have a 'validity', he declares, 'which is "psychological"; they "organise" human masses, and create the terrain on which men move, acquire consciousness of their position, struggle, etc.' (Gramsci, 1971: 376–7).

Ideologies are sets of ideas, meanings, and ways of behaving, furnishing practical rules to live by; what he calls 'common sense'. Ideologies can take different forms, from the systematic to the popular. This implies that at any one time there will be competing ideologies battling it out for consent. (Gramsci was especially interested in the ways in which popular – less systematic – knowledge and culture emerged and worked to ensure the involvement of the masses in the strategy of the ruling bloc.) For Gramsci, one of the ways in which class struggle is played out is ideologically. It is all about one bloc attempting to have its version of reality spontaneously accepted as natural and legitimate by others. When that happens, that bloc has achieved a hegemonic position. To reiterate: this does not imply passive subordination on the part of the masses but rather their active and practical participation. Unsurprisingly, as an active communist himself, he is particularly concerned with how the working classes ought to construct a hegemonic ideology. It is important to stress that no hegemony is ever secure but rather is always unstable. It has to be continually maintained. Gramsci's description of the state seems apt as a description of hegemony: it is 'a continuous process of formation and superseding of unstable equilibria . . . between the interests of the fundamental group and those of the subordinated groups . . . equilibria in which the interests of the dominant group prevail, but only up to a certain point' (1971: 182; see also Barker, 2000: 61).

A number of points are worth drawing attention to in respect of Gramsci's approach. First, the attention Gramsci paid to cultural leadership signalled the need for a rethinking of the Marxist idea of the superstructure. For many Marxists, following Marx's argument in *Contribution to the Critique of Political Economy* (1859), a distinction could be drawn between the economic base and the superstructure (the realm of politics, culture, law and ideology). The base was regarded as determinant. Everything that happened at the level of the superstructure merely reflected developments in the base. On this economistic reading (that is, one where economic factors are given priority), politics and ideology were secondary phenomena. They were understood as expressions of underlying economic change. Gramsci's account of hegemony challenged this deterministic account. The superstructure could no longer be theorised as a 'pale reflection of socio-economic organization' (Bates, 1975: 353). It was far more than that. Activities in this sphere could themselves affect what happened at the economic level. Politics and economics could not simply be regarded as entirely separate; they were interconnected. Gramsci's account thus implied a non-determinist theory of ideology (Mouffe, 1979: 178); that is, ideology was not merely a reflection of economics.

This leads on to the second point. Gramsci also challenged the claim that politics was principally concerned with control of the state. The superstructure had two significant dimensions: the state and civil society, each operating via different methods. By the state Gramsci means, quite simply, public institutions such as the government, the army, the police and the judiciary. These operate via coercion or direct domination. By contrast, civil society refers to 'private organisms' such as schools, churches, the media, cultural and voluntary associations (such as clubs) and political parties. These latter all contribute to the formation of social and political consciousness, to the production of ideological hegemony. Civil society was, as such, a key site of political struggle. The hegemonic class, for Gramsci, was the one that combined leadership of a bloc of social forces in civil society as well as leadership in the sphere of production and the state. This greater attention to society (over the state), as we will see, crucially informs the ideas of Laclau and Mouffe.

The final point to note is that Gramsci's principal (though not exclusive) focus is on ideology and *class*. As noted in relation to Foucault, however, the emphasis on class in Marxism has been subject to vigorous criticism from various quarters. Significantly, Gramsci's ideas about hegemony *implied* (even if they didn't emphatically demonstrate) that ideology might not necessarily be tied to class. Two important features of his work were, after all, the idea, first, that hegemony consisted in a series of alliances between classes and other social forces and, second, that ideology was the cement that bound together these classes and forces. This suggests that if an ideology was to become hegemonic it could not be simply a class ideology; it had to incorporate other non-class elements so as to produce a new 'common sense' that appealed to a range of social groupings. What is merely implied in Gramsci's theory about class is taken up explicitly in the work of Laclau and Mouffe. Rather than ditching the notion of ideology, as Foucault had, Laclau and Mouffe attempt to reformulate it, in the process severely diluting its class-related (and possibly its Marxist) elements.

Near the start of their book *Hegemony and Socialist Strategy* Laclau and Mouffe set out their stall on the future of socialism; they declare:

> What is now in crisis is the whole conception of socialism, which rests on the ontological centrality of the working class, upon the role of Revolution,

with a capital 'r' . . . and upon the illusory prospect of a perfectly unitary and homogeneous collective will that will render pointless the moment of politics.

(1985: 2)

Marxism, on their reading, is based upon a particular political 'imaginary' that sees class as central to political struggle and classes as pre-given and that regards History 'in the singular', that is, where History is understood as having one underlying purpose and a *telos*, or end – the attainment of communism in this case. This 'Jacobin imaginary', as they label it, invokes a very specific conception of society. Marxism, Laclau and Mouffe claim, considers society to be 'an intelligible structure' (Laclau and Mouffe, 1985: 2). In other words, Marxism assumes that the nature of society can be known and understood. On a Marxist reading, society is a class structure that is governed on the basis of class position (such that the ruling class 'rules' over society) and that can be recreated by an act of political will. Thus the proletariat – via revolution – will create a new society, one that is socialist or, ultimately, communist.

According to Laclau and Mouffe, this socialist (or 'Jacobin') political imaginary is currently 'at a crossroads' for two reasons. First, there have been a number of historical events that have cast doubt on the effectiveness of socialism and socialist struggle, 'from Budapest to Prague and the Polish *coup d'état*, from Kabul to the sequels of Communist victory in Vietnam and Cambodia' (Laclau and Mouffe, 1985: 1). All these events, they suggest, challenge the nature of socialism and the manner in which socialism was attained and maintained. Second, Marxism as a theory has been put into question by the emergence of various types of social conflict that are *not* based on class: 'the rise of the new feminism, the protest movements of ethnic, national and sexual minorities, the anti-institutional ecology struggles . . . the anti-nuclear movement . . .' and so on (Laclau and Mouffe, 1985: 1). Together these factors imply, for Laclau and Mouffe, that Marxism requires reformulating; it needs to address the challenge posed by the new social movements for a more egalitarian and democratic society and it needs to question what such a society will look like and how radical democracy may be attained. This in turn requires a rethinking of the nature of society. So what does their revised account of ideology and politics look like?

Noting that 'everything depends on how ideology is conceived', Laclau and Mouffe draw inspiration from Gramsci's account of ideology and hegemony. Two aspects are important: first, for them Gramsci challenges simple 'superstructuralist' readings of ideology as false consciousness by presenting ideology as a form of 'organic cement' that fuses together a historical bloc around certain principles or ideas. Second, Gramsci's account is anti-reductionist. That is, he does not see ideology as necessarily and inevitably tied to class. They note that 'political subjects' are not, strictly speaking, 'classes, but complex "collective wills"' and so the ideology of the hegemonic class does not have 'a necessary class belonging' (Laclau and Mouffe, 1985: 67). This allows Laclau and Mouffe to argue for a material conception of ideology that is, nevertheless, not simply and necessarily class-related. If the role of ideology is not class-related, protecting and promoting the interests of the ruling class (conceived in Marxist terms), then what is that role? Clearly, it is a way of forging a dominant understanding of society that the mass of people actively consent to. Why should this be necessary? Part of the answer lies in the way in which Laclau and Mouffe conceptualise society.

According to the version of society embedded in the 'Jacobin imaginary' sketched above, society was construed as a totality, that is, as an integrated whole that could be understood and analysed by analysing its class structure, mode of production and so on. (It could be treated as an outgrowth of economic laws of development, organised in such a way as to secure the interests of the ruling class – apprehended as those who own and control the means of production.) Laclau and Mouffe, by contrast, see society as 'impossible'. By this they mean that there is no single principle that fixes or organises the divisions or differences within society. Instead 'society' is made up of aggregates. Put another way, we might say that society cannot be understood merely in class terms, but that we must also attend to the ways in which gender, race/ethnicity, sexuality and so forth operate. Instead of arguing that society is underpinned by a necessary logic (the logic of capitalism), Laclau and Mouffe argue that arrangements are contingent (that is, accidental).

It is here that ideology becomes important. Because society is not a totality, the role of ideology is to attempt to impose closure upon it (to 'suture' it, to use their terminology): that is, it is to try to offer a way of making sense of the social world that treats it as if it is bounded and knowable, when it isn't. This is where hegemony comes into play. Recall that, for Gramsci, hegemony was itself insecure and uncertain, a constant struggle between competing blocs aiming to make their ideology dominant. This suggests to Laclau and Mouffe, in their radicalisation of Gramsci's ideas, that the social is characterised by cross-cutting antagonisms. Hegemonic projects attempt to create some form of social order out of this morass of antagonisms by bringing together and thereby modifying ('articulating', as Laclau and Mouffe put it), dispersed elements. Thus a radical democratic project might draw together feminist groups, the labour movement, anti-racist groups and so forth around the issue of equality; it might argue that society is currently unequal; and it might contend that democracy can be fully attained only once all anti-democratic elements in society have been persuaded of the rightness of democracy. In so doing it would generate an ideology (around equality, say) to sustain this project.

At the start of this section I noted that Laclau and Mouffe were post-Marxists in the sense that they merged ideas from post-structuralism within a revised Marxist framework. In order to complete this summary of their ideas, it is necessary to mention Laclau and Mouffe's account of discourse. This is important, since it underpins their account of ideology. Discourse refers to the idea that all objects and actions have meaning, and that this meaning derives from systems of rules that are themselves historically specific. So the discourse of radical feminism views women as oppressed by patriarchal institutions such as the family whereas the discourse of conservatism sees women as naturally suited to life in the family. Both these discourses set up a system of (contingent) relations between different practices and objects. Moreover, '*every* object is constituted as an object of discourse' (Laclau and Mouffe, 1985: 107, my emphasis). This does not mean, as some critics have contended (Geras, 1990), that Laclau and Mouffe reject the idea that there is a material world outside of discourse. All it means is that we cannot think of or understand that world or operate within it without using discourse (systems of socially constituted rules).

In an echo of Foucault, Laclau and Mouffe contend furthermore that discourses establish subject positions with which people can identify ('radical feminist', 'woman', 'mother', or 'conservative', to use my earlier example). For Laclau and Mouffe, as for Foucault, discourses are political constructions. They are attempts to organise meaning and to fix practices in particular ways. As David Howarth points out, 'the elements which make up a discourse, and the discourses themselves, do not have an unchanging essence, but can be constantly altered by political actions' (1998: 134). Discourses are contingent. Returning to the earlier point about ideologies attempting to fix meaning, it should be apparent now that ideologies are themselves discursive. We might see them as systems of meaning that produce social reality and guide political action (as in the earlier example).

Instead then of a Marxist account of ideology as economically determined, Laclau and Mouffe offer a post-Marxist account of ideology as contingent and discursive. They reformulate Gramsci's idea of hegemony by eradicating all class elements from it. For them, hegemonic activity is thus not tied to class, but articulates different subject positions and identities into a common political project. Part of this political project is the generation of a political discourse – or ideology – that attempts to determine the meaning of the social. It tries to account for the nature, that is, of society at any given time. Since Laclau and Mouffe's account eliminates most, if not all, of the features of Marxism, critics have argued that the epithet 'post-Marxist' is misleading; better to drop all pretence of Marxism (Geras, 1990). This is a moot point. What is clearer is that they do succeed in offering a persuasive reconceptualisation of ideology better suited to a political world where ethnic conflict appears more significant than class conflict and where all societies are fractured by competing divisions.

Conclusion

Questions about the future of ideological thinking have punctuated the history of ideology over the last half-century or so. One factor impelling this recurrent questioning of ideology has been the issue of the viability of socialism, and by extension of Marxism. When Daniel Bell declared the end of ideology in 1960 he was motivated to do so by the apparent failures and corruption of socialism. Likewise, when Francis Fukuyama confidently proclaimed not just the end of ideology but also the end of history almost thirty years after Bell, he justified his claims by pointing (among other things) to the dissolution of the socialist regimes of Eastern Europe and to events in China. Laclau and Mouffe also, as we saw in the last section, proposed their version of post-Marxism as a remedy for the historical deficiencies of socialism in practice. But it wasn't only actually existing socialist regimes that prompted serious questions about ideology; Marxism as a theory also came under scrutiny. Foucault cast doubt on the distinction in Althusserian Marxism between science and ideology and opened up for debate the question of truth and its relation to power relations. He queried the assumptions underlying Marxism's conception of history and its belief in progress towards a communist end, a view echoed by Laclau and Mouffe. Laclau and Mouffe, however, did not repudiate ideology as Foucault had done; they reformulated it. Whilst they argued that class ideology was in decline, drawing on Gramsci's account of hegemony, they regarded ideology as a politically useful and necessary medium: a means of organising popular consent. In this reformulation we can see the beginnings of what is becoming a more firmly established trend in ideology critique. It has been assumed that thinkers labelled post-structuralist are necessarily anti-ideological. Laclau and Mouffe suggest that another avenue is possible: where the critical questions raised by post-structuralism can be used to inform an alternative conception of ideology. After all, Foucault's conception of discourse could easily accommodate the notion of ideology as a particular kind of discourse. (For further discussion of this topic see Malešević and MacKenzie, 2002.) So, does ideology have a future or not? The answer depends, if the writers covered in this chapter are an indication, on one's conception of ideology and the historical conditions in which one writes.

Notes

1   Marx contended that the ruling ideas in every society served the interests of the ruling class. The working classes, however, were often unaware of this and assumed instead that capitalist values benefited everyone. They suffered from 'false consciousness' in the sense that they were unaware of what was really happening to them: that is, that capitalism exploited and alienated them.

2   By contrast, the 'new ideologies', to be found in Asia and Africa, are mass ideologies oriented around specific local concerns most usually relating to 'economic development and national power'. They are ideologies of 'industrialization, modernization, Pan-Arabism, color and nationalism' (Bell, 1960: 403).

3   The only other comparable occasion was the Japanese bombing of the United States Air Force base at Pearl Harbor, Hawaii on 7 December 1941, which took the US into the Second World War.

4   Specifically, knowledge was a system of production involving ideas (the raw materials) and a set of questions, concepts and methods labelled the problematic (the means of production). Through a 'symptomatic reading' – that is, focusing on the gaps and silences in a text – it was possible to discern the true questions and concerns behind the text. This was 'science'. (See Althusser, 1969: 161–218.)

5   'Hegemony' was a term that had been used by other Marxists prior to Gramsci (e.g. by the Russian Marxist Plekhanov and by Lenin) but it is Gramsci's formulation that has had the greatest influence on contemporary political thought.

Further reading

General

Adam Lent (ed.), *New Political Thought* (1998), provides a succinct introduction to the concept of ideology, particularly in relation to ideas such as post-Marxism and postmodernism. Gary Browning, Abigail Halcli and Frank Webster (eds), *Understanding Contemporary Society* (2000), is a useful supplement; this text-book surveys a number of the key debates that frame this chapter (such as post-history and post-feminism). (See also the further reading suggested in Chapter 1 for general texts on ideology.) On the topic of post-structuralism and postmodernism, in general, see Madan Sarup's *An Introductory Guide to Poststructuralism and Postmodernism*; this is a user-friendly and comprehensive textbook charting these complex ideas (1993). A good place to start for the reader already familiar with the broad terms of the debate but who is looking for a more critical assessment of the impact of postmodernism on political thinking, among other things, is Pauline M. Rosenau, *Postmodernism and the Social Sciences* (1992). This covers a wide range of material and includes a brief consideration of the relation of postmodern thinking to the end of ideology and of history debates. *Ideology after Poststructuralism*, edited by Siniša Malešević and Iain MacKenzie (2002), offers an important contribution to a largely neglected area of debate: the intersection between post-structuralism and ideology.

Bell and the End of Ideology

The classic text here is Daniel Bell's *The End of Ideology* (1960). For an examination of Bell's own reassessment of his ideas see his '*The End of Ideology* revisited' parts I and II (1988a, b). To explore the debate engendered by Bell's book see C. L. Waxman's edited collection of essays (many of them polemical), *The End of Ideology Debate* (1968), and for a more analytical and applied set of responses M. Rejai (ed.) *Decline of Ideology?* (1971).

Fukuyama and the End of History

The obvious starting point for an exploration of the ideas of Fukuyama is the essay that generated the initial debate, 'The end of history?' (1989). To fully appreciate the complexity of Fukuyama's account, I would recommend examining his book-length account of the same topic, *The End of History and the*

Last Man (1992). An early critical assessment of his book was Alan Ryan's review essay 'Professor Hegel goes to Washington' (1992). This has been followed by a number of other interventions. For a difficult but erudite piece exploring the end of history in general as well as in relation to Fukuyama see Perry Anderson's lengthy essay 'The ends of history' (1992). A collection of essays that considers the implications of Fukuyama's thesis from a left-wing perspective is *Has History Ended?* edited by Christopher Bertram and Andrew Chitty (1994). Another wide-ranging collection (that includes a response by Fukuyama) is Timothy Burn's edited book *After History?* (1994). A helpful overview of Fukuyama's account of the end of history, written with students in mind, is Krishnan Kumar's essay 'Post-history: living at the end' (2000).

Althusser and Foucault

The literature both by and about these thinkers is vast. The most useful sources by Althusser to read in relation to the concerns of this chapter are his edited collection of essays, *For Marx* (1969), and 'Ideology and ideological state apparatuses' (1971). Neither is easy and both require some prior knowledge of Marxism and of Althusser's own work. A good guide to Althusser's thought is *Althusser's Marxism* by Alex Callinicos (1976). For concise explanation of key terms in Marxism (including Althusserian terminology), *A Dictionary of Marxist Thought* edited by Tom Bottomore (2nd edn, 1991) is an excellent resource.

The piece where Foucault outlines, somewhat cryptically, his views on ideology and truth is 'Truth and power' (1980). It is worth the effort of reading. Michèle Barrett's comprehensive and stimulating account of the role of ideology in Marxist and post-structuralist thought, *The Politics of Truth* (1991), offers an overview of the relation between Althusser and Foucault, and considers in detail Foucault's critique of ideology and his alternative account of discourse, truth and power. Commentaries on and critical assessments of the work of Foucault abound. Alec McHoul and Wendy Grace provide a clearly written and accessible guide to Foucault in *A Foucault Primer* (1993). Lois McNay's *Foucault: A Critical Introduction* (1994) provides a more searching account of Foucault's thought that touches, albeit briefly, on the question of ideology. An example of an approach that combines Foucault's account of discourse, power and truth with ideology is Davina Cooper's essay 'Strategies of power: legislating worship and religious education' (1997).

Gramsci, Laclau and Mouffe

Given the nature of Gramsci's writings, his views on ideology and hegemony are not set out in a systematic fashion anywhere. For a taste of his views, it is necessary (and worth while) to dip into one or both of the collections used in this chapter: *Selections from Cultural Writings* (1985) and/or *Selections from Prison*

Notebooks (1971). The latter is perhaps the most useful in this context. Much has been written about Gramsci. A brief overview of his thought can be found in Roger Simon's *Gramsci's Political Thought* (1982). Anne Showstack Sassoon, *Gramsci's Politics* (1987), provides a broad-ranging and more demanding survey of Gramsci's work. A more recent critical account is James Martin's *Gramsci's Political Analysis* (1998). This is particularly worth exploring because it also traces the revival of interest in Gramsci's work (including that of Laclau and Mouffe).

The ideas of Laclau and Mouffe are set out in their now classic text, *Hegemony and Socialist Strategy* (1985). This is a dense and difficult book. The fullest commentary so far on and exposition of the ideas of Laclau and Mouffe (including their debt to Gramsci) is Anna Marie Smith's excellent book, *Laclau and Mouffe* (1998). A short piece tracing the contours of post-Marxism as an ideology is David Howarth's essay 'Post-Marxism' (1998). This can be usefully supplemented by David Howarth, Aletta J. Norval and Yannis Stavrakakis (eds), *Discourse Theory and Political Analysis* (2000). The introduction in particular is worth examining for its exposition of some of the key terms of analysis of Laclau and Mouffe. For a critical account of post-Marxism see the two essays (both previously published) on Laclau and Mouffe in Norman Geras, *Discourses of Extremity* (1990). For a convincing rebuttal of Geras's ideas see Laclau and Mouffe's 1987 essay 'Post-Marxism without apologies'.

References

Note. Dates in square brackets indicate date of original publication.

Althusser, L. (1969) [1965] *For Marx*, London: Verso.
Althusser, L. (1971) [1970] 'Ideology and ideological state apparatuses', *Lenin and Philosophy and other Essays*, London: New Left Books.
Anderson, P. (1992) 'The ends of history' in *A Zone of Engagement*, London: Verso.
Aron, R. (1957) [1955] *The Opiate of the Intellectuals*, London: Secker & Warburg.
Barker, C. (2000) *Cultural Studies: Theory and Practice*, London: Sage.
Barrett, M. (1991) *The Politics of Truth: From Marx to Foucault*, Cambridge: Polity Press.
Bates, T. R. (1975) 'Gramsci and the theory of hegemony', *Journal of the History of Ideas*, 36 (2), pp. 351–66.
Bell, D. (1960) *The End of Ideology: On the Exhaustion of Political Ideas in the Fifties*, New York: Free Press.
Bell, D. (1974) *The Coming of Post-industrial Society: A Venture in Social Forecasting*, London: Heinemann.
Bell, D. (1988a) *'The End of Ideology* revisited' I, *Government and Opposition*, 23, pp. 127–50.
Bell, D. (1988b) *'The End of Ideology* revisited' II, *Government and Opposition*, 23, pp. 321–31.
Bertram, C. and Chitty, A., eds (1994) *Has History Ended? Fukuyama, Marx and Modernity*, Aldershot: Ashgate.

Bottomore, T., ed. (1991) *A Dictionary of Marxist Thought*, 2nd edn, Oxford: Blackwell.

Browning, G., Halcli, A. and Webster, F., eds (2000) *Understanding Contemporary Society: Theories of the Present*, London: Sage.

Burns, T., ed. (1994) *After History? Francis Fukuyama and his Critics*, New York: Rowman & Littlefield.

Callinicos, A. (1976) *Althusser's Marxism*, London: Pluto Press.

Carter, B. (1997) 'Rejecting truthful identities: Foucault, "race" and politics' in M. Lloyd and A. Thacker (eds) *The Impact of Michel Foucault on the Social Sciences and Humanities*, Basingstoke: Macmillan.

Cooper, D. (1997) 'Strategies of power: legislating worship and religious education' in M. Lloyd and A. Thacker (eds) *The Impact of Michel Foucault on the Social Sciences and Humanities*, Basingstoke: Macmillan.

Foucault, M. (1972) *The Archaeology of Knowledge*, London: Routledge.

Foucault, M. (1978) [1976?] *The History of Sexuality*, Volume I *An Introduction*, Harmondsworth: Penguin.

Foucault, M. (1980) 'Truth and power' in C. Gordon (ed.) *Michel Foucault: Power/Knowledge. Selected Interviews and other Writings 1972–1977 by Michel Foucault*, London: Harvester Press.

Foucault, M. (1997) [1984] 'Polemics, politics, and problematizations: an interview with Michel Foucault' in P. Rabinow (ed.) *Michel Foucault. Ethics: Subjectivity and Truth. The Essential Works of Michel Foucault 1954–1984*, Volume I, London: Allen Lane.

Fukuyama, F. (1989) 'The end of history?' *The National Interest*, 16, pp. 3–18.

Fukuyama, F. (1992) *The End of History and the Last Man*, Harmondsworth: Penguin.

Geras, N. (1990) *Discourses of Extremity: Radical Ethics and post-Marxist Extravagances*, London: Verso.

Gramsci, A. (1971) *Selections from Prison Notebooks*, ed. Q. Hoare and G. Nowell-Smith, London: Lawrence & Wishart.

Gramsci, A. (1985) *Selections from Cultural Writings*, ed. D. Forgacs and G. Nowell-Smith, London: Lawrence & Wishart.

Hobsbawm, E. (1995) *Age of Extremes: The Short Twentieth Century, 1914–1991*, London: Abacus.

Howarth, D. (1998) 'Post-Marxism' in A. Lent (ed.) *New Political Thought: An Introduction*, London: Lawrence & Wishart.

Howarth, D., Norval, A. J. and Stavrakakis, Y., eds (2000) *Discourse Theory and Political Analysis: Identities, Hegemonies and Social Change*, Manchester: Manchester University Press.

Huntington, S. (1993) 'The clash of civilizations?' *Foreign Affairs*, 72, pp. 22–49.

Huntington, S. (1997) *The Clash of Civilizations and the Remaking of the World Order*, New York: Touchstone.

Kumar, K. (2000) 'Post-history: living at the end' in G. Browning, A. Halcli and F. Webster (eds) *Understanding Contemporary Society: Theories of the Present*, London: Sage.

Laclau, E. and Mouffe, C. (1985) *Hegemony and Socialist Strategy: Towards a Radical Democratic Politics*, London: Verso.

Laclau, E. and Mouffe, C. (1987) 'Post-Marxism without apologies', *New Left Review*, 166, pp. 79–106.

Lent, A., ed. (1998) *New Political Thought: An Introduction*, London: Lawrence & Wishart.

Lipset, S. M. (1963) *Political Man*, London: Heinemann.

MacKenzie, I. (1994) 'Introduction: the arena of ideology' in R. Eccleshall, V. Geoghegan, R. Jay, M. Kenny, I. MacKenzie and R. Wilford *Political Ideologies: An Introduction*, London: Routledge.

McHoul, A. and Grace, W. (1993) *A Foucault Primer: Discourse, Power and the Subject*, London: UCL Press.

McNay, L. (1994) *Foucault: A Critical Introduction*, Cambridge: Polity Press.

Malešević, S. and MacKenzie, I., eds (2002) *Ideology after Poststructuralism*, London: Pluto Press.

Martin, J. (1998) *Gramsci's Political Analysis: A Critical Introduction*, Basingstoke: Macmillan.

Marx, K. (1977) [1932] 'The German ideology' in D. McLellan (ed.) *Karl Marx: Selected Writings*, Oxford: Oxford University Press.

Mills, C. Wright (1968) [1960] 'Letter to the New Left' in C. L. Waxman (ed.) *The End of Ideology Debate*, New York: Funk & Wagnalls.

Mouffe, C., ed. (1979) *Gramsci and Marxist Theory*, London: Routledge.

Norris, C. (1991) '*The End of Ideology* revisited: the Gulf War, postmodernism and *Realpolitik*', *Philosophy and Social Criticism*, 17, pp. 1–40.

Rejai, M., ed. (1971) *Decline of Ideology?* Chicago: Aldine Atherton.

Rosenau, P. M. (1992) *Postmodernism and the Social Sciences: Insights, Inroads and Intrusions*, Princeton NJ: Princeton University Press.

Ryan, A. (1992) 'Professor Hegel goes to Washington', *New York Review of Books*, 26 March.

Sarup, M. (1993) *An Introductory Guide to Poststructuralism and Postmodernism*, 2nd edn, London: Harvester Wheatsheaf.

Sassoon, A. S. (1987) *Gramsci's Politics*, 2nd edn, Minneapolis MN: University of Minnesota Press.

Simon, R. (1982) *Gramsci's Political Thought: An Introduction*, London: Lawrence & Wishart.

Skinner, Q., ed. (1985) *The Return of Grand Theory in the Human Sciences*, Cambridge: Cambridge University Press.

Smith, A. M. (1998), *Laclau and Mouffe: The Radical Democratic Imaginary*, London: Routledge.

Waxman, C. L., ed. (1968) *The End of Ideology Debate*, New York: Funk & Wagnalls.

Zalewski, M. (2000) *Feminism after Postmodernism: Theorising through Practice*, London: Routledge.

Index

Page references for notes are followed by n